The Inimitable Dickens

The Inimitable Dickens

A READING OF
THE NOVELS

A. E. DYSON

MACMILLAN

ST MARTIN'S PRESS

© A. E. Dyson 1970

First published 1970 by
MACMILLAN AND CO LTD
Little Essex Street London WC2
and also at Bombay Calcutta and Madras
Macmillan South Africa (Publishers) Pty Ltd Johannesburg
The Macmillan Company of Australia Pty Ltd Melbourne
The Macmillan Company of Canada Ltd Toronto
St Martin's Press Inc New York
Gill and Macmillan Ltd Dublin

Library of Congress catalog card no 70–106204

Printed in Great Britain by
ROBERT MACLEHOSE AND CO LTD
The University Press Glasgow

Contents

For
Clifford Tucker

Preface

I should like to thank all the friends, colleagues and students with whom I have talked about Dickens over the years, and especially while I have been writing this book. They are in no way responsible for the opinions expressed here, but I have learned from them all. A special word of thanks is due to groups of M.A. students in the University of East Anglia over the past three years.

A few chapters have been pre-published in whole or part, and I must thank the editors of *The Dickensian* and *Novel*, and my co-editor of the *Critical Quarterly*.

A. E. DYSON

Norwich, 1970

1 The Inimitable

DICKENS called himself 'The Inimitable', and so he was; there is no other writer like him. At first it was an exuberant signature to 'Answers to Correspondents' in the *Miscellany:* 'The Inimitable Boz'. But Dickens kept it up throughout his life. 'Think of the unmitigated nonsense of an inimitable grandfather!' – this when his first granddaughter was presented to him in the 1860s, and after his marriage to Kate had broken down. It must be The Inimitable who wrote this letter from Broadstairs during the composition of *Martin Chuzzlewit*, even though the actual style does not appear:

In a bay-window in a one-pair sits, from nine o'clock to one, a gentleman with rather long hair and no neckcloth, who writes and grins as though he thought he were very funny indeed. His name is Boz. At one he disappears, and presently emerges from a bathing-machine, and may be seen – a kind of salmon-coloured porpoise – splashing around in the ocean. After that he may be seen in another bay-window on the ground floor, eating a strong lunch; after that, walking a dozen miles or so, or lying on his back in the sand reading a book. Nobody bothers him unless they know he is disposed to be talked to; and I am told he is very comfortable indeed.

Dickens larger than life, and enjoying every minute of it. Who could mistake the zest and showmanship for anyone else?

Naturally Dickens is very much more than a showman, and no attempt will be made to reduce him here. He is, for instance, our greatest English prose writer, with an amazing range and vigour of style. Rumbustious passages, celebrating common trials and enjoyments; great evocations, like the *Little Dorrit* prisons and the *Bleak House* fog; the Immortals, larger than life and correspondingly lively; powerful analyses of guilt and passion in Jonas Chuzzlewit or John Jasper; moments of deep

inwardness which Graham Greene described as 'delicate and
exact poetic cadences, the music of memory, that so influenced
Proust'. Dickens is one of our great comic writers, and a great
tragedian. He is both social reformer and social pessimist; a
man of boundless energy in creative affairs and practical
commitments, yet a deeply religious writer, too, of an un-
orthodox kind.

These aspects and others will present themselves in the
course of my reading, but The Inimitable seems the right place
to start. For one thing, its zestfulness saw Dickens through a
period of critical neglect in the earlier twentieth century, just
as it will see him through any reverse tendency at the present
time. No weight of Ph.D. theses could crush The Inimitable, or
put an end to Mr Micawber or Sairey Gamp. A certain un-
quenchable popular glamour hangs over them; indeed, a critic
can take heart from the thought that while he might help a few
more readers to enjoy Dickens if he succeeds in his task (very,
very 'umbly), he is unlikely to do a great deal of harm if he
fails.

Dickens's showmanship links him not only with the supreme
dramatic and literary entertainers of the world, but with a
select few among its very great men. Winston Churchill had
more than a touch of showmanship, and could have carried The
Inimitable as a name. It reminds us that even among his peers
Dickens was exceptional, a writer with an unusual aura of
greatness in his life. As showman he radiates that promise
which brings children wide-eyed to a circus, and really *is* what
his vaguely alcoholic Mr Sleary just fails to be. There is warmth
and courage in him as well as humour. No reader can doubt
how alive and large humanity is.

The celebration of life is a Dickensian hallmark, yet it was
a grim and in many ways evil world that Dickens saw. His
celebration always takes account of huge obstacles to optimism,
and is a triumph of will and energy as well as faith. In the first
place, he triumphed over his own adverse circumstances; The
Inimitable was made as well as born. Certain critics seem to
overlook, or at least to ignore this; they speak of Dickens as a
man crushed by suffering or as a manic-depressive, as though

his creative energy was some merely predictable reflex to pain.
His anguish is dwelt upon – the blacking factory at twelve,
unrequited passion for Maria Beadnell – as if these episodes
were a true and sufficient key to his art. Yet Dickens was never
a shrinking or sensitive soul, lacking in resilience; and the
blacking factory and Maria Beadnell, though 'sealed-off' areas,
were in no ways permitted to sour his life. He was never as
defeated by experience as his own David Copperfield; certainly
he was no Arthur Clennam or Pip. As early as *Sketches by Boz*,
low-life is transformed by exuberance; delight is more apparent
even than satire in the scheme. Dickens always moved in his
world as a god, shaping and mastering, not as a victim shaped
and mastered himself.

To call attention to this is not to deny the truth in Edmund
Wilson's theory that Dickens was manic-depressive, but it is to
question the importance of such a condition to his art. Many
men are, in a loose sense, manic-depressive, but how many of
them interest us as Dickens does? It is our modern reaction
against excellence that toys, I think, with such theories, in a
fruitless attempt to scale genius down. How reassuring if
Dickens really was just like ourselves in all important aspects,
with just a touch of extra suffering or freakishness to set him
apart! But energy and talent of Dickens's order are wholly
exceptional, and no good can come from pretending anything
else. Where he does differ from us, it is not in the direction of
illness or failure, any more than Philoctetes really was just one
more lame dog. Like all really great artists, he is a world away
from failure – whether the failure of the mentally sick, incapaci-
tated for creation by their depression or their delusions, or the
failure of men enslaved like John Jasper by passion and drugs.
No victim could call himself The Inimitable, and carry it like
Dickens; no victim could offer creation and wisdom on so
healing a scale.

II

My first purpose in this brief introduction is to draw attention
to Dickens's exuberance; my second is to explain a little more

the plan of this book. It is written as a sequence of studies of the novels from *The Old Curiosity Shop* onwards, but it is designed to be read as a whole. Each chapter is to some degree autonomous, and might be used as a Preface – or better, an Afterword – to the particular book. But I have also tried to avoid repetition, and the more general aspects of Dickens's art – his characterisation, symbolism, religious and political views and so on – are not discussed every time. Each topic is confined to one, or at the most two, chapters, with references backwards and forwards to the rest.

My main concern has been with the organic structure of each novel, and with the terms of reading prescribed by itself. This has seemed particularly important in a book on Dickens, since the 'loose baggy monster' theory has for so long held the field. The very homogeneity of Dickens's created world has led to oversimplification. While it is apparent (for instance) that Dickens's 'characters' appear in all the novels and that Dickens's 'London' appears in all but one of them, G. K. Chesterton was surely wrong to see each novel as a snipped-off length from the same rich cloth. In fact, the forty or fifty characters in any one novel always link more closely with each other than they do with similar characters in other books, and even 'London' takes on very distinctive colourings from the differing tales. The *Little Dorrit* London has more driving sleet and darkness, more weary distances, than the colourful, labyrinthine London of *Martin Chuzzlewit*; the sombre London of *A Tale of Two Cities* – a mere appendage, for once, to Paris – is not the sinister London of *Edwin Drood*. Artistic compression is by no means confined to those books where Dickens appears to be distilling essences – in *Hard Times* aridity, in *A Tale of Two Cities* violence – but exists equally in *Martin Chuzzlewit*, *David Copperfield*, *Our Mutual Friend*. I very much doubt whether paragraphs of mere padding could be found in any of the novels. I am certain that all of them are most subtly organised and knit through imagery and tone.

My method of arrangement has its own problems, some of them common to all criticism of a large body of work. While the ideal reader will have been long familiar with all Dickens's

novels, there is also an actual reader to keep in mind. No easy
solution to this dilemma suggests itself, since there is naturally
no substitute for reading the books. But I have attempted, I am
by no means sure how successfully, to make the chapters
generally intelligible, even to readers who may sometimes be
aware of a gap. It is to be hoped that gaps will be filled as
soon as possible, but I have tried to minimise the temporary
disadvantages as well as I can. This is chiefly because any
complete reading of Dickens depends on continuity, and there
is no novel which does not add something to our sense of his
work as a whole. *Barnaby Rudge* is the novel that most immediately comes to mind as an example. Though it is still read
less widely than the other novels, there is nothing in early
Dickens more fundamental to an understanding of his political
thought.

By quotation and other means, then, I have tried to make
this book readable as a sequence, and in the course of it a
complete assessment is suggested of Dickens's art. What I have
stopped short of offering, however, is plot summaries, since
these seem to me to cast darkness rather than light. For readers
determined to have them, they are available: in *The Charles
Dickens Companion*, edited by Michael and Molly Hardwick,
and in the older, out-of-print *The Dickens Dictionary*, edited by
Gilbert A. Pierce and William A. Wheeler. There are also
amazingly threadbare plot summaries in the *Oxford Companion
to English Literature*, which by some distinguished perversity
make all of Dickens's novels sound unreadable, but undeniably
name the chief characters and outline the plots.

My subtitle, 'A Reading of the Novels', runs into trouble
with Mr Eugene Wrayburn. 'By the by,' he tells Mortimer,
'that very word, "Reading", in its critical use, always charms
me. An actress's Reading of a chambermaid, a dancer's Reading
of a hornpipe, a singer's Reading of a song, a marine-painter's
Reading of the sea, the kettledrum's Reading of an instrumental
passage, are phrases ever youthful and delightful.' A whimsical
reminder, from Eugene, that sea and hornpipe outlive their
Readings, and that Reader is not greater than the Read. A
reminder, too, of the limits of criticism: since no reader can

wholly escape his temperament and predilections, his moment
in history, the objective quest is pursued against permanent
odds. But the corollary, more cheerful for a critic, is that without
Reading, sea or hornpipe are neglected; they exist, after all, to
be read. Just as the life of books is in the consciousness of
successive readers, so the books themselves must be picked out
by successive readers in order to endure.

III

My chief reason for writing on Dickens is that I have read
and reread him since my childhood, always returning with
expectations of pleasure, always finding new pleasures to
accompany the old. Naturally the old pleasures change a little
with adult understanding, but they never seem completely to
fail. The evergreen quality has been admirably described
by Robert Morse in his well-known essay on *Our Mutual
Friend*:

Perhaps it is because of the detachment of the poetic method
that Dickens's novels can be read again without loss of pleasure,
for, as in a well-loved poem, the sequence is largely independent
of the kind of time in which suspense draws us on. Since we
have never been invited to identify ourselves passionately with
the fate of the characters, and have not lived through their story
as if it were our own, we do not return to Dickens as we are
likely to return even to Tolstoy, with a sense of chill, of lost
magic and shrunken dimension. For there are certain books as
difficult to recapture in their essence as an old love, as difficult
to relive as a passage in our past, simply because they *were* our
love and past, and their truth for us has been assimilated and
has actually modified our present. Dickens's books are not of
this kind; like a sonnet, or Jack and the Beanstalk, their rewards
belong to a perpetual present.

It is true that we are never invited to identify passionately
with Dickens's people, which is doubtless one of the many
reasons why they remain so alive. If they are totally unsuitable
as vehicles for romantic self-indulgence, this is just one more
thing they have in common with most people in life.

  Enjoyment, then, is one reason for writing on Dickens, but

there is obviously very much more. Dickens remains present
even when his novels are back on the shelf and temporarily
forgotten; his events and people take themselves off the shelves
and into the streets. While reading him one enters his world,
of course, as one does with all compelling writers, suspending
'self' along with disbelief as far as one can. It is not a matter of
reducing or attempting to reduce him to 'our own experience',
but of expanding as far as possible to meet his world. Afterwards, he floats away from our immediate ken, again like all
other writers, to become one among many lanterns in the
perspectives of life. Some writers fail to interest us, and we are
hardly aware of them; some interest us, but nothing more.
Some shape our values and beliefs, becoming so interwoven
that they really are, or seem to be, 'part of ourselves'. And
there are others who glow with particular authority – Sophocles,
Shakespeare, Pope, Dickens, T. S. Eliot – brightening and
dimming to laws no longer anchored in time. We say, not 'Yes,
life is like that' but: 'Yes, this *is* Life' – the highest tribute
payable to art. It may be that young readers are more liable to
jump in and out of such relationships than older ones, but by
middle age there are four, five, six such writers in most of our
lives.

For me Dickens is such a writer, so that when I read him
literary criticism reaches out from its usual sphere to somewhere beyond. I realise that this statement is open to question;
some critics might detect in it the betrayal of literary discourse
for ulterior ends. They would see their own role more simply
as dealing with artistic artefacts – with the analysis of structure,
tone, imagery and so forth in a closed verbal world. If further
obligations were envisaged, these might be to a somewhat
impersonal view of language or literary tradition, still insulated
from direct commentary upon life. A critic might feel it his
duty to applaud fine uses of language and to rebuke sloppy
uses without necessarily endorsing, or refusing to endorse,
what the language *does*.

And there is much to be said in favour of such impersonality,
which at least avoids the grosser errors of critical rape. It is
academically useful and indeed respectable to direct attention

to works of literature as artistic objects, existing toughly and durably, and with a healthy independence of the reading proposed by ourselves. *Not* 'Dickens our contemporary', but 'Dickens everyone's contemporary', a much larger and more challenging thing. There is much to be said for analysing Dickens's language also as a transpersonal value. If the flexibility and purity of language are always threatened and always precious, then the great classics are the life-blood in more than a purely metaphorical sense of our world.

Yet impartiality, though useful and admirable, cannot be the whole story; there are two converging objections to be faced. The first is that however useful impartiality is as a corrective to subjectivism, it is unsuitably lifeless as a total ideal. The impression conveyed may be not of equal respect, but of equal disrespect for all great writers, if the critic is, or seems to be, totally free. How can he remain free – neither fired, angered, saddened, converted nor even engaged deeply – unless he is implicitly superior, in such detachment, to the writers themselves? And this is a direct pointer to the second objection. Although writers create art and approach us as artists, they are not themselves indifferent to their raw material back in 'life'. No writer would want to be only an artist (though no writer would want to be less than an artist): no writer, that is, who cares what he writes. Dickens of all writers meant to engage his readers. He would not have seen the death of Jo as a text, in the first instance, for literary debate.

But the most simple point is that great art is, and always has been seen to be, a source of wisdom, and this vision is needful to the health of the culture to which it belongs. It is worth recalling that the older classicists founded an academic discipline on the study of great authors chiefly because they revered such authors, also, as teachers of truth. 'Education for life' is such cant now that one hesitates to use it, yet the classicists really did embody the ideal in its sanest form. Their belief was that great authors are the crowning glory of a culture, and its mode of transmission; expose boys and students to them, and the effect must be good. To my mind this remains the simple truth on which all literary education is founded, and a permanent

rebuke to any narrower notion, however sophisticated, of the
importance of books. It is this which encourages me to claim
for Dickens status as a classic writer : an assumption that will
be pervasive, though I hope not tedious, in the chapters
ahead.

IV

It would be redundant to anticipate here the themes touched on
later, but I must admit that my discussions often focus on the
'characters' themselves. This is because I believe that Dickens
did not create characters to illustrate theses or to chart abstrac-
tions, but as an extension of his boundless sense of the richness
of life. The energy of his novels is pre-eminently in their
characters, and all the technical triumphs – tone, symbolism,
imagery – bring us back to the characters time and again. Even
ideas, religious and political, are of secondary importance.
Dickens's ideas evolve from his continual engagement, through
people, with life.

To say this is not to mistake fictional people for real people,
one's own friends and colleagues; but then, what literary critic
ever did ? We all know that Dickens's characters exist in novels
and are illusions; we know their births are not registered in
government offices like our own. But they are illusions so
massive and vital, so vividly unforgettable, that we very
naturally carry them, with all the insight and inference we
can muster, back to 'life'. A critic is not essentially a technician
manqué, sitting in the stalls but brooding on greasepaint; he is
Audience, and meant to respond as such. There can be no
separate no-man's-land for him between creation and response
to creation. Not until he is carried into the world of the art
deeply and totally will his own expertise be of use. The
expertise may be what makes him a *professional* reader, but he
remains a reader, and on the reader's side of the great divide.

It will be noticed that I have little to say in this book about
the history of Dickens's critical reputation and trends in modern
criticism, and this is because I have already discussed these
themes elsewhere. They are the subject of my Introduction to

Dickens in the Modern Judgements series, published by Macmillan, where my personal debt to other readers and critics is also made clear. Only one work requires to be picked out here for special mention. This is Edgar Johnson's two-volume biography, *Charles Dickens: his tragedy and triumph*, essential reading for all Dickensians, which readily explains those episodes in Dickens's life to which most critics refer.

v

It will be seen that I start with Dickens's fourth major novel, and perhaps this requires a note. The first three novels are all amazingly vital, but they speak very directly for themselves. *Pickwick Papers* was the tale with which he made his great reputation, and it has remained the most popular of his books to this day. Funny, idyllic, timeless, it yet has many sombre undercurrents, the intimation of much to come in the later books. The praise of *Pickwick* needs no rehearsing, though two modern critics deserve mention: G. K. Chesterton in his brilliant, erratic little book on Dickens, W. H. Auden in an essay reprinted in *The Dyer's Hand*.

Dickens's next novel, *Oliver Twist*, was astonishingly different, an exploration of the cruelty of criminals and of middle-class legislators alike. There are several fine essays on this novel – notably Graham Greene's 'The Young Dickens' (reprinted in my 'Modern Judgements' on Dickens), John Bayley's essay (reprinted in the Twentieth Century Views volume on Dickens), Arnold Kettle's chapter in his two-volume *An Introduction to the English Novel*, and Angus Wilson's Introduction to the Penguin Classics edition. *Oliver Twist* is a dark, frightening tale, with a pattern of fear close to nightmare, and perhaps related, in its obsessive terror, to *Edwin Drood*. Oliver is pursued by Fagin's gang until no place is safe for him; as Graham Greene has it:

We know that when Oliver leaves Mr Brownlow's house to walk a few hundred yards to the bookseller, his friends will wait in vain for his return. All London outside the quiet, shady street in Pentonville belongs to his pursuers; and when he escapes again into the house of Mrs Maylie in the fields beyond Shepperton, we know his security is false. The seasons may pass, but safety depends not upon time but on daylight. As children we all knew that: how all day we could forget the dark and the journey to bed. It is with a sense of relief that at last in twilight we see the faces of the Jew and Monks peer into the cottage window between the sprays of jessamine. At that moment we realise how the whole world, and not London only, belongs to these two after dark.

Monks is of course the crowning horror; behind Fagin, terrible enough, is this other shadowy figure, dedicated to Oliver's destruction in the world. No persecution nightmare could surpass it: yet Dickens persuades us that this is indeed a small boy, not untypically helpless, for whom starvation is a mere curtain-raiser to horrors to come. As we know, Oliver is born to higher things than appear on the surface, and, in contrast to more vulnerable child-heroes to follow him, at least he survives. But the presence of powerful, irreducible evil is what stays with us. Just as Oliver asking for more remains one of the few episodes in the English novel that everyone knows about, so his terrors haunt the night side of our minds.

The third novel, *Nicholas Nickleby*, is a sprawling, picaresque work, in many aspects close to the eighteenth-century novels on which the young Dickens had nourished himself, and the only real loose baggy monster in the *œuvre*. In other words it is the only Dickens novel which either has no clear organic unity, or which has one that the present reader has failed to find. Very little has been written about it; yet if we judge it by Dickens's own standards a minor masterpiece, a masterpiece it is, all the same. It is still read, and widely popular; it has, again, one event and one character known to everyone (but of what Dickens novel could one say less?).

My decision has been to bypass these three first novels, and to start with the two which open the brilliant decade of the 1840s. *The Old Curiosity Shop* had a tremendous success when it first appeared, but declined in favour afterwards; *Barnaby Rudge* was less successful on publication and has remained so since. They are both, in my view, major novels of classic status;

and they both give the lie to oversimplified accounts of the development of Dickens's art and his ideas. Without further preamble then, let us pass on to the old man Master Humphrey, and to those London streets which Dickens and his people so often walked.

2 *The Old Curiosity Shop*
innocence and the grotesque

And lastly, there was the girl;
Beauty under some spell of the beast.
      (from R. S. Thomas's 'On the Farm')

I

The Old Curiosity Shop opens with the never-ending feet of London as a sick man might hear them, imagining the people, the faces, the destinies, 'the stream of life that will not stop, pouring on, on, on, through all his restless dreams, as if he were condemned to lie, dead but conscious, in a noisy churchyard, and had no hope of rest for centuries to come'. This vision of London is the narrator's, the old man (bequeathed to the novel by *Master Humphrey's Clock*) who sets the tale in motion and then withdraws. The opening chapter sets a tone which is to pervade the novel. As Dickens said later in his Preface, the story came from a deep region of his mind:

I had always in my fancy to surround the lonely figure of the child with grotesque and wild, but not impossible companions, and to gather about her innocent face and pure intentions, associates as strange and uncongenial as the grim objects that are about her bed when her history is first foreshadowed.

The grotesque is always strong in Dickens, but here in *The Old Curiosity Shop*, it is the organising principle of his art. The characters are grotesque: Quilp and Kit, Dick Swiveller and Sally Brass, old Mr Trent and the Marchioness – and so is the setting: the curiosity shop, the Brass *ménage*, Quilp's riverside hideout, the picaresque world of giants and dwarfs, freaks and travelling showmen, bargees and outcasts through which Little Nell and her grandfather flee. The morality is grotesque: good and evil, tragedy and comedy exist as in a distorting glass. Even the humour is grotesque. 'I don't eat babies,' says Quilp, 'I don't like 'em' (a wisecrack midway between Swift and sick

comedy) – and there are discussions like this, in the Jolly
Sandboys :

'How's the Giant?' said Short, when they all sat smoking
round the fire.

'Rather weak upon his legs,' returned Mr Vuffin. 'I begin to
be afraid he's going at the knees.'

'That's a bad look-out,' said Short.

'Ay! Bad indeed,' replied Mr Vuffin, contemplating the fire
with a sigh. 'Once get a giant shaky on his legs and the public
care no more about him than they do for a dead cabbage-
stalk.'

'What becomes of old giants?' said Short, turning to him
again after a little reflection.

'They're usually kept in caravans to wait upon the dwarfs,'
said Mr Vuffin . . .

. . . 'What about the dwarfs when *they* get old?' inquired the
landlord.

'The older a dwarf is, the better worth he is,' returned Mr
Vuffin; 'a grey-headed dwarf, well-wrinkled, is beyond all
suspicion. But a giant weak in the legs, and not standing up-
right! – keep him in the caravan, but never show him, never
show him, for any persuasion that can be offered.'

The worlds of Lewis Carroll and Franz Kafka both seem near,
as a sense of strangeness spreads back from this mingling of
homely atmosphere and ruthless logic into our more normal
world. What race produces such a wisdom, so familiar and
alien? Caricature is fundamentally serious, as in Hogarth; Mr
Vuffin's freaks exist for public mirth and private profit, but in
The Old Curiosity Shop most of the characters are freaks. Yet
there is some resilience in the humour, a reminder of Kit and
his strange, misshapen family, as well as of Quilp. Dickens, said
Chesterton, 'could only get to the most solemn emotions
adequately if he got to them through the grotesque'. Perhaps :
but equally, only through the grotesque could certain of his
artistic effects be achieved. When Dickens holds up his distorting mirror, we see, surprisingly elongated or shrunken,
ourselves – behaving much as we normally do. There is satire,
but also something else than satire here; the figures are caught
in the mirror as in a spell. It is in a spell, too, that we meet

the heroine, as the narrator first creates her for us, in an image hauntingly present long after he himself has bowed out:

But all that night, waking or in my sleep, the same thoughts recurred, and the same images retained possession of my brain. I had, ever before me, the old dark murky rooms – the gaunt suits of mail with their ghostly silent air – the faces all awry, grinning from wood and stone – the dust, and rust, and worm that lives in wood – and alone in the midst of all this lumber and decay and ugly age, the beautiful child in her gentle slumber, smiling through her light and sunny dreams.

But this is the narrator, not the author; the 'light and sunny dreams' turn to waking nightmare, and there is no fairytale prince but Kit. In many respects *The Old Curiosity Shop* is the least sentimental of novels; Little Nell's innocence is shadowed with ironies from the first.

    The Old Curiosity Shop (1840) belongs, in my view, with two other early Dickens novels, all of which stand among his greatest achievements, although only one of them has had its proper due. These are *Oliver Twist* (1837–8) and *Barnaby Rudge* (1841), two other virtuoso exercises in the grotesque. It is hard to fit them into the conventional view of Dickens's development, and this may be one reason why *The Old Curiosity Shop* and *Barnaby Rudge* have suffered comparative neglect. The conventional view assumes that there are two, or possibly three, phases in Dickens's career, with *Dombey and Son* (1846–8) (or *David Copperfield*, 1849–50) as the watershed, and an authorial progress from simplicity to complexity, optimism to pessimism, inspired slapdash to Art. Naturally there is some truth in this, but the novels I am now grouping together do not easily fit. All three are remarkably unified in mood and tone, and their artistry is nearer to *Great Expectations* (1860–1) than to *Nicholas Nickleby* (1838–9) and *Martin Chuzzlewit* (1843–4) on either side. The notion that *The Old Curiosity Shop* is 'sentimental' and *Barnaby Rudge* dull and badly organised except for the Riots, can have developed only through a remarkable tradition of critical neglect. At the risk of paradox, therefore, I want to by-pass the ending of *The Old Curiosity Shop*, which has hogged so much attention, and to look at the

work as a whole. Only two critics seem to me to have written
well on this novel : Edgar Johnson in his admirable biography
Charles Dickens: his tragedy and triumph, and Steven Marcus in
Dickens: from Pickwick to Dombey. Like all good critics, they
give the impression of opening a debate, not of closing it;
certainly they make the high opinion of this novel held by many
of Dickens's distinguished contemporaries, including Tolstoy,
seem far more understandable than it normally does.

My own method will be to examine three characters, one evil,
one good, one morally unclassifiable, and then to proceed to
some central themes. But, first, a few facts about the composition of the novel may be helpful. From the germ of Dickens's
idea, first announced to Landor in February 1840, progress
was extremely rapid. Rapidity was forced upon Dickens by
circumstances. The newly founded weekly *Master Humphrey's
Clock* made a splendid start, but sales slumped badly within a
month. Clearly, the public wanted another full-length novel,
and would let Dickens off with nothing less. Dickens, with his
unerring mixture of business acumen and actor's clairvoyance,
decided to oblige. The much-deferred *Barnaby Rudge* was once
more shelved, and the new tale started before any detailed plans
for it were complete. At first, Dickens still envisaged something much shorter, scarcely more than a moral fable or a sketch.
But his own imagination took fire along with his public's; from
the very first chapter a truly organic growth seemed to flower.
The author's chief delight in the early stages was with Dick
Swiveller, whose 'behaviour in the matter of Miss Wackles', he
wrote to Forster, 'will, I hope, give you satisfaction'. Up to
half-way through, Little Nell's fate seems to have hung in the
balance. Forster claimed this, anyway, and gave himself the
credit for her death. But the creative logic was ruthlessly
pointing in one direction; as soon as Dickens became conscious
of this, Nell was instinctively identified with Mary Hogarth, and
he looked forward to writing the ending with intense dread. 'All
night', he wrote, 'I have been pursued by the child; and this
morning I am unrefreshed and miserable.' And again, 'I am
breaking my heart over this story.' The death of Little Nell
required as much courage of him as anything in his writing

career, and the general verdict in his lifetime confirmed his own
feeling of success. The sales, by now, were enormous; when the
crowds waited to learn Nell's fate on the quayside of New York,
one hundred thousand copies were being sold. This was the
largest number on first publication that any of his major novels
ever achieved, though the Christmas books and stories later set
up records of their own.

This was the first of the novels that Dickens wrote for
weekly instead of monthly instalments, and he groaned endlessly
about the restrictions thereby imposed. It was the same with
Barnaby Rudge (the other *Master Humphrey's Clock* novel), and
with *Hard Times* later in *Household Words*. The weekly space,
he complained, gave him too little elbow-room; how could he
develop the numerous characters and plots in such a space?
Nonetheless his art seemed in many ways more compressed and
telling for the discipline; *Great Expectations* was also published later in weekly parts. *The Old Curiosity Shop* is characterised, too, by all of Dickens's early gusto; one senses here, as in
Pickwick, the sheer delight which he took, in these early days, in
his work.

II

To turn, then, to the characters. First, evil: and, in addition
to the Brasses, Dickens gives us the unforgettable figure of
Quilp:

The creature appeared quite horrible, with his monstrous head
and little body, as he rubbed his hands slowly round and round,
and round again – with something fantastic even in the manner of
performing this slight action – and, dropping his shaggy brows
and cocking his chin in the air, glanced upwards with a stealthy
look of exultation, that an imp might have copied and appropri-
ated to himself.

Quilp, says Chesterton, 'is precisely the devil of the Middle
Ages; he belongs to that amazingly healthy period when even
lost spirits were hilarious'. But hilarious for whom, one wants
to ask: for Mrs Quilp? – for Little Nell and her grandfather?
– for the normal readers of the book? For the latter, certainly,

in that we, at least, are protected by the normal barriers of art. Yet Chesterton's comment, despite its element of truth, can hardly satisfy. Isn't the 'hilarity' of Quilp largely the exuberance generated by all great art? And hasn't *this* great art a distinctive exuberance, more obviously peculiar to Dickens himself? It is in part an aesthetic quality, an Hogarthian energy of disorder and breakdown transcending the satiric impulse from which it starts. But it is also demonic exuberance straight from exper- ience – from that area of experience where Dickens's artistry seems always to thrive. Quilp's vitality, and our own vitality drawn out in answer to it, is nearer to fear than to joy. If we laugh, this is partly to tame the demonic with incredulity; isn't Quilp, after all, a game with the reader, an example of that Dickensian talent for exaggeration which we are only too eager to admire? Doubtless Dickens realised this and took pains to circumvent it, for Quilp creeps back in the uneasy silence following laughter, or joins all too horribly in the laughter himself. His relish for evil is almost creative, as though he were a Manichean devil, with a whole world to be made out of malice and spite. His very ugliness is attuned to inventiveness: we see him tormenting his wife with false endearments, ugly grimaces, threats to bite her, and making from this an evening of pure boredom transmuted, for him, by her fear. His eating and drinking are prodigiously horrible, an outrage on nature. His one relationship of mutual 'liking' – the motives of which, Dickens says, are 'to no purpose' – is the strange give-and-take of blows and defiance with Tom Scott.

Quilp's humour and malice cannot be distinguished or separated, as he stage-manages his various horrific appearances throughout the novel – grimacing in mirrors, hanging upside down from the roofs of stage-coaches, standing on windowsills, or carefully arranged as a crowning detail of the grotesque:

he soon cast his eyes upon a chair, into which he skipped with uncommon agility, and perching himself on the back with his feet upon the seat, was thus enabled to look on and listen with greater comfort to himself, besides gratifying at the same time that taste for doing something fantastic and monkey-like, which on all occasions had strong possession of him.

So he lurks, a gothic voyeur of secrets and suffering; and so in due season he dies, his body swollen with water, and is buried at a cross-roads, with a stake through the heart. As, of course, he would have wished; Dickens extends his own relish in melodrama to crown Quilp's end. It is, indeed, the creative relish in mischief and destruction for which we remember Quilp – that source in him of the mingled fear and laughter which is the tribute of Little Nell's innocence to his life. We remember the moment when Quilp talks to Brass about his plan to make Little Nell – at this time fourteen – his second wife, and dwells with revolting sensual relish on her charms. It is the scene where he is forcing Brass to smoke tobacco frenziedly 'against infection from fever', and Brass's comment, gasped out in the midst of this torture, 'What a remarkably pleasant way he has with children!' is quintessential – funny and horrible at once. There is also the splendid scene when Quilp has made Dick Swiveller drunk, and Dick, forgetting Quilp's presence, drops into maudlin soliloquy:

'Here's a miserable orphan for you. Here,' said Mr Swiveller, raising his voice to a high pitch, and looking sleepily around, 'is a miserable orphan!'
　　'Then,' said somebody hard by, 'let me be a father to you.'

Quilp still there, laconic and malicious – and the serious glance at father-and-son relationships enhances the well-judged cynicism of his remark. The timing is perfect, both Quilp's and Dickens's; the reader knows that Quilp has been making Dick drunk for a purpose, but he shares Dick's surprise that Quilp is still there. The pure humour is helped by our knowledge that Dick is a fair match for Quilp in all matters, including resilience; Mr Swiveller's tipsy self-pity is as zestfully creative as Quilp's relished false friendship and sinister charm. More genuinely sinister, because the victim is so much more vulnerable, is Quilp's taunting of poor Mrs Quilp with inventories of torments, when she makes her last pathetic attempt to approach him as his wife:

'I'll keep watch-dogs in the yard that'll growl and bite – I'll have mantraps, cunningly altered and improved for catching

women – I'll have spring guns that shall explode when you
tread upon the wires, and blow you into little pieces.'

Like Shakespeare, Dickens endows some of his most evil
characters with humour, energy and inventiveness; the paradox
of Iago is interestingly parallel to Quilp. Like Shakespeare, too,
he is more concerned to present evil than to explain it. 'How
could you be so cruel?' sobs Mrs Quilp, and 'How could I be
so cruel!' mocks the dwarf. 'Because I was in the humour. I'm
in the humour now. I shall be cruel when I like.' This reminder
of the irrationality of pure evil, its terror, goes beyond analysis.
Its force is wholly in its truth.

It is no new observation to point to similarities between
Quilp and his creator, but Quilp could indeed be a partial self-
portrait, Quilpishly drawn. His ogreish geniality is close to
Dickens's: is it Dickens or Quilp who writes of Sally Brass like
this?

In face she bore a striking resemblance to her brother Sampson
– so exact, indeed, was the likeness between them, that had it
consorted with Miss Brass's maiden modesty and gentle
womanhood to have assumed her brother's clothes in a frolic
and sat down beside him, it would have been difficult for the
oldest friend of the family to determine which was Sampson
and which Sally, especially as the lady carried upon her upper
lip certain reddish demonstrations, which, if the imagination
had been assisted by her attire, might have been mistaken for a
beard. These were, however, in all probability, nothing more
than eyelashes in the wrong place, as the eyes of Miss Brass
were quite free from any such natural impertinences. In complexion Miss Brass was sallow – rather a dirty sallow, so to
speak – but this hue was agreeably relieved by the healthy glow
which mantled in the extreme tip of her laughing nose. Her
voice was exceedingly impressive – deep and rich in quality,
and, once heard, not easily forgotten . . .

And so on . . . The mingling of cruelty, playfulness and deadly
accuracy is decidedly Quilpish, and while it is true that Dickens
himself always looked for women who were fair game before
tormenting them, when he found one – the mannish and
shrewish Miss Brass, Cleopatra in *Dombey and Son*, almost any

woman over twenty who tried to look young or who wore make-up – he had about as much mercy as Quilp. It is even possible that Kate Dickens had cause to remember poor Mrs Quilp in the years ahead, as Dickens dragged her over the ocean and across America one year, through hair-raising exploits in Europe the next. Dickens's account of his daily life was a saga of restless energy. From the obsessive walks at night in the streets of London, through endless amateur theatricals, to the fatal readings of his later years, he sought violent excitement as a daily food. All this side of him is mirrored in Quilp – which is perhaps why the dwarf's macabre imagination is so Dickensian. There is the morning when Quilp wakes up in a hammock in his riverside hideout, and ponders a possible metamorphosis in the night:

The first sound that met his ears in the morning – as he half opened his eyes, and, finding himself so unusually near the ceiling, entertained a drowsy idea that he must have been transformed into a fly or bluebottle in the course of the night – was that of a stifled sobbing and weeping in the room.

This pressure towards symbolism is as prophetic of Dickens's later techniques as it is of Kafka; it is a further reminder of how completely Quilp eludes 'explanations' of a normal kind.

Not, of course, that there are *no* explanations; Quilp's psychology is partly understandable in Freudian terms. The driving power of his life is hatred, and hatred is one classic response – perhaps the most spirited, certainly the most spontaneous – of the freak. Quilp is not content to be exploited like Mr Vuffin's dwarfs in a freakshow, and prized for his wrinkles; he is content only with punishing, and when possible destroying, the world where he must be a freak. Since revenge is the basic motive, he uses his freakishness as the weapon most appropriately to hand. The torment is in the inescapable consciousness of a world alien to him; if the world solves the problem of coping with him by way of circuses, he will find an answering solution to the world. Where could his energy turn, if not to rage and destruction? The only completely full-blooded alternative is sanctity, but does the world take kindly to a

sanctified dwarf? It is the triumph of Dickens's art that though
he does not analyse, he creates understanding; Quilp's greatest
hatred is reserved, surely incontrovertibly, for another grotesque, who responds to his predicament in the opposite way.
One of the most powerful scenes occurs when Quilp destroys a
ship's figurehead in a fit of uncontrollable malice, seeing in
its ugliness not his own image (as Brass does), but Kit's.
The intention, analysed, becomes a kind of sympathetic magic,
but Quilp does not analyse; he acts, and enjoys a sense of
release.

Our last view of Quilp in death is scarcely less effective; his
appearance is a fitting crown to his life, and Dickens is left,
now that Quilp himself is no longer able, to relish its flavour of
irony and spite: 'The hair, stirred by the damp breeze, played
in a kind of mockery of death – such a mockery as the dead man
himself would have delighted in when alive – about its head.'
Though Quilp's character is evil, he remains hilarious for the
reader; in this, Chesterton was undoubtedly right. He belongs
with a range of other characters – almost peculiar in English
literature to Shakespeare and Dickens – in whom we meet the
same striking paradox: that though they originate in satire,
and are in varying degrees wicked, they establish themselves
for very many readers as 'friends for life'. How does this come
about? – certainly not by any perversity on the part of the
readers, who are surely responding to an exuberance in the
creation itself. Yet it is not wholly the alchemy of art that
accounts for this paradox, though that must be part of it; for
whereas Pecksniff, Mrs Gamp, Joe Bagstock, Mr Micawber,
Podsnap, even Silas Wegg would be high on anyone's list of
such characters, there are other vivid characters in Dickens – Sir
John Chester, Jonas Chuzzlewit, Carker, Uriah Heep for
instance – for whom no such claim could be made. Tentatively,
my own feeling is that this is to do with creativity. In various
ways, no matter how twisted, Quilp, Pecksniff, Mrs Gamp, Joe
Bagstock, Mr Micawber are among the great creative artists
in Dickens's work. Their creations are often far from agreeable,
yet they all take pleasure in creating; they convey the genuine
energy and exuberance of the creator himself. In contrast,

Chester, Carker, Jonas Chuzzlewit, Uriah Heep have only the cold simulacrum of artistic creation – a devious, purely intellectual resourcefulness, wholly dedicated to self: the Gorgon's bloodless alchemy against life. We remember these latter characters with all the pleasure created by Dickens's own artistry, but they do not light up with their own additional warmth from within.

The Old Curiosity Shop offers this kind of paradox in good measure, since it also contains another of Dickens's great creative characters, Dick Swiveller.

III

But before turning to Dick, let us look at the character who most nearly balances Quilp, and who bears the main burden of virtue in this novel (if we exclude the heroine): Kit Nubbles. Quilp evil, Kit good: but Kit scarcely less of a grotesque. His role is a fascinating cross of Knight and Fool; though his first appearance is as 'the comedy' of Little Nell's life, he is to carry Dickens's main perception of disinterested love. It is significant that he, like Quilp, makes use of his ugliness, but to produce laughter and happiness in the child:

The lad had a remarkable manner of standing sideways as he spoke, and thrusting his head forward over his shoulder, as if he could not get at his voice without that accompanying action. I think he would have amused one anywhere, but the child's exquisite enjoyment of his oddity, and the relief it was to find that there was something she associated with merriment, in a place that appeared so unsuited to her, were quite irresistible. It was a great point, too, that Kit himself was flattered by the sensation he created, and after several efforts to preserve his gravity, burst into a loud roar, and stood with his mouth wide open and his eyes nearly shut, laughing violently.

This is not without its cost; Kit is one 'whose laugh had been all the time one of that sort which very little would change into a cry', and his destiny is far removed from the lady he serves. His family lives in an 'extremely poor and homely place', with an 'air of comfort about it'; it is 'rather a queer-looking family:

Kit, his mother, and the children, being all strongly alike'.
Kit's 'good-humour' is more a virtue than a mood; it is closer
to eighteenth-century 'cheerfulness' than to romantic *élan*.
There is a delightful and healing moment when Kit comes home
with Little Nell's bird, which Quilp has made him fight for,
and an infectious gaiety spreads back from the immediate
situation to the family group :

Kit laughing so heartily, with his swollen and bruised face
looking out of the towel, made little Joseph laugh, and then his
mother laughed, and then the baby crowed and kicked with
great glee, and then they all laughed in concert : partly because
of Kit's triumph and partly because they were very fond of each
other.

'Healing' this certainly is; its effect runs directly counter to the
evil world of the Brasses and Quilp. Kit's is a good magic, which
defines the limits of nightmare and keeps hope alive. It is as
though Dickens were resolved to depict the reality of chivalry
with none of its trappings – an undertaking profoundly subversive, in that Kit's class, appearance, social uncouthness seem
at the opposite pole to chivalry, and clearly he couldn't have
married Little Nell, even had she lived. He is a kind of polar
opposite to Chester in *Barnaby Rudge*, whose perfect manners
and frozen heart Dickens depicts with cold hatred. Kit, with
none of the appearances of chivalry, has all the reality – which
is why he is so central to a novel where the conflict of appearance
and reality is a central theme. 'Codlin's the friend, not Short,'
says Codlin – and his phrase links with similar professions of
false friendship throughout the book – Quilp to Dick Swiveller,
Sampson Brass to Kit. The theme is inverted in Kit's tribulations, first when he is represented to Little Nell's grandfather
as an enemy (by Quilp), and then when he is gaoled as a thief
(at the instigation of Brass). Throughout such scenes, the evil
are articulate and the good puzzled. In a world where the
language of virtue is stolen by vice, what is virtue to say ? This
theme links the novel (it is one of several links) with *King Lear* :
like a more agreeable Cordelia, Little Nell becomes a touchstone
of moral reality in a world of lies. For all the grotesquerie and
deceitfulness, she knows the difference between friend and foe.

In spirit she is protected by her virtue, even though her body is subject to more tragic laws. She trusts Kit, despite all the appearances against him, and he is rewarded by her trust (it is, properly speaking, his only reward, since Barbara belongs well outside the ambience where Kit is a knight).

The lower-class boy is not in fact a disguised or incognito nobleman; his ugliness is not an irresistible romantic magnet, like Mr Rochester's; his devotion to Little Nell points to none of the conventional romantic rewards. Dickens does not sentimentalise *here*, and he does not oversimplify; he offers, in defiance of conventions, the simple truth about virtue like Kit's. Kit imagines that his honesty will protect him against false accusations, but though Little Nell understands him, the rest of the world is unimpressed. Kit is hauled trembling into court and found guilty; 'it's all one now', says the Turnkey, 'whether he did it or not'. Even Mrs Nubbles is not wholly sure of Kit, despite her loyalty, since her moral judgement is distorted by a puritanical and joyless religion which Kit, like his creator, hates. Yet Dickens achieves one of his most distinctive effects when Kit cries out in his innocence to know who doesn't trust him. While socially naïve, this is morally challenging; trusting Kit is excellent insight in a wicked world.

Kit offers Nell his home, when she is homeless; his loyal protectiveness (unbeknown to her) when she is threatened; his cheerfulness when she is downcast. The effect is marvellously positive because it is so simply realistic; it stands up in a novel dominated by Quilp. Of course Kit's future bride must not be Little Nell, but Barbara: poor Barbara! – so loyal and silly, so teased by Kit's obtuseness, so inferior to Kit in moral stature, so exposed by Dickens to avuncular winks, pinches and nods. What Barbara has to put up with! – not least, Kit's endless recitals of the virtues of Nell. But she puts up with it and wins through to marry Kit and cherish him; and she is exactly the kind of person that someone like Kit would, with luck, marry in actual life. It is this aspect of the novel which most jars today (except for the ending), yet Dickens's realism is scarcely at fault. The whole episode of Kit's courting – Mrs Nubbles's prompting, the visit to Astley's, the authorial gloatings – rings

B

as true now as it ever did. The author simply steps into the
shoes of a favourite uncle, and depicts courtship as if it were a
supernumerary Christmas. Which, often enough, is what it is
– even for an Arthur Seaton, one suspects, after the wild oats
have been sown. The main thing in common is a blessed suspension of normal criticism; the underprivileged count their
blessings, and Aunt Jane hears that she is the grandest old lady
in the world. The good things of life are enjoyed – food,
shelter, drink, family and friends; and an evening out at Astley's
is just as innocent as Dickens describes it, whatever Thackeray's
worldlings, to take a contrary instance, would find.

There is something childlike in such times, the recapture
of wonder; it is the good intoxication of the virtuous poor.
The secret behind it Dickens knew as well as anyone; by his
passionate crusade against poverty he had earned the right to
celebrate it; by his refusal to use such terms as 'virtuous poor'
in cold analysis, he could afford to let the reality be seen. And
which of us can be called a social realist if we refuse this kind
of reality? The human heart is not a sophisticated sport.

Kit marries Barbara, and it is right that he should, but I think
that Dickens was uneasy about him, for somewhat different
reasons, all the same. Did he realise that though Kit is so much
more valuable than Quilp, he is also much less interesting?
Perhaps he wished a better destiny for Kit's virtue than life
could possibly offer; perhaps he felt that allowances must too
explicitly be made. By means of Barbara, he at least avoided
the more serious embarrassments (serious aesthetic embarrassments) that confronted him later with Tom Pinch. Barbara is
admirable for Kit, and Dickens is right to show this; but would
Kit and Barbara have been among his own 'friends for life'?

I V

Quilp evil, Kit good, Dick Swiveller neither – simply one of the
most splendid creations in the world. 'At length there sauntered
up . . . a figure conspicuous for its dirty smartness' . . . and Dick
saunters into the novel, 'merry, but not wise'. As he cheats,
lies, drinks, charms, loves and looks after himself ('Love-

making yes, Promising no,' said Dick. 'There can be no action for breach') he seems a perfect prototype for the anti-hero of today. His specious lies to creditors, his growing list of streets he can't risk being seen in, his plan to write a letter to his aunt covered with 'tears', his grandiloquent, half-rhyming soliloquies, his abortive wooing of Sophy Wackles – all these things exist in a world that Kingsley Amis has coarsened, brutalised and made his own. Like all good rogues, Dick Swiveller jests with himself. ' "Marchioness," said Mr Swiveller, rising, "the word of a gentleman is as good as his bond – sometimes better, as in the present case, where his bond might prove but a doubtful sort of security." ' He is lured into evil by Quilp, for reasons of vanity, poverty, self-interest and thoughtlessness, all of which the dwarf fully understands and exploits. But we never feel that he is essentially evil. He toys with evil only when he doesn't bother to imagine it : or rather, when his particular exuberance of imagination converts it into the innocence of farce. Given a real situation, and someone in need, he will always ring true. He is a hero as exempt from normal moral criteria as the third son of a fairytale, who is fated to make errors, get into scrapes, suffer for his sins, win our hearts, come out right in the end. It is no surprise to find Dick brooding on his destiny; we see ahead of him what his destiny is to be. So he decides to shield the Marchioness from the fairly serious crime of which he suspects her; and the Marchioness saves his life, and marries him.

Dick Swiveller is miles removed from Little Nell, and the novel rightly insulates them; but he is well placed to make on Quilp, in comic vein, the comment that Little Nell could also make :

'I not a choice spirit!' cried Quilp.
'Devil a bit, sir,' returned Dick. 'A man of your appearance couldn't be. If you're any spirit at all, sir, you're an evil spirit. Choice spirits,' added Dick, smiting himself on the breast, 'are quite a different-looking sort of people, you may take your oath of that, sir!'

Predictably, Dick fits admirably into Brass's ménage, when Quilp's malevolence has delivered him up to it; bemused by Sally Brass, and by her 'intolerable headdress', he nonetheless strikes up a manly *bonhomie* with her fairly soon. His initial temptation to knock the headdress off with a ruler he *just* suppresses; but only by gazing fixedly at her until almost hypnotised by the sight. When she leaves the room, his fullness of joy expresses itself in a 'manic hornpipe' – and, later, in characteristic verbal embroideries of his predicament, where everything is comedy – his unspoken rejoinders to Sally, cocky and irreverent; his taunting of his personal destiny 'as heroes do', says Dickens, 'when in a mess'. The whole Brass household becomes tinged with the comic-sinister; the arrival of the eccentric 'single gentleman' as lodger is like a projection of Dick's mind. 'She-dragons in the business, conducting themselves like professional gentlemen,' Dick reflects to himself, 'plain cooks three feet high, strangers walking in and going to bed without leave or licence in mid-day . . .' It is a fitting *milieu* for his humour to transform. Dick is a healing force in this world, as Kit is in Nell's – neither can alter evil, but each alleviates it in a distinctive way. Sally Brass, mediated by Dick, is at her most grotesque but her least unpleasant; it is possible to see her, suddenly, simply as a mannish and bossy old maid. Certainly Dick brings out the best in her, not necessarily for sexual reasons; she finds him attractive for his vigour and health. He presides for a time as a Lord of Misrule, and his flamboyant misrule almost transforms the deeper evil of the house. This may be one reason why Dickens's very bitter and unusually badly written dismissal of the Brasses in his final chapter comes as a shock: it is obviously justified, yet Dick's imagination has very nearly converted the Brasses into a lighter frame.

Dick's function in the novel is purely natural – a sunny interlude in stormy weather. He lights up in the warmth of Dickens's approval – a force for good, outside all social conventions and in defiance of most of them: as incontrovertibly good as the superficially similar Sim Tappertit in *Barnaby Rudge* is bad. To an even greater extent than Quilp, he may strike us as a partial self-portrait, an embodiment of that side of Dickens's manifold nature which loved to drink in convivial company, visit the theatre, play pranks, and sport in the light.

It was Longfellow who, seeing this side of Dickens in America, said that he had 'a slight dash of the Dick Swiveller about him'; the 'slight dash', in clothing and social manner as well as mood, was the reason, no doubt, why Dickens remained an outsider, for all his fame. There is an episode recorded in Edgar Johnson's biography which catches Dickens in his Dick Swiveller mood:

Once, when the Hogarths were all quietly sitting in the family drawing room, 'a young man dressed as a sailor jumped in at the window, danced a hornpipe, whistling the tune, jumped out again, and a few minutes later Charles Dickens walked gravely in at the door, as if nothing had happened, shook hands all round, and then, at the sight of their puzzled faces, burst into a roar of laughter.'

Dick is full of vitality and zest, of creative ingenuity as spontaneous as Quilp's, and harnessed to spontaneous goodwill. No wonder he is closer to his author than Kit – Kit who doesn't create, doesn't aspire, can't transform Sally Brass into a she-dragon and a kitchen-maid into a Marchioness, can't rise totally out of his background and class. Dickens loved Kit, admired him, fought his battles, extolled his virtues, but he spent his life escaping from Kit – from everything for which Kit ultimately stood. Kit might have irradiated a blacking factory with virtue, and almost redeemed it; it is Dick Swiveller who would have whistled himself up and away.

v

The various grotesques in *The Old Curiosity Shop* are interestingly contrasted, but one thing they have in common; they are not so much explained by their author as exhibited. Explanations appear and disappear, but our main impression of them deepens all the time.

It is sometimes assumed, even by Dickens's admirers, that there is something inferior in this method; George Eliot's novels, in particular, caused later Victorian critics to see psychological analysis as a *sine qua non*. Yet the triumphant exhibition of characters and events is one of the many things which Dickens has in common with Shakespeare, and in the very greatest art perhaps it must always come first. We have

only to think of real life and its interesting people to realise
that explanations take a very second place. Naturally, complex
acts have many sources, but the sources hardly exhaust the acts,
while 'explanations' can degenerate into the merely polemical
exercise of friend or foe. If we ponder on Gladstone or Disraeli,
Lloyd George or Winston Churchill, is there not first a
memorable image, clear-cut and ineffaceable, with strong
intimations of richness beneath? So it is in fiction, with Dickens's
great characters – who have also, again like Shakespeare's, a
distinct tinge of heaven or hell. 'Will you, I pray, demand that
demi-devil', cries Othello, 'Why he has thus ensnared my soul
and body?' But Iago is silent and the critics are baffled; there
are too many explanations, all plausible, all conflicting, none
adequate to explain the horror we see. But the horror is real,
and we cannot doubt it; in Iago, Goneril, Regan, Shakespeare
enacts the mystery of iniquity, just as in certain other characters
he enacts the mystery of good. In Coleridge's terms, such art
moves on the plane of Reason rather than of Understanding;
certain supreme realities are imaginatively realised to the full.
To try to recapture such art for 'Understanding' can be deeply
misleading; it has led certain critics of Dickens to mistake his
central greatness for some kind of peripheral defect. We have
heard of his 'Calvinism', his fatalism, his caprice, his use of
'coincidence', his propensity to 'caricature' or 'melodrama', all
offered as excuses for quite non-existent faults. His characters
have been quite particularly maltreated – to hear certain critics
talking of extravagant humours, or repetitive verbal rhetoric,
you would think they had never seen Mrs Gamp passing down
the street.

My own view is that Quilp, Kit, the Brasses, Dick Swiveller
exist because Dickens has created them; they radiate reality,
lighting up the world and the people we know. In their prime
reality, they are incontrovertible; who can say that Quilp
wouldn't have treated his wife as he does, or that Dick Swiveller
would have been less thoughtful about Kit? The world is full of
Dickens's people because he created people; he looked at the
world in its strangeness, and made what he saw.

This is not to assert that there are no rational explanations of his people; but simply, that rational explanations are as little complete for them as they are for ourselves. We are reminded in the greatest art that only by dulling our perceptions, hardening our morality, donning blinkers and muzzles, can we ever persuade ourselves that we 'fully understand'. This, again, accords with Coleridge's theory, which allowed the importance of rational understanding, but subordinated it to intuitive perception of the wonder of life. I suppose this is why, looking round us at friends and acquaintances, we so often feel: yes! – there to the life is Hamlet or Falstaff, Quilp or Dick Swiveller, in a way that we never quite feel: yes! – there is Elizabeth Bennet or Dorothea Brooke. The latter characters are deeply revealing to sensitive reflection, they are fine parables and *exempla*, but it is the former who have the unique unexpectedness of life. Indeed, it is because they remain unique that they seem universal; it is because we know, like Prufrock, that we are not Prince Hamlet nor were meant to be, that Prince Hamlet remains the mirror of us all. That, I take it, is why such figures are always highly idiosyncratic, in life as in literature; they are real with the full courage of their reality – the courage so easily whittled away by introspection and analytical thought. The universality of Jane Austen's characters is in their range of moral experience; the universality of Dickens's is in their unfailing illusion of life.

When critics maintain that Jane Austen's world is more 'real' than Dickens's, they usually seem to mean one of three things. The first is that the 'real' world consists only of middle-class, respectable people, and that any other kinds of people do not really exist. Surprisingly often this turns out to be the underlying assumption, if Jonas Chuzzlewit, or Miss Mowcher, or Jenny Wren is declared less 'real' than Fanny Price. The second is that such people do exist, but ought not to be depicted; that only a small range of humanity, suitably reduced by explanation, belongs to the province of art. The third, which I take to be the most sophisticated (if one leaves aside formal literary theory), is that literature exists as a kind of superior social reporting, in which ideas can be complex, but people have to be morally analysed, generalised and judged.

Jane Austen is much greater than people holding any of these assumptions usually realise, but she does not offend their assumptions in any too flagrant way. Dickens, on the other hand, does offend them; he offends the instinct for complacent and comfortable recognition which all these assumptions to some degree serve. His world is one which intelligence and sensitivity cannot plumb, cannot very radically heal or alter; it is a world where openness to experience, however sophisticated or unsophisticated, is a prerequisite to any other virtues there may be. The world of Quilp and Kit, Dennis the Hangman and Gabriel Varden, Captain Cuttle and Joey Bagstock, the Murdstones and Betsey Trotwood, Miss Havisham and Joe Gargery, Jenny Wren and Silas Wegg may be far removed from rational explanations and panaceas; it is not, however, removed either from real experiences that we might at some time encounter if we have eyes for them, or from the two or three apocalyptic explorations of human destiny that have shaped our lives. It accords very well with the grand melodrama of heaven and hell depicted by the Christian tradition, and with the grand inner melodrama depicted by Freud and Jung. It accords very much less well, as its author was the first to proclaim and realise, with the sober speculations of Jeremy Bentham, the *laissez faire* utilitarians, and the earlier Mill.

VI

In *The Old Curiosity Shop* such dramatic contrasts of character are heightened by the alternation of scenes of good and evil; the reader is frankly amazed by a world where such contrasts can be. How can Quilp's treatment of Mrs Quilp exist in the same universe as Nell's treatment of her grandfather, or Sampson Brass's spirit co-exist with Dick's? Dickens did not invent this world, but he did transform it. His creative energies both reflect the world, and make it anew.

We notice how characters and their backgrounds interact and interrelate with each other, in this grand exhibition of the grotesque. Mr Trent is so assimilated to the old curiosity shop that he seems like an extension of it. He carries it with him, until the whole world becomes the shop, and the novel's title remains true to the end. He emerges from the shop at the very start of the novel on his mysterious mission, and is swallowed up in the labyrinth of London streets. Is he a miser, a criminal, an extreme eccentric? – we see him driven by restlessness like an ancient mariner, his compulsions reflected in the night-long anxieties of the child. He merges, in the night watches, into the child's reveries; she fancies ugly faces peering from the crooked chimney stacks, and would have to assure herself 'that everything was in its place and hadn't moved'. When men pass with a coffin, she thinks of someone lying dead; after the normal goodnight kiss, she lies awake in her bed, fearing suicide as the old man's end.

As in *Oliver Twist*, a child's consciousness seems merged in its destiny; unlike the other main characters in this novel, but like Oliver, she is mainly passive in her role. Though she sets out on her wanderings, and guides the old man through peril, it is surprising how little active impression we have. Our sense of her grows through our response to her predicament, not through a direct view of her thoughts, or her motives for choice. There is a curious trap here for the hostile reader – a trap which also exists, and for the same reason, in *Oliver Twist*. In all Dickens's later novels, children are presented differently. Florence Dombey, David Copperfield, Pip, Lizzie Hexam mature through suffering; Paul Dombey is a unique study of the mind of a sensitive and doomed child. But in *Oliver Twist* and *The Old Curiosity Shop*, the child's role is passive. Men and circumstances act upon the child, and are in turn judged by their effects. We are asked to imagine the plight of a human being in a particular setting; the setting itself is richly presented and the child is a normal, vulnerable human like ourselves. The trap for the reader, therefore, is to find Nell and Oliver 'wooden' – which amounts to an imaginative failure to enter into the experience of the book.

In *The Old Curiosity Shop* the setting has the intensity of myth, as well as its realism. ' . . . let us wander barefoot through the world', says Little Nell, as they set off on their wanderings; 'we will be happy'. They will be 'as free and happy as birds',

agrees her grandfather, and the words resonate like symbols
from a different world. Quilp likes *his* birds in cages, and Kit
barely rescues Little Nell's bird from death. The surrounding
omens are all unpropitious. Little Nell is deliberately romanti-
cising, to rally her grandfather; like a more humane Cordelia,
she adapts strict truthfulness to the weakness of a grandfather-
child. The old man's reply is tinged with senility. His vision of
new happiness waiting for them is no more sanctioned than
Lear's image of two birds in a cage. Yet this exchange is no
more simply ironic than it is simply sentimental. The vision of
idyllic wanderings through nature, far from cities, far from
enemies, recalls old dreams of nature's love for a favourite child.
The effect, in this darkened world, is close to the Epistle to the
Hebrews : here we have no abiding city, but we seek one that
is to come. The wanderers are indeed exiles, in search of a
kingdom; though Dickens is seldom explicitly Christian in his
earlier works, the myth of pilgrims and strangers had an early
hold on his mind. (This is one reason why the ending of *The Old
Curiosity Shop* ought not to be dismissed as 'religiose' until its
claims to be religious have been understood first.) The setting
out of the travellers is surrounded with enigma. As they pass
out of sight, we return to Quilp, presiding over the destruction
of their former home.

On the journey the old man's senility emerges in the feverishness with which he seeks to escape from his enemies, in his
childlike pleasure in Punch and Judy and the travelling showmen,
in the increasing complacency with which he accepts their
reversal of roles. ('It is true', he admits long before this, 'that
in many respects I am the child, and she is the grown person.')
Nell is not a grown person, and he knows it; but this knowledge
is altogether too painful to bear. The psychology of his gambling
is wonderfully attuned to this moral escapism; Dickens's
analytical insight receives a larger setting, as usual, than itself.
Mr Trent knows that he gambles solely for Nell's sake, so is
not Providence bound to favour his cause? This half-super-
stitious, wholly home-spun reasoning makes 'luck' respectable;
and places the onus of bad luck squarely on Providence itself.
So Providence can both be blamed, and freshly invoked, through

each catastrophe; and meanwhile the fever in the blood, the compulsion, thrives on this hope beyond hope. With its simulacrum of reasoning and its irresistible compulsiveness, the old man's vice resembles delirium, or the borderline between sleep and waking in a troubled dream. Quilp's malice is a hard, external spotlight upon it, but Nell's suffering lights up the horror from within.

So gambling becomes part of the novel's prevailing grotesquerie, and seems more a symbol of evil than its ultimate cause. It is part of the web in which Nell finds her destiny, a Cordelia accompanying old age on its path of ruin and death. There is the harrowing progress of the old man's failure under his sufferings; his intermittent bouts of gambling, with their erosion of dignity; and the final descent into plaintive despair. 'Nothing to fear', lies Nell, in her role of more humane Cordelia – and 'No-one is true to me,' whines the old man, 'not even Nell.' The old man's physical and moral weakness are sadly familiar, but his words latch on to the novel's central theme of 'true' *versus* 'false'. As in *King Lear*, the reality of 'true' becomes increasingly real to its audience, but in no obvious manner does it operate healingly inside the tale. The child's heroism and love are refracted by the context; if they have a meaning, it must lie beyond tragic suffering in the human world.

VII

Some of the greatest writing in the novel is to be found in chapters 43 to 45, when the first clear signs of Nell's illness appear. She has rescued her grandfather from his most terrible temptation – again by lying – and they are once more on their way.

In the pale moonlight, which lent a wanness of its own to the delicate face where thoughtful care already mingled with the winning grace and loveliness of youth, the too bright eye, the spiritual head, the lips that pressed each other with such high resolve and courage of the heart, the slight figure firm in its bearing, and yet so very weak, told their silent tale . . .

It is now that the travellers strike the industrial Midlands, and

Dickens describes for the first time in his work (*Hard Times*
was the next) a scene that had very powerfully affected him on
the Birmingham to Wolverhampton road. In this novel the
scene is depicted through the consciousness of the senile man
and the tubercular girl; the feverishness of their vision turns it
to nightmare as they stagger on, desperately tired and fright-
ened, the girl fulfilling her parental responsibility to the last.
The phantasmagoric quality seems distinctly 'modern'; perhaps
their fevered vision mirrors a social reality, but no simple
equation is allowed. It is a clear literary progenitor of the Circe
episode in *Ulysses*, of the scene in Orwell's *A Clergyman's
Daughter* when the heroine, down and out, spends a night
among the derelicts in Trafalgar Square. It is artistically more
honest (if not necessarily more powerful) than Eliot's vision of
London in *The Waste Land*, where a sick vision of the city is
too simply translated into cultural myth.

Whether Dickens fully understood his own technique is,
however, doubtful. The relevant passages are too long to quote
in full, and selective quotation is bound to diminish the effect.
They are reminiscent of certain other passages in Dickens when
some nightmare vision of evil is imposed upon – or discovered
in – scenes of squalor or violence: the riots in *Barnaby Rudge*,
Jonas Chuzzlewit's night walk with murder, the railway passages leading up to Carker's death, the Terror in *A Tale of Two
Cities* – at least one example springs to mind from every book.
There are reasons to believe that Dickens aimed fairly directly
at social and psychological realism in such scenes, and that he
was more preoccupied with simple, powerful moral effects than
with the process of art. In a letter to Forster, who had been with
him on his journey through the Black Country, Dickens
expressed some slight dissatisfaction with what he had achieved.
He had sworn to strike 'the heaviest blow in my power' on
behalf of the industrial victims, and this experience was already
set aside for a novel at some later date. He seems to have felt
that his depiction in *The Old Curiosity Shop* fell short of the
whole truth. This can hardly be because the pages fail in horror
and misery; it must be that Dickens intended some more
penetrating analysis of the social forces and philosophies which

had brought such horror about. It was not until *Hard Times* that he expressed this 'truth' as he fully understood it – and there the didactic intention, the determination to confront utilitarian impoverishments of the spirit starkly and challengingly, produced a novel rich and powerful, but oddly removed from the normal resources of his strength. In *The Old Curiosity Shop* he moves in his more usual ambience; the description resonates more subjectively and suggestively than it does in the later book. Perhaps Nell's vision *is* that of a girl feverish and slowly dying; but if her images ring true to experience, is this not more disturbing, even, than a social tract? The social point is made glancingly; it is as little underlined as the relevance of Mr Trent's vice to the stock-jobbing and fraudulent financial empires in the City of London. But symbolic echoes are set up in the grotesque world – which seems poised, aesthetically, between Hogarth's Gin Lane and Dante's Hell.

It is in the middle of these fevered visions that Dickens produces one of his most memorable images of good. Little Nell and her grandfather are succoured by a coarse, poor, simple-minded workman, who offers them his god: the great blast-furnace fire where his life is passed. Nell is carried, saturated and ill, to the fire he has always worshipped, and, lying beside it, she hears the strange tale of his life, and the pictures he sees in the flames. She falls, finally, into a deep and easy sleep, and the next day passes out of his life. The workman, anonymous, halting in communication, shut in his anxious melancholy, has made his offering to one less fortunate than himself. He is an astonishing, profoundly moving creation; he belongs to the creative region where Dickens is set wholly apart. Though the ending is slightly spoiled for sophisticated readers by some explicit moralising, the real power of the episode is beyond formulation at all. But the moralising, too, is the mark of Dickens's greatness; for all his fantastic creative insight, he does not forget the majority of simple readers who also hung on his words.

The novel ends with Little Nell's death, and her grandfather's sorrow. The great crux of sentimentality I am avoiding here, though I think that an examination of the squeamishness

of our own century about such real and life-giving emotions as
sentimentality and heroism is long overdue. The ending of the
novel is not as good as most of the rest of it, but is far from
failure. My purpose has been with the underlying unity of the
rest.

3 *Barnaby Rudge*
the genesis of violence

THE original title of *Barnaby Rudge* was *Gabriel Varden, the Locksmith of London*, and it should have been Dickens's first published novel; instead, it turned out to be his fifth. The idea had been in his mind since 1836, when he entered into a contract for it with Macrone, the publisher of *Sketches by Boz*. The terms agreed became unsatisfactory, however, with the huge success of *Pickwick* (1836–7), and after angry scenes *Gabriel Varden* was transferred to Bentley. In the meantime, other creative projects had intervened, first *Oliver Twist* (1837–8) and then, overlapping with *Oliver* for several months, *Nicholas Nickleby* (1838–9).

Not until the winter of 1839, when these two major novels were finished, did Barnaby's turn seem to have come. The first ten pages were written, and Dickens hoped to complete the rest at speed. But at this very moment new obstacles presented themselves. There was a move of house to be attended to, and a new weekly publication *Master Humphrey's Clock* to be prepared. Bentley, moreover, had made the mistake of trying to force Dickens's hand by advertising the forthcoming novel in the newspapers, and this determined the author to take his time. When *Master Humphrey's Clock* made an uneven start early in 1840 and needed rescuing, Dickens embarked upon a supposedly short tale, which turned itself into *The Old Curiosity Shop*. So 1840 was devoted to Quilp, Dick Swiveller and Little Nell, and *Barnaby* once again had to wait.

It was not, however, waiting fruitlessly. There was Grip, for instance, a pet raven in Dickens's household, who took the author's fancy at this time, and inspired his affectionate wit in several letters. And in July 1840 the public hanging of the murderer Courvoisier joined Grip in that area of Dickens's mind where Lord George Gordon, riding Londonwards on his horse, took clearer shape. By now further impressive displays of Dickens's wrath against publishers had intervened, and the Shandyan embryo of *Barnaby* had been transferred once again, from Bentley to Chapman & Hall.

At last, with Little Nell dead and triumphant, and Quilp exorcised, *Barnaby* could no longer be delayed. Yet right on the threshold Dickens hesitated. 'I didn't stir out yesterday,' he wrote to Forster early in 1841, 'but sat and thought all day; not writing a line; not so much as the cross of a t or the dot of an i.' What, this time, was the difficulty? Had his exhausting struggles with publishers affected, slightly, his creative exuberance, casting a sombre colouring, even, over the work to be done? Or might it have been that he sensed just ahead of him more ambitious possibilities, more exacting challenges, than any he had known before? Whatever the explanation, this eleventh-hour delay was also conquered. On 13 February 1841 *Barnaby Rudge* started appearing, in weekly parts, and as the successor to *The Old Curiosity Shop* in *Master Humphrey's Clock*, all previous arrangements and contracts notwithstanding.

Once he had started, Dickens settled down to composition in his usual style. 'I was always sure I could make a good thing of *Barnaby*,' he wrote to Forster, 'and I think you'll find that it comes out strong to the last word . . . I am in great heart and spirits with the story.' It is clear that the idea of the 1780 riots had powerfully influenced him, and that he had undertaken detailed research on his historical theme. The day-by-day events are faithfully charted, and the setting is accurate. Dickens's Gordon is a plausible, if colourful, interpretation of his deranged original, and even minor figures like the Lord Mayor of London are made vividly alive. Naturally Dickens adds and embroiders, and just occasionally he alters history slightly for his ends: the historical Dennis, for instance, was reprieved. His main concern, however, was with the accurate depiction of civil violence, from its earliest inception in individuals and in social situations, to its dramatic denouement in riot and flame. Naturally the relevance of this to all similar political upheavals would have concerned him, and particularly

its relevance to his own England of the early 1840s, with its
Chartist uprisings, and its simmering hostilities to the Catholic
Church. *Barnaby Rudge* includes his first, and perhaps his
greatest, study of mob violence. For this reason alone it has a
place of great importance among his early works.

II

Why, then, did *Barnaby Rudge* fail in popularity? Any critic is
bound to ponder this problem, since of all Dickens's novels it
has been the most consistently underrated and ignored. During
publication, sales dropped from 70,000 to 30,000, a great set-
back, particularly after the 100,000 who had attended the
obsequies of Little Nell. It was the moment, said enemies, when
Dickens's sky-rocket exploded, and the stick began its fall back
to earth. But why were the first readers disappointed? Perhaps
they missed the zestful humour and sentimentality of his
previous novels, or hankered after characters with whom they
could personally laugh and weep. Perhaps they missed the
'exposure' of specific social abuses, or alternatively were
annoyed with Dickens for choosing public hangings as an abuse
to expose. But another explanation of the defection is also
possible. It could be that Dickens's art was moving, now,
towards a complexity incompatible with the particular kind of
popularity enjoyed by his earlier works.

Whatever the explanation, Dickens's next novel, *Martin
Chuzzlewit* (1843–4), proved even less popular, and one of the
complaints made about it – that most of the characters are
unpleasant – applies with equal force to *Barnaby Rudge*. After
Martin Chuzzlewit Dickens's sales started to rise again, and
there were no further setbacks during his life. With *Edwin
Drood* in 1870 he had climbed back to 50,000 readers, and an
unsurpassed record of public acclaim. But his later works,
though popular, were manifestly more strenuous. Readers who
no longer expected the powerful simplicities of *Pickwick* or
Oliver might have felt less inclined to blow hot and cold from
book to book. *Barnaby Rudge*, however, never recovered favour,
as *Martin Chuzzlewit* did, in Dickens's lifetime, and it has been

the least read and discussed of his novels since his death. Even
Edgar Johnson failed to make amends. 'Among its defects', he
writes, in his splendid biography, 'are a clumsy and broken-
backed plot, with which the feeble-witted Barnaby, its central
character, has no organic connection.' Only recently has the
novel been treated as a work with a high degree of organic
unity, by Steven Marcus in a fine chapter of his *Dickens: from
Pickwick to Dombey*, and by Jack Lindsay, in a contribution to
Dickens and the Twentieth Century (edited by Pearson and Gross).
This still leaves *Barnaby Rudge* in that rare but perceptible
category of more-or-less-neglected masterpieces, where the
Cinderella works of very great writers sometimes fit.

Barnaby seems to me to mark an advance in Dickens's
artistry, and in exactly the respects where it is usually said to
fall short. It is more coherently planned than his previous
novels, with important connections and ironies developing
through both of its parts. Though not formally divided into
two, as *Little Dorrit* was later, the parts are clear enough to see.
Chapters 1 to 32 are set in 1775, chapter 33 brings us, after a
five years' silence, to 1780, the riot year. Both parts begin in
the Maypole, the first serenely (though violence follows), the
second on a night of mystery and storm. In the first part all the
seeds of the second are planted. When Lord George Gordon at
last rides in on his horse in 1780, appearing as suddenly in the
pages of the novel (says Dickens) as he appeared in fact on the
stage of history, everything needed to explain his impact is in
place. His pious supporters are familiar to us, notably Mrs
Varden with her moneybox for offerings from virtuous protestants like Miggs; and so are his militant supporters: Sim
Tappertit with his Prentice Knights, Hugh, and Barnaby himself.
There is also John Chester – Sir John Chester M.P. as he has
become in the interval – who without any absolute commitment
will, nonetheless, find Gordon useful to himself. And most
importantly, there is a general ambience of violence, a climate
where turbulence is held in check more by custom and lethargy
than by any strong, traditional defences against its sway. If any
reader of the first part of the novel has found the development
a little slow for him, this may be one of the effects most carefully

devised. With hindsight, the first part becomes altogether more
significant; *Barnaby Rudge* is one of those novels like Graham
Greene's *The Quiet American* which more or less demands a
second reading to complete the first.

Indeed, the main new characters in the second part are in
some sense prefigured. Gashford and Dennis seem missing
links almost, the grim sense in much that has already taken
place, whilst Gordon himself proves a mere catalyst for events.
It becomes clear that the Rudge plot is not the main plot,
despite appearances: the main plot, which certainly centres
upon Barnaby, culminates in the chaos of June 1780. These
clarifications happen, however, only in the light of Dickens's
implied reading of history. The liberal myth of political stability
as the fruit of long progress and constitutional development is
not allowed to us. We are shown, rather, a rootless and drifting
society, where civilisation is at best a very thin ice.

III

Dickens is famous for his prodigal fathers, but no novel provides
a richer crop of these than *Barnaby Rudge*. John Willet may be
judged the least culpable in this company, in that he at least sins
in ignorance: but he cripples his son emotionally, whether he
intends to or not, and Joe's lost limb is a fitting obsession for
his own subsequently crippled mind. Much more sinister than
John Willet are Rudge and Chester: Rudge, who leaves his son
maimed at birth and pursues him with hatred; Chester, who
curses one son and helps the other to hang. There are still more
ominous aspects to these relationships. Barnaby lurks at night,
hoping to kill Ned Chester's assailant; the situation is potentially that of Oedipus's encounter with Laius. Chester threatens
Hugh, and later helps to destroy him: though the two are
ignorant of their relationship, a disturbing current of intimacy
between them is always conveyed. These sombre themes illum-
inate the still more prevalent sin of spiritual slaughter – John
Willet's of Joe (though Joe survives), Chester's of Ned,
Haredale's of Emma. Mrs Varden casts a gloom over her home,
which even Gabriel's vitality cannot dispel.

Underlying these situations, and the whole novel, is hatred, as a fermenting and destructive power. 'I don't hate anyone,' says Gabriel Varden during one of the crises, and this simple truth sounds almost unnatural. Who else in the novel could say as much? Even Dolly and Emma are forced into hatred by their destiny; even John Grueby hates Bloody Mary, as far as in him lies. Hatred infects individuals, situations, the entire Body Politic; it is as ubiquitous as selfishness in *Martin Chuzzlewit* and pride in *Dombey and Son*. There is open hatred in Rudge and Hugh, brooding hatred in Haredale, mindless hatred in Barnaby, psychopathic hatred in Dennis, and hatred barely concealed behind a façade of politeness or servility in Chester, Miggs, Gashford, Stagg and Sim. Often, hatred finds a focal point, as if by accident. Is there any reason why Haredale, a malcontent himself, should become the chief target of Rudge, Chester, Hugh and Gashford? – or that Joe should attract the particular malice of Sim and Hugh? We cannot be certain whether hatred spills over from these ill-fated individuals to the rest of society, or whether they are mere lightning conductors, attracting hate.

The problem confronting us seems more religious than social; there is a *mystery* of hatred, in the flagrant disproportions between cause and effect. Rudge, it may seem, is the easiest example to analyse : his hatred is the fear of a murderer fleeing from justice, with the guilt of murder still festering in his heart. But why, in the first place, did he become a murderer? And why are his wife, and her idiot son, reserved for his special hate? Most of the other characters can be 'explained' in terms of social underprivilege or thwarted energies, but the explanations challenge, chiefly, by their ultimate failure to convince. A single girl, fending for herself, may become edgy and bitter, but need she seem as much a warped force in nature as Miggs? A blind man, living alone in poverty, may develop opportunism, but is the relish for persecution which we find in Stagg not different in kind? Even if we assume, as Dickens did not, that affliction must always sour and embitter, there remain abysses of positive hatred – of creative evil (to risk the Manichaean formula) – to be plumbed. Why are Chester and Gashford so consumed with hatred, behind their peaceable exteriors; how does piety turn so inevitably to malice in their mouths? Hugh, in his very different way from Miggs, seems a warped force in Nature – a dangerous animal, perhaps, transmuted into a man. And Barnaby's hatred, whilst comparatively innocent in its mindless-ness, is hardly less dangerous : he is a 'natural', in one authentic usage of the term.

We are forced to suspect that hatred not only lies deeper than its social occasions, but that it requires social occasions to feed on; that it is a poison working outwards from man to society even before it is a poison returning, in this or that injustice, this or that affliction, from society to man. Already, in fact, Dickens's distinctive analysis of evil is fully apparent – the analysis which led him away from belief in any purely social or political panaceas to human suffering at the same time as it led him towards belief in passive and wholly other-worldly people – Agnes, Little Dorrit, Joe Gargery – as the only authentic images of good. A modern reader is bound to be impressed by the degree to which all the characters in *Barnaby* (as in most of Dickens's later novels) are uprooted, with no home, no mean-ingful religion, no hierarchy or traditional 'place'. And this is not simply an opposition between rural and urban : just as the rural village in *Martin Chuzzlewit* produces nothing more life-enhancing than Mr Pecksniff and his daughters, so in this novel the very symbol of Merrie England – the Maypole – slumbers under the indolent idiocy of John Willet, whilst England splits into factions all around.

The revolutionary forces that will destroy the Maypole are loose indeed, unsuspected, within its doors. And as we survey this cast of characters, we find the same basic condition of rest-lessness in all of them, from Chester, who will sacrifice Ned, Hugh and all the world to his own comfort, down to Hugh the bastard, Barnaby the idiot, both free to come and go in the Maypole like cat or horse. Stagg is a blind man, consigned by society to rot in a cellar; Miggs's only point of reference is her married sister, 'Golden Lion Court, number twenty-sivin, second bell-handle on the right-hand side'. Sim comes from a class which will breed greater discontents and greater subversions.

All belong to a society where violence and irrationality will
hold increasing sway. It is no wonder that certain scenes of
restless wandering resonate in this setting : Rudge's midnight
appearances here, there, everywhere, until superstitious terror
surrounds him; Gordon's bizarre entry into London on a horse.
Society first creates and then ignores these haunted figures : or
they create themselves, in their bitter fight with society, and
wander restless through the world, disturbing men with their
image and their deeds. We see them seeking refuge, or opportunity, until the currents of their obsessions and hatreds come
closer together, mingle, start moving slowly towards an as yet
unguessed moment in time.

IV

Before I turn more directly to the individual characters, an
aside may be in order. The reader of Dickens is constantly
teased into comparisons across the novels, especially when he
is confronted with as richly idiosyncratic a cast as this. No other
novelist has managed to suggest so many moral and spiritual
affinities between characters of vastly different temperaments
and backgrounds whilst preserving, and even enhancing, their
individual roles. Chester calls to mind Carker in one direction,
Skimpole and Turveydrop in another; Gashford has the slimy
and venomous feel of Uriah Heep. John Grueby is a half-way
house between Sam Weller and Mark Tapley, the strong,
faithful servant who has become detached from his 'natural'
master (surely Varden?), and is doomed to a minor, somewhat
uneasy role where fate decrees. Gabriel Varden, of course, is a
successor of Pickwick, taken further into adversity (some would
say reality) than his great original. Dolly Varden and her father
foreshadow Bella Wilfer and the Cherub (though Mrs Varden
fails to compete with Mrs Wilfer among Dickens's portraits of
really memorable awfulness in the home). So one could go on,
surprising fresh similarities in these richly particularised people,
and appreciating Dickens's mastery of this most familiar and
elusive feature of ordinary life.

  Such speculation can be illuminating as well as compelling,

but it does less than full justice to Dickens's art. In *Barnaby Rudge*, as in all Dickens's novels, the characters are more importantly linked inside the novel where they belong than outside it. Certain groupings emerge, with a significance underlined in the imagery, symbolism and the progress of the plot. We notice first that there is an array of madmen, idiots, and otherwise socially alienated people: Barnaby, Hugh, Gordon and to some degree Dennis and Sim. And then there are the sane, but wholly cold-hearted predators: notably Chester, Gashford, Miggs and Stagg. All these characters, sane and insane, are passionate and egocentric; all contribute to the great explosion of hate to which the novel moves. And set against them, alone in this novel, is Gabriel Varden, whose genial sanity stands at bay, first in his home, and then at the novel's fiercest moment, at the Newgate door.

v

It is in the context of these general groupings that the novel unfolds, and in the light of them that we come to see why Barnaby rightly acquired the title of the novel from Varden. First, then, the madmen and defectives, who take us directly towards the novel's heart. We know that at one time Dickens thought of having the riots led by madmen loosed from Bedlam, a horrific idea, which he would no doubt have achieved splendidly; but Forster was against this, and Dickens agreed with him: the creative logic pointed to something subtler, if scarcely less horrific, than the original idea. So when the novel's action culminates in June 1780, it is not 'madmen' in some general sense who lead the chief mob, but Barnaby, flanked by Dennis and Hugh. The other mobs are led by Gordon himself, and by Sim, with Gashford manipulating, and Chester deviously adding his mite.

I want to start with Sim, who though he isn't mad is certainly irrational, and whose delusions of grandeur are introduced at an early stage. Neat, dandified, a vain and bumptious little malcontent, he is as ludicrous to his allies as to his foes. Dickens captures Sim's type with the cruellest accuracy. Personal

exhibitionism, which in the subversive Dick Swiveller had been
so attractive, becomes odious in this cold-hearted man. We
easily see that Sim is oversexed, though not as oversexed as he
would like to be; and that he is too self-absorbed to have any
clear understanding of the world. Other people's reactions
mean nothing to him: he fails to sense even such distinctive
tones towards himself as Stagg's, Chester's and Hugh's. Indeed,
he is only marginally aware, for her nuisance value, of the
encroaching Miggs. No doubt he is extremely lucky in his
circumstances: Gabriel Varden is altogether too kindly a master
to 'come down' on him, while Miggs, Stagg, Hugh and Chester
find it easier, or more amusing, to give him his head. Hugh's
relationship with Sim is indeed remarkably authentic: there is
delight as well as malice in his mock-servile tone. So Sim lords
it over his Prentice Knights in the Barbican cellar, creating a
little image of anarchy near the novel's start; and his cherished
little legs carry him unscathed through the main action, almost
as far as the end.

Sim's 'spiritual essence or soul', says Dickens, fumes 'within
that precious cask his body . . . until, with great foam and froth
and splutter, it would force a vent, and carry all before it'. The
depiction of the Barbican meeting is full of interest. A comic,
often facetious tone plays around the grotesquerie – Sim's
hatred towards Joe, the oaths and commitments of the new
initiates, the silent menace emanating from Stagg. How
seriously is the scene to be taken? Perhaps Dickens deliberately
leaves this fluid. The Prentice Knights are, in part at least, a
working-class parody of Young England (still in its early days:
Disraeli's *Sybil* was not published until 1845). The apprentices
want freedom, including freedom to marry their masters'
daughters; they hark back to the good old days when apprentices
enjoyed 'ancient holidays and rights' under a constitution that
has been allowed to lapse. Dickens's view of all this is naturally
contemptuous. His own myth of the old days ran to consistent
pessimism, and he interpreted the 'freedoms' sought by the
apprentices in much the manner of Arnold's *Culture and Anarchy*
(1869): freedom to march, burn, pillage and destroy. The
apprentices' designs against their masters' daughters are

rendered doubly ridiculous, by the tawdry initiation ceremonies of their conspiracy, and by the moral as well as physical repulsiveness of the lads themselves. It would be easy to see this chapter as a mere exercise in facetiousness, but Dickens's tone fluctuates away from this several times. Disruptive forces can be sensed as much in the whole situation as in Sim's little body; the image of violence fermenting inside Sim is seminal to the book. The cellar is underground and full of vermin; the meeting takes place, like much in *Barnaby Rudge*, at the dead of night. If we simply laugh, we join Stagg in his amusement; which we only do if we overlook, among other features, Stagg himself.

To turn from Sim to Barnaby is to emerge into daylight – though daylight too bright, too blinding as it strikes us, too fraught with sudden suggestions of change. Barnaby is altogether nicer than Sim, as well as being altogether madder; he is a unique figure in the crowded Dickens world.

He was about three-and-twenty years old, and though rather spare, of a fair height and strong make. His hair, of which he had great profusion, was red, and hanging in disorder about his face and shoulders, gave to his restless looks an expression quite unearthly – enhanced by the paleness of his complexion, and the glassy lustre of his large protruding eyes. Startling as his aspect was, the features were good, and there was something even plaintive in his wan and haggard aspect. But the absence of the soul is far more terrible in a living man than in a dead one; and in this unfortunate being its noblest powers were wanting.

Barnaby has no intellect, no nobler portion of the 'soul' – a fatal lack, yet he is happy, innocent, blissful for much of the time. As he roams about, leaving and returning home unpredictably as the mood takes him, he presents an archetypal romantic occasion; Mrs Rudge and her idiot boy are Dickens's most extended depiction of a Wordsworthian theme. Barnaby is in several important aspects a romantic hero : spontaneity, vigour, the most touching heroism and loyalty are abundantly his. Dickens endows him, even, with his own most precious gift of fancy : and of fancy at the point where 'imagination' might seem the more appropriate term. Barnaby's world is richly and continuously animate; in his idiot's perceptions and his colourful, primitive speech, he is constantly breaking down, diffusing, and recreating the world :

'Look down there,' he said softly. 'Do you mark how they whisper in each other's ears; then dance and leap, to make believe they are in sport? Do you see how they stop for a moment, when they think there is no-one looking, and mutter among themselves again; and then how they roll and gambol, delighted with the mischief they've been plotting? Look at 'em now. See how they whirl and plunge. And now they stop again, and whisper cautiously together – little thinking, mind, how often I have lain upon the grass and watched them. I say – what is it that they plot and hatch? Do you know?'

'They are only clothes,' returned the guest, 'such as we wear; hanging on those lines to dry, and fluttering in the wind.'

'Clothes!' echoed Barnaby, looking close into his face, and falling quickly back. 'Ha! ha! Why, how much better to be silly than as wise as you.'

With this, we may compare one of the most famous of the *Sketches by Boz*, 'Meditations in Monmouth Street', where Dickens's fancy, working on second-hand clothes in a tailor's window, conjures up character after character to fit. It represents, indeed, one of the most distinctive features of Dickens's writing, the perception of a universe strangely, sometimes ominously alive. The view from Todgers's has become a famous example since Dorothy van Ghent's notable article, but there is scarcely a novel where 'things' do not become complexly and particularly active. For Dickens such moments were clearly closer to mystical vision than to 'mere' literary technique. They are part of his consciousness of the world.

Between Barnaby and Dickens, however, there is one all-important distinction; Barnaby cannot distinguish between perception and creation, his rioting fancy has no perspective beyond itself. His choice of his own 'silliness' against the world's mundane 'wisdom' is, therefore, especially ironic, since without intellect his silliness lacks the true wisdom it might otherwise have. He moves from Heaven to Hell by all too casual compulsions; his fears, of blood for instance, are as total as his joy. He can be utterly cowed, as well as exalted to bravery, since his consciousness, at its most idyllic even, is reason's defect. Because he learns nothing, he is at the mercy of everyone; because he cannot associate ideas, he can have no moral guidance or ideals. The loss of the past leaves him as vulnerable, in his unrelated present, as the smallest child. His love of gold drives him on a destructive search that leads to Gordon; his very virtues – love, tenderness, loyalty – impel, in this company, to disastrous ends.

At the same time he cannot grasp the reality of other living beings, including those as dear to him as his mother and Grip. Who is Grip? – perhaps really the kettle, the teapot, the Polly, the devil he proclaims himself, but Barnaby puzzles over the riddle to no effect. Who is Barnaby's mother? Her hopes and fears are a closed book to him in their concrete particulars, though he senses her extraordinary capacity for expressing terror, which he shares. He remains sure throughout the riots that she is proud of him, for all her pleas that he should not take part. Who is Hugh? Hugh is Barnaby's friend, who can always be trusted; whatever Hugh says and orders must be right. And Gordon, in Barnaby's eyes, is a natural leader; the scenes between the two defectives are among the most memorable in the book. Barnaby, in the world's term, which Dickens also uses, is a 'natural'; the world is therefore right to see his happiness, vitality, innocence as an affliction, a tragic curse, to him, and to itself.

Yet Dickens depicts idiocy with delicate insight; Barnaby's courage and loyalty remain true, and because true moving, whatever their commitments and their ends. His closest friends are animals (like Hugh, he is made free of the Maypole as though he were an animal himself). With Grip, he seems joined in an alliance of two types of sharpness, almost above reasonableness; and Grip, of course, is a full Dickensian character before Dickens is through. Grip, Barnaby and Hugh seem almost like a hierarchy ascending between the brutes and the humans; one wonders if the talking beast is even higher in this scale than the idiot man. Yet Barnaby's place in the community is fixed by his capacity for tragic suffering. When he is forced to flee with his mother, leaving behind the dog who has become his favourite, his words have the music of a Chekhov or a Synge: 'O mother,

mother, how mournful he will be when he scratches at the door,
and finds it always shut.' He has some of the finest prose in the
novel, and its tenderest insights. Dickens finds pathos, tenderness, tragic truth in him even, but no wisdom. We are not,
finally, offered the paradox of wisdom in the fool.

In Barnaby, Dickens develops one kind of romantic hero; in
Hugh another, equally anti-social, though different in almost
every other way. The complexity of Hugh's characterisation is
of particular interest, since though an unusual figure in Dickens,
he is of particular importance to the modern world. He lends
himself – and surely Dickens intends this – to revealing over-
simplifications; to half-baked responses, or questions too easily
asked. Is he a Byronic hero (we might wonder), with Richard-
son's Lovelace among his remoter ancestors? – or a satanic
hero, manifesting human energy released from control? Is he a
criminal hero, descended from Jonathan Wild and the eighteenth-
century popular broadsides? – or a primitivist hero, the Natural
Man rejected and victimised by the timid and weak? To the
student of politics, he might seem a most dangerous working-
class malcontent, whose true nature the French Terror, as well
as the Gordon Riots themselves, had by the 1840s abundantly
shown. Certainly he represents a vision of manhood which the
Brontës were soon to embellish, a sexual magnet dangerous,
wicked and fascinatingly alive. Our own century, also, has
perspectives for Hugh of tempting simplicity. Isn't Dolly
merely prudish to reject the chance of being raped by him?
Isn't he, in embryo, every tough-guy intellectual's campus
ideal?

Hugh tempts us, in short, to be 'for' him, or 'against' him, or
'interested' in him as a moral enigma, but Dickens expertly
refuses to make things as simple as this. Though Hugh is a
magnificent and dangerous animal, he is also a magnificent and
dangerous man. Inarticulate or incoherent for the most part, he
is far from being unintelligent; he rises to noble and convincing
eloquence at his death. This eloquence is in no simple tradition
of criminal swagger. Hugh rebukes his hearers justly, and
morally diminishes them, even though his death at their hands
is finally endorsed. A bastard by birth whose mother was

hanged for the offence of stealing to feed him, his life among animals has been all that society allows. His preference for horses and dogs to his fellow men is based on experience; he has found them more loyal and tender in their ways. He is loyal and tender himself, to his mother's memory, and to his one friend, Barnaby – though since he holds all life cheaply, this does not prevent him from squandering Barnaby's life along with his own. Give him a scuffle, a chance to pay off old scores, and he doesn't mind the outcome; his courage is recklessness in its quintessential form. In sex, his drives are instinctively brutal. There is no tenderness here, only aggressiveness, and Dolly's terror merely feeds his lust. But though he wouldn't formulate this, or even recognise it, his sex is partly political; it includes both masculine mastery and class revenge. This insight, more familiar to us since Strinberg's *Miss Julie* than it was earlier, is conveyed very clearly. It accounts for Hugh's hatred of Joe, as well as for his pursuit of Dolly herself.

Hugh fears no man but Chester, and then it is the smooth graces of his dark angel which defeat him; he fears instinctively, as a lion may fear a snake. He is fully human enough to resent his degradation at the hands of society, and to turn his reckless destructiveness into conscious revenge. His views on revolution are, therefore, fully explicable, and function in the novel as social criticism as well as psychological truth. But if he seems, at times, admirable, it may be in much the same manner as Barnaby. At least he is incorruptible, and true always and wholly to himself. Like Barnaby, he lacks the normal social instinct for reason and order. Akin to the brute, he is also larger than life. Like a lion, he can be admired for courage and defiance. When caging him, we recognise our vulnerability, our inferiority even, in the social good sense.

The magnitude of Hugh's strength, as of his grievances, is finally revealed when he and Barnaby go into action, in June 1780, side by side. As they hurl themselves over banisters, burn down prisons, ride invulnerable through danger, they are heroes in the traditional meaning of the term. Dickens is glancing, of course, at the absurdity inherent in heroism, none the less menacing as they ride 'like hideous madmen' to destroy. Yet there are distinctions between them, in their heroism: Hugh's courage is more real than Barnaby's, in that he, at least, has human reason and moral sense. Barnaby, for all his quick momentary empathy with animals and humans, has no real insight into what they are. Since he cannot envisage the sufferings of his victims, or even his own sufferings, his stance in the condemned cell remains vacant, however moving it is. Hugh, in contrast, is fully aware of suffering, his own and other people's, and has the full, if desperate, courage of a man.

What Hugh images is violence unleashed from restraint or reason; his open hatred balances the carefully hidden hatred of Chester and Gashford, Stagg and Miggs. Made by society, and to the degree that society has made him its nemesis, he is disorder and lawlessness operative in society and writ large. It is precisely because order and lawfulness themselves are so grossly parodied in their supposed embodiments, like Chester, that Hugh has some claim to sympathy from ourselves. The effect may be slightly blunted for modern readers by the very general discredit into which gentlemanly virtues have since fallen: Chester is now the standard image for many people of a 'gentleman', and Hugh has been apotheosised into a familiar British and American ideal. It would be interesting to know what Dickens would have made of Hugh's temperament in a society disposed to admire and accommodate him. Perhaps the notion would have seemed to him simply unthinkable; or perhaps he would have seen Hugh's resentment, energy, violence and residual nobility as the product of his own society at its most hypocritical – understandable, but inherently flawed. Undeniably, Dickens was less sentimental about uncouth violence than we are in our century, less charmed by toughness as a quality admirable and acceptable *per se*. We are left in *Barnaby Rudge* with an image of Hugh and Barnaby linked in affection, in disturbing vividness, outside society; two powerful and dangerous forces, given their hour.

In the second half of *Barnaby Rudge* we are introduced to Dennis, another astonishing character, though more recognisably 'Dickensian' than Barnaby or Hugh. Dennis is the most horrible, in certain suggestions of perversion, of all Dickens's villains, just as he is, in his own estimation, and even society's, the most respectable : is it not conscientious, indeed admirable, for the public hangman to be so dedicated to his task? By profession he is a fringe figure, guarding social order at its most extreme reach of legal sanctions, and given status only in association with violence and horror. As we see him recalling his victims with affection if they died bravely, and dressed from head to foot in their clothes, the ghastliness of the image becomes oppressively real. The public hangman had traditionally received the clothes of his victims, but to sell, as part of his stipend; Dennis's adaptation of the custom is of a piece with his obsessive interest in people's necks.

The horror is intensified by Dennis's absolute unawareness of hidden motives. He accepts his social respectability in total good faith. There are fifty capital offences in the Protestant Constitution, and if 'any man, woman or child does anything against any of them fifty acts, that man, woman or child shall be worked off by Dennis'. Dennis is a righteous man, a Pharisee of the Pharisees, the ultimate safeguard of England against criminals. Dickens's irony is all the more intense for its total context; Dennis is the perversion of something incontestably true. If we are to be protected by law, by *whom* are we to be protected? – against our neighbour, and occasionally perhaps against ourselves? Yet the protection can surpass in evil its *raison d'être*, or can boomerang into a *fons et origo* of evil itself.

In Dennis the vicarious violence of the law-abiding is vested; his image justly reflects the mobs who throng to witness his work. The people he kills are mere things to him, despite his pleasure in killing them; and the more 'things' the better, for a public servant so characterised by zeal. Dennis's anti-catholicism is based solely on fears for his office. The papists will 'boil and roast instead of hang', and then where will England, and Dennis, be? That boiling and roasting may also deter does not occur to him; nor (of course) that there can be any deterrence short of death. Yet Dennis half senses the immense anarchy of his public *persona*. When Hugh responds to 'No popery' with 'No property', and is unctuously corrected by Gashford, 'All the same,' says Dennis, 'down with everybody,

down with everything! Hurrah for the Protestant religion!'
Dennis's very guile is as simple as his integrity. He believes
that he is protected against suffering with the other rioters not
only because he tries to conceal his identity, but because he *is* the
law. How should the hangman be hanged?

Because Dennis sees his victims as things, and misunderstands
his pleasure in killing, he 'belongs' among the sub-human
hierarchy with Barnaby and Hugh. But, since he is far more
horrible than Barnaby or Hugh, or than any animal, it is
correspondingly the more startling that he alone is accepted by
society on his chosen terms. It might be more proper to call him
a monster than an animal – or a devil, since his obsessions have
a framework, wholly perverted, of logic and sense.

And finally among the defectives is Gordon, the almost
innocent spark who starts the blaze. He is kindly, as Dickens
sees him, but deluded, a weak and vain fanatic, too easily led.
In skilled hands he is clay to the potter. Gashford plays on his
vanity, piety and messianic delusions until 'something wild and
ungovernable gets out'. It gets out of Gordon, and through him
is loosed on London. He is the catalyst for tensions that have
been building up in the diverse people and scenes.

One of Dickens's happiest strokes is the meeting between
Barnaby and Gordon, when each becomes concerned with the
other's sanity and good repute. For Barnaby, Gordon is exactly what he appears, a natural leader; for Gordon, Barnaby is
too enthusiastic an ally to permit of doubt. In these two
defectives, drawn together by their mutual inability to compre-
hend each other, much of the novel's grotesquerie is caught up.
As Barnaby ponders aloud the mystery of Grip, puzzled to think
him 'only a bird' ('He's my brother, Grip is – always with me –
always talking – always merry – eh, Grip?') Gordon also
pauses in the midst of other burdens to consider the raven.
Meanwhile, Grip's demoniac liturgy of identity proceeds in full
spate: 'I'm a devil, I'm a Polly, I'm a kettle, I'm a Protestant,
No Popery!' ('Having learnt this latter sentiment from the
gentry among whom he had lived of late', says Dickens, 'he
delivered it with uncommon emphasis.)'

VI

The face of violence in *Barnaby Rudge* is the idiot's grin; it is
also the predator's smile. With his usual flair, Dickens makes
the predators as varied as the madmen. When Dolly Varden
remarks on similarities between Chester and Miggs, she is
right to sense that the vulgarly obsequious and the poisonously
polite are near neighbours. But her observation is surprising all
the same. Chester enjoys his duping of Mrs Varden much as
Miggs does; both despise their victim in the admiring enact-
ment of self. The tone they work by is pre-eminently respectable. It implies moral esteem for Mrs Varden, admiration,
disinterested concern for virtue – all too strongly, too honestly
felt, to be held in check. It includes flattery, but is worse than
flattery in its deviousness. The whole of society is vulnerable to
it, and not only Mrs Varden: protestantism has sold out to it,
and conventional morality, as they appear in this book. All
social order is unsurped and degraded by Miggs and Chester.
The language of virtue *is* now this servant, and this knight.

   With hindsight, we see similarities, in a wholly different
direction, between Chester and Hugh. Though one is all art, the
other all nature, they share the courage of boredom and recklessness combined. Both are highly sexed and wholly self-
centred. Both are nourished by the taste of a victim's fears. But
Chester, choosing money, prestige and comfort, becomes an
insider and, unlike Hugh, preys on society in society's own
terms. With Lord Chesterfield as his text-book, he thrives on
dissimulation, and becomes one variation on a most important
Dickensian theme. Like Mr Pecksniff, he is an artist in decep-
tion; like Harold Skimpole, he avoids the expression of ageing
emotions, and so remains as ageless as time can be persuaded to
allow.

   Gashford is also, of course, of this company of predators,
behind the bland face he presents to the world. Though his overt
tone, unlike Chester's, is obsequious flattery, the overtones
of each are strangely alike. Both he and Chester manipulate
and enjoy manipulating; both, under pretence of respectability, let chaos loose. Both cultivate a tone of good-humoured
C

serenity which torments, and therefore satisfies, by its very
flawlessness. When used on someone as obtuse as Sim or Mrs
Varden, there is the pleasure in such a tone of superior intelligence; when used on a fellow conspirator like Dennis or
Stagg, the pleasure of complicity; when used on an intelligent
enemy like Haredale or Varden, the pleasure of insolence too
oblique to be either evaded or pinned down. It is a marvellous
tone for a vicious malcontent, but its edge of hatred cannot be
wholly concealed. This hatred is the Achilles' heel of both
Chester and Gashford, the fire which will burn away, eventually,
their careful façades. Only once in each does the mask slip, to
reveal naked reality – in Gashford when he allows the rioters
to see his clear intention for Haredale, and in Chester, when he
has his final meeting with Haredale near the novel's close. Yet
this is enough to reveal the inner corrosion, which is always
working; and in the end, Chester's predicament is also Gashford's. For all his talent for social privilege he is handicapped
by poverty, and driven to stratagems like any toady or crook.

The similarity of Stagg to Chester and Gashford in his inner
hatred is also apparent; he enjoys his evil in very much their
way. But in Stagg's pursuit of Mrs Rudge, Dickens uses one of
his most distinctive perceptions of the cat-and-mouse mentality :
Stagg becomes a fairytale figure horribly reversed. When Mrs
Rudge accepts him as a blind man in need of food and hospitality,
she might be entertaining an angel unawares. Stagg's sudden
epiphany is to this degree the more horrifying (Betty Higden,
much later, will encounter Riderhood in *her* hour of need).
Throughout *Barnaby Rudge*, similar powerful archetypes underlie the social realism. Our sense of Rudge as Cain, Haredale as
Knight Avenger, Gordon as Wandering Jew, reinforces the
dark atmosphere of impending doom.

VII

In *Barnaby Rudge* Dickens is not yet ready to confront the
place of Money in his society directly, but we can already see
why his later horror of capitalism never led him to revolutionary
political views. Dickens's vision of the past was uniformly

disenchanted, but some slow progress had, he saw, been made. The London of 1775 is depicted as being worse, in every way, than the London of the 1840s, and the forces of change were as much in scientific progress as in anything else. 'Merrie England' for Dickens is John Willet and the Maypole – pleasant enough, and not to be lightly dismantled, but closer to Marx's rural 'idiocy' than to, say, Morris's notion of paradise lost. The Catholic past, of course, Dickens always detested: it is remarkable that he should have been as generous to Haredale and his Church as he is. At the same time, Protestantism appeared to him even meaner and more odious than Catholicism: Mrs Varden, Miggs, Gordon and Gashford can be matched by canting or murderous Protestants throughout his work, from Mrs Nubbles's pastor in *The Old Curiosity Shop* through (to take just a few examples) the Murdstones and Chadband to Mrs Clennam.

This disillusionment with the past and its traditional religious resources itself told, however, against facile optimism for the future. The main snag in both Catholicism and Protestantism was human nature, and Dickens was the last man to suppose that changes in social organisation or structure would alter *that*. Most of the current panaceas or ideologies struck him as far more dangerous than the ills they were supposed to eradicate, and particularly those which on any pretext of social improvement threatened to let violence and revolution loose. In *Barnaby Rudge* the sources of violence are found in hatred, a mystery of evil deep and ineradicable in the human heart. The riots themselves are a disaster, and a continuous warning: Dickens must have sensed in 1841 – nearly everyone did – the imminent possibility of revolution on a larger and more terrible scale. The Chartist risings provided the most obvious occasion for concern, much more so, certainly, than the essentially middle-class Anti-Corn-Law League. But it should not be forgotten that the Oxford Movement was exciting new and widespread anti-clericalism, and that despite the emancipation reluctantly conceded to Catholics in 1829 – or more possibly because of it – hostility to the Catholic Church was still very likely to erupt. Dickens, who fully shared this anti-Catholicism, might have

been preaching as much to himself as to his readers; the psychology of mob violence, with its gravitational pull on whatever
members of society are most uprooted, violent, mad and disruptive, was a force he had come most of all to fear.

Barnaby Rudge shows the explosion of 1780 subsiding without
full-scale revolution, but there is no cause for complacency in
this. The most dangerous leaders – Hugh and Dennis – are
hanged for their activities, but in an atmosphere where violence
and injustice are still rife. Gordon lives on, but in increasing
derangement, until he finally acts out (and Dickens follows
history here) his fantasy of becoming a Jew. Barnaby is rescued,
by the valiant efforts of Mr Varden, but he can be restored,
with Grip, only to his exuberant, precarious life. Haredale and
Chester act out their bitter hatred as an aftermath to the riots,
and the survivor goes off to finish his darkened life as a penitent
in a religious house abroad. For Sim, Dickens reserves a
particular cruelty; after the loss of his cherished legs in battle,
he marries a shrew, who takes his wooden legs away from him
as a periodic punishment, and exposes him to the jeers of urchins
in the street. Miggs is shown to Mrs Varden at long last in her
true colours and expelled from the household, but she finds a
new niche for herself as female turnkey for the County Bridewell.
In society at large, no more optimistic conclusions are discernible. Violence has been quelled, but not extinguished; the
riots remain as the culmination of a cycle which will return, no
doubt, when the historical soil is again prepared.

Where, then, is virtue in *Barnaby Rudge*? – its one great
embodiment is Varden, who stands out from the surrounding
darkness, inviolable, but alone:

From the workshop of the Golden Key there issued forth a
tinkling sound, so merry and good-humoured, that it suggested
the idea of some one working blithely, and made quite pleasant
music. No man who hammered on at dull monotonous duty
could have brought such cheerful notes from steel and iron; none
but a chirping, healthy, honest-hearted fellow, who made the
best of everything, and felt kindly towards everybody, could
have done it for an instant. He might have been a coppersmith,
and still been musical. If he had sat in a jolting waggon, full

of rods of iron, it seemed as if he would have brought some harmony out of it.

Tink, tink, tink – clear as a silver bell, and audible at every pause of the street's harsher noises, as though it said, 'I don't care; nothing puts me out; I am resolved to be happy.' Women scolded, children squalled, heavy carts went rumbling by, horrible cries proceeded from the lungs of hawkers; still it struck in again, no higher, no lower, no louder, no softer; not thrusting itself on people's notice a bit the more for having been outdone by louder sounds – tink, tink, tink, tink, tink.

It was a perfect embodiment of the still small voice, free from all cold, hoarseness, huskiness, or unhealthiness of any kind; foot-passengers slackened their pace, and were disposed to linger near it; neighbours who had got up splenetic that morning, felt good-humour stealing on them as they heard it, and by degrees became quite sprightly; mothers danced their babies to its ringing; still the same magic tink, tink, tink came gaily from the workshop of the Golden Key.

Who but the locksmith could have made such music? A gleam of sun shining through the unsashed window, and chequering the dark workshop with a broad patch of light, fell full upon him, as though attracted by his sunny heart. There he stood working at his anvil, his face all radiant with exercise and gladness, his sleeves turned up, his wig pushed off his shining forehead – the easiest, freest, happiest man in all the world. Beside him sat a sleek cat, purring and winking in the light, and falling every now and then into an idle doze, as from excess of comfort. Toby looked on from a tall bench hard by; one beaming smile, from his broad nut-brown face down to the slack-baked buckles in his shoes. The very locks that hung around had something in their rust, and seemed, like gouty gentlemen of hearty natures, disposed to joke on their infirmities. There was nothing surly or severe in the whole scene.

The entire morning is irradiated by Varden, and redeemed by him; he transforms it, from his own unquenched resources, into spring. For all the power of this, however, and for all its truthfulness, it stands outside the body of the novel itself. In *Pickwick* the whole world is transformed by such a person: Pickwick's radiancy keeps the darkest shadows at bay. *Pickwick*, for the first and last time in Dickens, is idyll; after *Pickwick*, never glad confident morning again. Varden's role in this novel is a very

different one : he keeps the citadel of virtue alive, but in a
darkened world. His image remains undimmed, and he isn't
harmed by the action, but there are limits set to what he can do.
In part I, we see him beset by a shrewish wife, with Miggs as
servant and Sim as apprentice : at best he can tolerate the world
which these three create. His most active role is in a kind of
conspiracy of happiness with all that is best in his daughter – a
more robust version of the situation of Mr Wilfer in *Our
Mutual Friend*. In part II of the novel he is brought to the gate
of Newgate and surrounded by enemies : even this does not
touch him, but his life is saved only by outside intervention, and
he has no positive role to play. At the end of the book he is able
to save Barnaby, and his patience with Mrs Varden is rewarded.
Yet Mrs Varden's conversion is not really his doing. She is
brought to her senses only by violent events.

What we are left feeling about Varden, I think, is that he is
immensely real, but also alien; an image of goodness no longer
at home in the social and political world. He cannot be destroyed
by the world, he cannot be qualified, but he cannot assume a
genuinely saving or hopeful role. He remains as a witness, an
alleviation on certain sunlit mornings. After this, goodness will
be more and more pressed in Dickens's novels towards alienation
and social powerlessness, and no unambiguously good man of
Varden's vitality and stature will again emerge. Between the
novel's inception in 1836 and its publication in 1841, the title
changed : and it *is* Barnaby's novel, as Dickens then knew.

4 *Martin Chuzzlewit* howls the sublime

The difficulty for criticism that *Martin Chuzzlewit* and all of Dickens's subsequent novels present is to be found in their surprising combination of expansiveness and compactness. Again, the comparison with Shakespeare is useful; in any one of Dickens's mature novels scarcely a page goes by which does not in some way further the central course of development; no detail is too small or by-the-way for it not to be discovered as elaborating some larger organic theme – even as it stands by itself, as a locally justified detail. *Martin Chuzzlewit* is the first of Dickens's novels in respect to which criticism, if it is to remain reasonable, must settle for suggestive commentary and fragmentary analysis. (Steven Marcus, *Dickens: from Pickwick to Dombey*.)

THIS is admirably said, and a text with comfort for all Dickens critics; and I would only wish to add that the 'difficulty' defined by Steven Marcus is a recognition, also, that Dickens's place is firmly among the great. It is the law of life in great literature to elude its critics, and to mock those who imagine they can defy this law. Dickens's critics will be wise, surely, to accept Steven Marcus's dictum and to settle for suggestive analysis, whilst noticing the high standard for this activity which he sets.

Even so, *Martin Chuzzlewit* (again like the later novels) sets some quite distinctive problems. How can a 'loose baggy monster' be so highly organised and sophisticated? How can the funniest book in the language be so consistently grim? It looks backward to *Nicholas Nickleby* and forward to *Bleak House* in almost equal measure; certainly it appears wholly different from *Barnaby Rudge*, the novel immediately before. Is its organisation conventionally picaresque or daringly symbolist? It is the first of Dickens's novels to send critics off happily and illuminatingly towards Kafka, but also the first to bring anti-Kafkaesque critics baying at their heels. 'I can truthfully say', Barbara Hardy tells us, grimly, or possibly sadly, 'that the *Martin Chuzzlewit* of Jack Lindsay (*Charles Dickens*), Dorothy

Van Ghent ('The Dickens World: a view from Todgers's', in
Sewanee Review, LVIII (1950) and J. Hillis Miller (*Charles
Dickens*), is a novel – or rather, three different novels – which I
should like to read.' At the same time, *Martin Chuzzlewit* is the
first of Dickens's novels to produce an array of critics each
proudly bearing a Key, but each confronting a different door, or
at least a remarkably different-shaped lock. We are most
familiar with this phenomenon when we turn to the later novels:
to *Little Dorrit* for instance, where critics with the Prison Key
line up alongside critics bearing the False-Gentility Key, the
Childlike-Versus-Childish Key, the Anti-Capitalist (or Pro-
Marxist) Key, the Prodigal Father Key, until criticism itself
resembles a Turnkey presiding over dozens of doors. *Martin
Chuzzlewit* is not as seminal in this respect as *Little Dorrit*, but
it still attracts something of the same kind of attention. I am
tempted myself to propose, for instance, a 'principle of doubleness', of the kind which Robert Morse writes about in his
brilliant essay on *Our Mutual Friend*. Mrs Todgers's face as she
stands gazing at the Miss Pecksniffs 'with affection beaming in
one eye and calculation shining out of the other' reminds us,
surely, of Mr Scadder, who sells Martin his share in Eden:

Two grey eyes lurked deep within this agent's head, but one of
them had no sight in it and stood stock still. With that side of
his face he seemed to listen to what the other side was doing.
Thus each profile had a distinct expression, and when the
movable side was most in action, the rigid one was in its coldest
state of watchfulness.

There are two swindlers in the novel, both with similarities in a
context of notable differences – the English Tigg, with his
Anglo-Bengalee Disinterested Loan and Life Assurance Company
attuned to expanding English capitalism, and the American
Scadder, a very incarnation of all that is most radical and idyllic
in the American myth. There are also strikingly parallel scenes
of moral exposure – Tom's rejection first by the moral Pecksniff,
and later by the saddened Martin, both times on the grounds of
his hypocrisy. The 'principle of doubleness' would make, in fact,
an interesting key, but I prefer to think of it as a marginal insight, a single instance among many of that subtle incorporation

of local details into an organic structure to which Steven Marcus drew attention in the quotation from which I began.

A critic must produce some explanation, however, of the felt unity behind such incredible diversity of scenes and effects. The moral theme of selfishness extends, of course, to a great many of the characters, but this hardly distinguishes *Martin Chuzzlewit* from *Dombey and Son*. In my view, the' really distinguishing feature is a mode of treatment; in its inner essence, *Martin Chuzzlewit* is like no other book. It is the most purely sparkling of Dickens's novels, not even excepting *Pickwick*, yet its themes are among the darkest he ever produced. It comes close in fact to creating a holiday out of evil: with the exception of Jonas (to whom I shall be returning) and Jonas's victims, everyone is brought, in the end, into a comic frame. This amounts to an exercise of creative tact unparalleled except by Shakespeare, whose comedies – *A Midsummer Night's Dream*, *As You Like It*, *Twelfth Night* – also alchemise savage possibilities in a golden world.

Martin Chuzzlewit is no more 'like' any of these comedies, however, than they are themselves like *Hamlet*: the analogy rests simply on the perception that they all transmute strangely painful material into a sparkling whole. Material potentially satiric or tragic, people in varying degrees ill-fated or wicked, are kept poised in a world of bubbling inventiveness and mirth.

The essential framework is provided by the two Martin Chuzzlewits, each in a distinctively different way. Martin *grandpère* is one of those infuriating but enormously useful, and highly respectable (indeed Shakespearean) *deus ex machina* figures, who can disguise his nature, play games, put people through tests and trials of their virtue, himself tottering, bad-temperedly enough, between black cynicism and incipient good-will. His essential role is to expose evil, vindicate whatever is good, and set things right. If the ending includes rough justice for a Caliban or a Sairey Gamp, then this merely reminds us of the necessary limits of a comic world. Old Martin lacks, it is true, the suggestion of divinity, or at the least magic, which hangs about his Shakespearean counterparts, but makes up for this by being exactly the sort of rich, bad-tempered old man who

C2

might just conceivably act like this. The younger Martin, meanwhile, enacts another traditional comic pattern, in that he exemplifies in a heightened form, and is finally purged from, a notable failing : through suffering, ridicule and his own basic decency and intelligence, he comes to see and renounce his own selfishness, in time to marry the heroine and live happily on. This broadly comic framework is reinforced – again if we except Jonas and his victims – by the fact that no-one suffers fatally in the book. Pecksniff's pupils and Sairey Gamp's patients have a difficult time, and we cannot envy them, but somehow (we assume) they usually survive. Martin and Mark Tapley suffer a great deal in Eden and nearly die, but they both recover, and later marry appropriately, so moral therapy outweighs merely physical ills. The damage done to Charity by Mr Pecksniff seems more serious, yet Dickens hated women like Charity, and her final humiliations from the unfortunate Moddle are in the tradition of savage unchivalry towards unattractive oversexed women which pervades his novels, from Sally Brass in *The Old Curiosity Shop* through Charity, Mrs Skewton and many more, to old Lady Tippins in *Our Mutual Friend*. It will be noticed that even the resilient Bailey is restored from the dead to a rapturous welcome from the effeminate but gentle and kindly Poll Sweedlepipe, and that the still more resilient Pecksniff and Sairey Gamp survive their moral exposure with unaffected aplomb. The only real victims are Tigg and Mercy, both through Jonas, and Jonas himself – in whom the prevailing exuberance of the novel becomes feverish, so that Dostoevskian insights into murder counterpoint, without altogether suspending, the prevailing mood.

The comic framework explains why the novel's darkness and savagery only once or twice, and always when Jonas is there, makes a bid for the tone. The amazing thing, indeed, is how close darkness and savagery are to the surface; there is hardly a page where they might not have broken through. The accumulated abuses represented by Pecksniff, the Chuzzlewit family in general, Sairey Gamp and Betsey Prig, Scadder and Tigg, and the general condition of America as Martin experiences it, are the stuff of continuously bitter indictment or even despair. Yet the tone never deepens, as it frequently does in *Oliver Twist* and *Barnaby Rudge*, into pure savagery: Dickens's unleashed inventiveness, at its most extravagant, remains in command. This, to my mind, is the distinguishing feature of *Martin Chuzzlewit*, a high and rare triumph of mood and tone. Only once after this, in *Our Mutual Friend*, did Dickens again unleash his full comic extravagance: from *Dombey* onwards, he more normally held it in check.

The comic triumph in *Martin Chuzzlewit* extends both to its organic unity and to its most localised parts. It is the secret of its two most triumphant characters, Pecksniff and Sairey Gamp (Sairey takes over from Pecksniff in the second half of the novel as the centre of virtuosity, but without eclipsing him), and of its most triumphant inset, Martin's voyage to, and adventures in, the U.S.A. These two characters and the American episode all contain material for very bitter satire, but become, instead, the crowning achievement of Dickens's comic art. The transmutation is already at work, however, in the novel's opening chapters, before the main actors have even appeared.

II

Take, for instance, the first chapter – that delightful exercise in pseudo-scholarship in the tradition of Swift, Sterne and Peacock. It starts playfully and progresses to outrageously funny punning, but the underlying ideas are grim. The Chuzzlewit family is presented as a tightly knit aristocracy stretching back in England (by its own pretensions) to the Conquest, and stretching back before that to Adam and Eve. This final claim to pre-eminence is, in one glorious over-reaching, a final levelling: as men, it appears, we are all Chuzzlewits too. At no stage in the unfolding saga does evil originate: for the origin, we are returned to the prime, general taint. Go back to William the Conqueror, and you find a king rewarding his friends with other people's land; go back to Eden (the scriptural original of Martin's investment) and you find Cain, Abel and the usual human routine. It is amusing to compare with this Disraeli's expository chapters in *Sybil* (1845), published a year after

Martin Chuzzlewit was complete. For Disraeli the ills of
England were a catastrophe post-dating the Middle Ages; you
could point to Henry VIII's sack of the monasteries in the 1530s
and to the rise of capitalism during the Whig oligarchy of
(roughly) 1720 to 1760 as the twin villains in an historical
decline. From feudal harmony between masters and servants
to the two nations of the 1840s, a clear and well-charted path
could be traced. Dickens, writing a year or two before Disraeli,
presents a very different picture : though he is far from entertaining a Whig myth of progress, he is still further from entertaining the primitivist myth of an historical decline. The
Chuzzlewit family in its entire history, real or imaginary,
reveals only depraved humanity up to its tricks. This insight is
mediated decisively, but with unfailing playfulness : the trans-
muting power of unleashed humour is already at work.

The second chapter opens with a set-piece of landscape
description where similar transmutations are at work. After a
brief, illusory moment of spring in autumn (Martin with
Scadder ? – Pecksniff with Tigg ?) a boisterous night settles in.
The wind descends on the peaceful rural village with dangerous
vitality; it races around the houses, torments the Dragon, sends
the leaves flying, overturns (with his own front door!) the
majestic Pecksniff : then off it goes, rampaging far out to sea
after its pranks. Dickens's zest suggests parody, but the description is excellent, and the element of parody is hard to pin down.
The reader is left with the fallen Pecksniff, on the novel's
threshold : when Pecksniff is raised and rallied by his charming
daughters we accompany them, past the brazen plate upon the
door 'PECKSNIFF, ARCHITECT', 'which, being Mr Pecksniff's, could not lie', and into the parlour, for our first clear
view of the family hearth. This masterpiece of family complicity
proceeds through the arrival of Tom Pinch on the scene to the
departure of Westlock, a marvellous demonstration of Pecksniff at work. Mr Pecksniff indeed – like Sairey Gamp – cannot
lie because his lies are inviolable : his moral world must be at
least as consistent as Truth. He keeps it up – as Anthony
Chuzzlewit rightly supposes – even with his daughters, so that
only Merry's giggles (inexplicable) and Cherry's sourness

(also inexplicable) remind one that the Pecksniff house is a triumph of Art rather than Life. The result is that we are delighted from first to last by its sheer creativity, pursued on a scale commensurate with Dickens's own. Pecksniff's morality has all the vitality of a great comic actor playing Pecksniff: which is what it is, and why it has authority – who could cavil at such an actor's merely private life? Dickens not only endows Pecksniff with wonderful comic images, but makes him a source of them: we sense that Pecksniff's artistry is even more important, to Pecksniff, than his moral repute. This, I fancy, is why Pecksniff's really evil moments – his lust with Mary Graham and greed with Tigg – seem almost out of character: it is as though the real Pecksniff had just for a moment been deprived of his life. It is also why Mr Pecksniff's 'quest for identity', as some recent critics have called it, seems so robust. Mr Pecksniff is, of course, continually creating himself, but the creation comes from assured and unfailing strength.

What then *is* Pecksniff? – the novel's distinctive tone is pinpointed by a question like this. The 'real' Pecksniff, we say, is shabby and degraded, a sham and – of course – a hypocrite. He swindles his pupils, he ruins the lives of his daughters; he is drunken; he is greedy; he is treacherous; he is machiavellian; he becomes, through lust, a horrible old lecher, shrunken and diminished just for one moment even to himself. All this is Pecksniff, but is not Pecksniff: does anyone seriously bracket him as an evil father with William Dorrit, or even with Jenny Wren's sordid and horrible Mr Dolls? When John Westlock says of Pecksniff to Martin 'he is the most consummate scoundrel on the face of the earth', and backs up this judgement with an ample indictment, we acknowledge the justice of it, but reflect that this is not exactly the Pecksniff we know. The 'real' Pecksniff, then, is a creature transformed, like Sairey Gamp and Mr Micawber: he is transformed until we value him more, it may even be, than we value Tom Pinch. And this is partly because his audacity in being Pecksniff is constantly being tested, and constantly reasserted: from the moment we meet him, floored by his own front door and the wind's caprice, he is a favourite sport of the fates. He is always in one scrape or

another that would be death to a lesser Pecksniff – colliding with
Tigg in the dark outside old Martin's keyhole; cowering on the
floor where he has collapsed as young Martin upbraids him;
drunk and disorderly in Todgers's until he has to be locked in and
guarded by the delighted young Bailey; warned off the grass
by Ruth Pinch's employers; hiding in a church pew like a jack-
in-the-box as Tom and Mary Graham discuss him; tricked by
Tigg in the Anglo-Bengalee investment; shown up by old
Martin as part of the comic denouement: this list of mishaps is
impressive, and by no means complete. To all of them his
energy is equal: he transforms them, just as Dickens transforms the book. If he were warm-hearted like Dick Swiveller
instead of cold-hearted and Pecksniff, we should almost think he
deserved to succeed. Even his most outrageous moments, like
the dismissal of Tom Pinch, have a certain gaiety: his hair on
end still, his arm raised piously, his tone unassailable, 'See the
moral Pecksniff!' he continues to say. His status among the
literary immortals is as assured as Falstaff's, that other old
reprobate whom we thrive on as *he* thrives on defeat.

The transformation of Pecksniff is central to *Martin Chuzzlewit*, which is why he and Sairey Gamp seem like incarnations of
its creative force. The qualities I have noted in the opening two
chapters continue with old Martin's arrival at the Blue Dragon,
and acquire new dimensions in chapter 4. This is Dickens's
account of 'the strongest and most agreeable family in the
world', and is one of the moments in his work – most frequent
perhaps in the novels between *Martin Chuzzlewit* and *Bleak
House* and then in the three marvellous last novels from *Great
Expectations* on – when sheer richness of style and texture leaves
a critic disarmed. Short of quoting most of the novel verbatim,
how is one-tenth part of its richness to be conveyed? This
particular chapter of *Martin Chuzzlewit* is one where the
satiric material basic to such a depiction is transcended by
humorous inventiveness quite titanic in scale. The richest life
is in the images, which combine unprecedented extravagance
with sharp accuracy of observation and mood. When Pecksniff
collides with Tigg outside old Martin's keyhole, he finds
himself 'collared by something which smelt like several damp

umbrellas, a barrel of beer, a cask of warm brandy-and-water,
and a small parlour-full of stale tobacco smoke, mixed' . . .
Quintessence of Tigg here, even before that last, clinching,
'mixed': then we proceed to our first intimation of Tigg's
friend and patron, Chevy Slyme, whose distinction it is to be the
least attractive member, *pace* Jonas, of the Chuzzlewit clan:
'Mr Chevy Slyme, whose great abilities seemed one and all to
point towards the sneaking quarter of the moral compass.' And
then comes the moment when we see the family steadily and see
it whole, caught in a kind of snapshot as it waits, with un-
accountable suspicion, to be addressed by the moral Pecksniff:

First there was Mr Spottletoe, who was so bald and had such
big whiskers that he seemed to have stopped his hair, by the
sudden application of some powerful remedy, in the very act of
falling off his head and to have fastened it irrevocably to his face.
Then there was Mrs Spottletoe, who being much too slim for
her years and of a poetical constitution, was accustomed to
inform her more intimate friends that the said whiskers were
'the lodestar of her existence', and who could now, by reason of
her strong affection for her uncle Chuzzlewit, and the shock it
gave her to be suspected of testamentary designs upon him, do
nothing but cry – except moan. Then there were Anthony
Chuzzlewit and his son Jonas, the face of the old man so
sharpened by the wariness and cunning of his life that it seemed
to cut him a passage through the crowded room as he edged
away behind the remotest chairs, while the son had so well
profited by the precept and example of the father that he looked
a year or two the elder of the twain as they stood winking their
red eyes, side by side, and whispering to each other softly.
Then there was the widow of a deceased brother of Mr Martin
Chuzzlewit, who being almost supernaturally disagreeable and
having a dreary face and a bony figure and a masculine voice,
was, in right of these qualities, what is commonly called a
strong-minded woman, and who if she could, would have
established her claim to the title and have shown herself,
mentally speaking, a perfect Samson, by shutting up her
brother-in-law in a private madhouse until he proved his complete sanity by loving her very much. Beside her sat her spinster
daughters, three in number, and of gentlemanly deportment,
who had so mortified themselves with tight stays that their
tempers were reduced to something less than their waists and

sharp lacing was expressed in their very noses. Then there was
a young gentleman, grand-nephew of Mr Martin Chuzzlewit,
very dark and very hairy, and apparently born for no particular
purpose but to save looking-glasses the trouble of reflecting
more than just the first idea and sketchy notion of a face which
had never been carried out. Then there was a solitary female
cousin, who was remarkable for nothing but being very deaf,
and living by herself, and always having the toothache. Then
there was George Chuzzlewit, a gay bachelor cousin, who
claimed to be young but had been younger and was inclined to
corpulency and rather overfed himself, to that extent, indeed,
that his eyes were strained in their sockets, as if with constant
surprise, and he had such an obvious disposition to pimples that
the bright spots on his cravat, the rich pattern on his waistcoat,
and even his glittering trinkets seemed to have broken out upon
him and not to have come into existence comfortably. Last of all
there were present Mr Chevy Slyme and his friend Tigg. And
it is worthy of remark that although each person present disliked
the other, mainly because he or she *did* belong to the family,
they one and all concurred in hating Mr Tigg because he didn't.

There is tremendous life in the adverbs, adjectives and asides:
'irrevocably', 'nothing but cry – except moan', 'remotest',
'gentlemanly deportment', and that splendid 'comfortably' in
which George Chuzzlewit's description culminates. This snapshot achieved, the family proceeds to action, with Pecksniff
triumphing as usual in adversity, and everyone dispersing in a
mood of highly articulate hatred as news of Pecksniff's treachery
arrives. Pecksniff's hypocrisy rides through all this to the crest
of a wave, and the crest is purest and happiest Dickens. It
remains, therefore, only for Dickens, in his epilogue to the
affair, to cap Pecksniff's tone, as though in demonstration of the
degree to which he is authorially entitled to it himself:

Mr Pecksniff had, in short, but one comfort and that was the
knowledge that all these his relations and friends had hated him
to the very utmost extent before and that he, for his part, had
not distributed among them any more love than, with his ample
capital in that respect, he could comfortably afford to part with.

The zest of this is a kind of innocence, Pecksniff's kind; as we
see if we compare it with the superficially similar but far more

sombre hypocrisies of Sir John Chester in *Barnaby Rudge* or Carker in *Dombey and Son*. Pecksniff outsoars our own moral censure, as he outsoars old Martin's; he belongs with those other Dickens characters who, in transcending a satiric framework, tend to sweep the whole framework upwards along with themselves: Mrs Nickleby, Sairey Gamp, Joe Bagstock, Mr Micawber, Skimpole and Turveydrop, Flora Finching, and (a more dubious case?) Silas Wegg. But these characters do more than capture the novel, they capture the author; and this is especially apparent in *Martin Chuzzlewit*, the novel preeminently exuberant in tone.

III

I have tried to point to a distinction of tone in the first few chapters and in the creation of Pecksniff, and to suggest that it amounts to a radiance in which nearly everyone except Jonas and Jonas's victims becomes bathed. The radiance is not reserved only for the two 'immortals': it plays around Mark Tapley and Mrs Lupin, Tom Pinch, the numerous Americans, Mrs Todgers and Todgers's, Young Bailey, even Scadder and Tigg. It plays very particularly around the American chapters, which would surely have been among the most savage satire in English if they had existed in any other novel than this. The material for satire is at least as prolific as it is in the affairs of Pecksniff and Sairey Gamp, and Dickens was in no mood, personally, to hold himself back. His own pride had been hurt, since while he swallowed very few myths and panaceas in his life he had swallowed America, and expected to find it really the land of the free. There had also, of course, been his extreme and often expressed indignation at American copyright piracy, and possibly some further indignation at the American reception of *American Notes* (1842). American radicalism had turned out in Dickens's experience to be at least as hollow as Pecksniff, and no laughing matter to anyone who took his radicalism as seriously as Dickens did. Martin's Eden seems a very exact and bitter idea and symbol for the context: all the more remarkable then that these chapters, too, are sparkling and alive with

humour, and that Martin's America endears itself to us almost
as much as Pecksniff himself. As Steven Marcus has very well
written : 'Although it is true that Dickens did not like what was
happening in America, it was also true that he fell in love with
America and its rhetoric in the same way that he did with his
great wicked or foolish characters, like Quilp or Pecksniff or
Flora Finching.' This is certainly true, and particularly relevant,
on my reading, to *Martin Chuzzlewit*, where the tendency in
Dickens which Steven Marcus calls attention to and which we
must all have noticed becomes the controlling principle of the
book. America's Eden is saved from Dickens's naked bitterness
only by that other Eden of perfected art. In its sheer commitment to insensitive hypocrisy America achieves its own kind of
radiance. Satire is transplanted to Illyrian soil.

The last and no doubt the greatest example of transformed
satire is Sairey Gamp, surely the most perfect creation in the
book. Like Pecksniff, she started from a real-life original.
Pecksniff was based on Samuel Carter Hall (1800–89), author
and editor, whom Dickens referred to, in company with his wife,
as 'the most terrific humbugs known on earth at any period of
its history'. Sairey Gamp had her origin in a nurse hired by
Angela Burdett-Coutts to look after her friend Miss Meredith.
'Pray tell Miss Meredith', Dickens wrote to Angela Burdett-
Coutts on 16 September 1843, 'that I have written the second
chapter in the next number, with an eye to her experiences. It
is specially addressed to them, indeed.' This was chapter 25
in the October number, which depicts Mrs Gamp in the sick-
room – already settled in with her tray of pickled salmon, fennel
and cowcumber, her gin-and-warm-water, her Brighton Old
Tipper ale for the night if she feels 'so disposed', and already
treating her unfortunate patients with the admixture of philosophy and sternness for which she is famed.

Part of Dickens's greatness as a novelist lies in his power of
creating very distinct speech rhythms for his characters, and
Sairey Gamp is a most notable instance of this. Prodigal in his
powers of observation and mimicry, he could create distinctive
speech even for the characters on the sidelines of life – Barkis,
Mrs Guppy, Mr F's Aunt, a waiter who serves Arthur Clennam

once and hasn't even a name. For more important characters, he could produce far more complex speech habits: consider Uriah Heep, Rosa Dartle, Peggotty, Dora Spenlow, Betsey Trotwood, to take five notable examples from just one book. And beyond these, again, are the still more famous characters who are lifted, as much as anything by their speech, into popular mythology: Quilp, Pecksniff, Micawber, William Dorrit, Flora Finching, above all Sairey Gamp.

How is this done? It is easy to oversimplify. To say that Sairey Gamp and Flora Finching are perfect illusions, but that no-one ever 'really' talked like them is as misleading as the crudely realist theory that they come directly from life. Speech like theirs represents, no doubt, some distillation, but this is not simply a matter of shedding the 'ums and 'ers of 'ordinary' speech and adding pattern instead. Not everyone 'ums and 'ers, and not all pattern is literary: most ordinary speech is a patterned, even a weirdly patterned, affair. The speech of Sairey Gamp is best thought of not as a construct of twisted syntax and highly stylised cockney, but as a triumph of style. It belongs with the speech of Dr Johnson, or Oscar Wilde, or Sir John Falstaff – and this mixing of real and fictitious people is, I hasten to add, intentional, since the phenomenon is an overlapping one for literature and life. By 'style', I mean an activity always intelligent and almost always histrionic, which cuts across social class and formal education, but is more likely to be found in dialect or in highly idiosyncratic conversation than in standard speech. Among fictional characters we most often encounter it in plays or novels where readers are likely to sense realism and artifice in almost equal degrees: Hardy's rustics, Synge's peasants, Dickens's cockneys, James Baldwin's Negroes, the people of Llareggub in *Under Milk Wood*. Such speech, though naturalistic, is not simply 'reported'; it is heightened, but in a manner as often encountered in life as in art. We must all have met West Indians, Irishmen, Welshmen, Scotsmen, cockneys, West Countrymen, in pubs or on coach trips, or just relaxing together, whose speech might have come 'straight from a book'. The conditions needed are precisely those that one finds in a local, where banter takes on the suggestion of a ritual or game.

The people are friends, linked by mutual liking or at the least mutual tolerance; the atmosphere is relaxed but highly intelligent, with much nudging of life, through mimicry, in the direction of art. The mimicry is as often as not self-mimicry, all zest and no malice, recreating personality a little larger than life. It is easy to see why formally educated people are often disqualified; they are deprived of a natural and instinctual relationship with speech. There is the barrier of standard speech, with its calculated sacrifice of colour to logic, and the barrier of diffidence or self-absorption, to which the 'educated' are prone. Sairey Gamp, in contrast, 'acts' herself with a panache and a total conviction inaccessible to most of her middle-class superiors. The educated man who remains colourful nearly always does so with some edge of defiance or conscious rebellion, and is far more likely to be the product of conscious artifice than of instinct alone.

Such generalisations, it will be readily conceded, fall short of perfection, but they seem to me broadly, and for my present purpose sufficiently, true. In fiction, whether Dickens's or Hardy's, James Baldwin's or Pinter's, the most colourful speech usually belongs to peasants or workers, to outsiders, to the technically illiterate, and in recording this the writers are being broadly true to life. Yet 'recording', again, is a misleading word if left unqualified: in creating Mrs Gamp, Dickens is faithful to her pre-eminent skill in creating herself. Few characters from fiction can challenge her pre-eminence among the immortals. She has the uniqueness and universality natural to myth.

One further aspect of Mrs Gamp's highly idiosyncratic speech habits is a certain elusiveness, in the teasing suggestion of things unsayable, or unsaid. Her tone when she is being pious is peculiarly elusive. Is she being consciously ironic, or does the irony come wholly from elsewhere? A little of each, but how much of each is hard to determine. Sairey on this 'wale of tears' is in very obvious ways incongruous, but our chief impression is of a real guardian of the mysteries, birth, marriage and death. She is timeless by her continuing vitality as well as by the art which preserves her: in her creative resilience, her

survival, she is heroic and true. And this is because she is real
before she is mythic – an ordinary old woman, poor in purse,
alone in the world, living in rooms at Poll Sweedlepipe's, and
surviving on minimal talents dynamically employed. Her moral
character, good and bad mixed, is fascinating, but not in itself
remarkable; the remarkable thing is her colour and life. She is
both a social scandal and a hope for humanity; there would be
a gap in nature if she finally ceased to live down the street or
just around the block. And this is because, though her speech
rhythms are important, they are not everything; the really
important thing about Sairey Gamp is *what* she says, and who
she is. She is a hope for humanity because she is more than vivid,
she is authentic : against the growing complexity of her rhetoric,
as she becomes established in the novel and Dickens takes flight
with her, her presence simply and massively grows. For every
tough, vivid, coarse, inventive and unpredictable old woman,
a patron saint has been born. God bless thee, Sairey Gamp! – as
Dickens, or Pecksniff, would say.

I V

Pecksniff and Sairey Gamp are at the heart of *Martin Chuzzlewit*,
but what of Tom Pinch? He is the one indisputably good
character, and we see a lot of him, since he keeps appearing,
though his direct influence upon the plot is very small. Tom is
a fascinating enigma, not so much in himself but in what we
make of him, and in what Dickens may be assumed to have
wanted us to make. At first, Tom seems a grotesque like Kit
Nubbles, shambling and vaguely ageless because always old :

'Come in!' cried Mr Pecksniff – not severely, only virtuously.
'Come in!'
An ungainly, awkward-looking man, extremely short-sighted
and prematurely bald, availed himself of this permission; and
seeing that Mr Pecksniff sat with his back towards him, gazing
at the fire, stood hesitating, with the door in his hand. He was
far from handsome, certainly, and was dressed in a snuff-
coloured suit of an uncouth make at the best, which being shrunk
with long wear, was twisted and tortured into all kinds of odd

shapes; but notwithstanding his attire and his clumsy figure, which a great stoop in his shoulders and a ludicrous habit he had of thrusting his head forward by no means redeemed, one would not have been disposed (unless Mr Pecksniff said so) to consider him a bad fellow by any means. He was perhaps about thirty but he might have been almost any age between sixteen and sixty, being one of those strange creatures who never decline into an ancient appearance, but look their oldest when they are very young, and get it over at once.

Tom is like Kit in general uncouthness, and like him in being disqualified from marrying the woman he loves. Why? Because she is engaged to Martin: but then, Tom is morally superior to Martin, and it seems odd that he should never stand a chance to compete.

I think Dickens was uneasy about Tom for all kinds of reasons, and it might be as well to start with a prosecution case. Consider the tone in which Tom is exalted in chapter 5 : this is the chapter following the famous Chuzzlewit family gathering, and my present quotation follows the superb description of Mr Pecksniff's horse :

Blessings on thy simple heart, Tom Pinch, how proudly dost thou button up that scanty coat, called by a sad misnomer, for these many years, a 'great' one, and how thoroughly as with thy cheerful voice thou pleasantly adjurest Sam the hostler 'not to let him go yet', dost thou believe that quadruped desires to go and would go if he might! Who could repress a smile – of love for thee, Tom Pinch, and not in jest at thy expense, for thou art poor enough already, Heaven knows – to think that such a holiday as lies before thee should awaken that quick flow and hurry of the spirits in which thou settest down again, almost untasted, on the kitchen window-sill, that great white mug (put by, by thy own hands, last night, that breakfast might not hold thee late), and layest yonder crust upon the seat beside thee, to be eaten on the road, when thou art calmer in thy high rejoicing! Who, as thou drivest off, a happy man, and noddest with a grateful lovingness to Pecksniff in his night-cap at his chamber-window, would not cry: 'Heaven speed thee, Tom, and send that thou wert going off forever to some quiet home where thou mightst live at peace, and sorrow could not touch thee!'

This is pure Pecksniff, whatever Dickens intended – and Dickens had more of Pecksniff in him, certainly, than he had of Tom. We have only to examine the rhetoric, addressed apparently to an exclusive audience of Pickwicks and Brothers Cheeryble, to feel that only Pecksniff could rise to such heights. Then, a little later, we come to this : 'But there was more than this. It was not only the married people and the children who gave Tom a welcome as he passed. No, no . . .' That 'No, no' is even purer Pecksniff : how can we miss the serene smile and piously uplifted hand ? Yet Dickens is not being consciously hypocritical about Tom (No, no!) : it is much more a matter, in this sparkling context, of protesting too much. Tom's virtue has flavours difficult enough at any time to stomach : he is uncreative, uncritical, unambitious, and attuned to patronage, as Dickens makes clear. We are teased into pondering how virtue can overcome such handicaps, and indeed whether handicaps of this order may be virtues themselves, since Tom's joy in living, his rich human consciousness, all rewards for virtue, are too evident to doubt.

The problem of Tom must have been at least as acute for Dickens, however, as for most of his readers, since his energetic villains were obviously so very much more akin to himself. His depictions of virtue nearly always include the withdrawal of certain kinds of commitment, whether the withdrawal of Pick- wick and the Brothers Cheeryble from worldliness (despite their careers as businessmen) or the more profound withdrawal of Agnes Wickfield and Amy Dorrit from ambition or any hint of self-assertiveness. In the later novels, virtue is usually sacrificial, and it is Tom Pinch's destiny to live in a richly comic book. But aspects of the deep problem of virtue are already evident – for instance, is happiness anti-critical, even anti- intelligent, *per se*? Tom himself is a hedonist in the mood and genre of Father Christmas, and Dickens, who was writing *A Christmas Carol* concurrently, would clearly have approved this. But Christmas demands a radical suspension of normal judge- ment. The presents are all just exactly what one wanted, and from the best family and friends in the world. The exercise requires euphoria, or a very high degree of willed delusion,

with total idiocy an undeniable aid. Dickens of all men understood the predicament. Few Victorians were more instinctively
critical and subversive, and as a novelist, he was the reverse o
Pinchlike : had he not just produced the Chuzzlewit family
gathering in chapter ɪv ? Yet true hedonism may require a Tom
Pinch rather than a Dickens, as Dickens would wryly have
known. Tom's knack of suspended awareness is indeed remarkable. In Pecksniff's house he serves the best and kindest of
masters, the sweetest of mistresses, as though it really were
Christmas all the year. When Pecksniff and his daughters go
off to London, leaving for Tom and Martin the most grisly
scraps from the previous night's feasting, Tom enjoys the best
and heartiest of meals. All very well, except that Martin laughs
at him : and here Dickens's real difficulties begin. Anyone
would laugh, we are assured, even Diogenes, but some would
laugh at Tom, some with him, and here is the great divide.
Martin laughs at Tom, and so reveals his selfishness – a quality
apparent enough in all that he says and whatever he does.
Later, when John Westlock and Martin discuss Tom, the moral
gulf is further indicated. For John, Tom is a good man at precisely the points of obtuseness which arouse Martin's contempt.

   Yet surely Martin is right, at least in principle ? We may
feel affection for Tom in his extreme enjoyment (and Martin
feels affection), but hardly respect. Curiously, Martin is made
to seem unnaturally selfish even when he accepts the normal
Victorian conventions – that Tom is a servant, and therefore
his inferior; that marriage must be based on something more
than love in an attic; and matters like these. Perhaps the
Victorian ideal of romantic love as a sufficient basis for marriage
was already winning, and Martin's realism about marriage, as
it would have seemed to an earlier generation, already strikes
Dickens as cynically tinged. And perhaps Dickens himself was
suffering from an unease about egalitarianism – the American
chapters certainly suggest this – which caused him to over-
compensate about Tom. Nevertheless, an inescapable question
looms behind such writing. Whatever Tom's virtue, and whatever the theory, is Tom really Martin's equal in any meaningful
sense ?

The problem becomes more acute in matters involving human judgement. We may accept Tom's delight in stale scraps and dregs of food as evidence of virtue, but can we accept Tom's delight in Pecksniff as well? Tom exists to be patronised and he thrives on patronage; it is the secret of his success with Martin as well as with Pecksniff himself. A sharper truth about patronage is later expressed by Dickens through Skimpole and William Dorrit; there is a sharper truth here, indeed, in Chevy Slyme. Slyme differs from Tom in that he is unutterably lazy and that he despises his patrons, but like Tom he lives on scraps from richer men's feasts. Then there is old Chuffey, who revolves around Anthony Chuzzlewit much as Tom does round Pecksniff. Given old age, illness, and the erosion of inner resources by senility, what is to prevent Tom from ending like this?

Tom's obtuseness is not purely personal in its implications; it has inescapable repercussions on the world. Pecksniff regards Tom as a social asset even while he despises him; Tom's enthusiasm is an important aspect of Pecksniff's repute. So it is not enough to endorse Tom as a holy fool who sees precious truths hidden from the cunning, since though he may be this, he also fails to see glaring moral distinctions between true and false. There are many characters in Dickens who have a sure instinct of moral discrimination – Little Nell is an early example, while a late and very remarkable one is Jenny Wren. But Tom Pinch wholly lacks this instinct, or has it only selectively; his own habit – perhaps equally valuable – is to think the best of everyone until decisively proved wrong. But what would happen if the world were nine-tenths Pinches and one-tenth Pecksniffs? – the Pecksniffs would have a field day, as Pecksniff does. Certainly the Pecksniffs would get away with being Pecksniff indefinitely, losing only the pleasure of adversaries worthy of their skill. It is interesting that old Martin Chuzzlewit is at first convinced that Tom is a toady, and treats Tom's deference with suspicious contempt. But then, Martin is soured by life, and mistrusts everybody, and learning to distinguish between Pecksniff and Tom is a lesson for *him*. Nonetheless, his initial suspicion is not unnatural. Tom's *tone* could hardly be bettered, even by Uriah Heep, for 'umble designs.

Later, Dickens tries to get round this problem by calling Pecksniff Tom's 'delusion', and showing – very convincingly and affectingly – how much Tom suffers when he has to see the truth. But Tom's Pecksniff is not really an aberration, he is a symptom; Tom tends to think well of all men whenever he can. And here, the difficulty again presents itself acutely: Tom's simple trust is delightful, and delightful especially to its recipients, but would it not be still more delightful (I am still with the prosecution case) if it included judgement and tact? A dog's affection is pleasing, but not really flattering; and Tom's insight into Pecksniff is hardly greater than a dog's. Tom, again, is one of nature's Tories, a godsend to his superiors; he knows – who better? – that he should be duly grateful and know his place. A case could be made out even for Tom as the victim of social injustice, were this not so clearly unintended. Whatever Tom is, he is not a victim, not in any manner degraded or crushed.

So one circles around to another, and better place of starting; to see Tom's virtue, including the virtue of thinking well of Pecksniff, we must perceive good and evil on a spiritual plane. The prosecution case blames Tom for being virtuous in a manner that some people cannot stomach; but the matter cannot quite rest here. A world of Toms and Pecksniffs would give the temporal advantage to the Pecksniffs, but so much the worse, perhaps, for such a world? Tom is far more rounded as a character than has yet been suggested. He is wholesome, dependable, courageous, hard-working; he enjoys a rich consciousness, and is glad to be alive. All this is something, if it is not quite everything, and if we find it nauseous, the disorder may conceivably be in ourselves. There must be people in the world who are not particularly clever, talented and creative, in whom virtue can yet exist and take lovable forms. Not everyone can be as intelligent and energetic as (say) Dickens, and Dickens need not have been patronising, merely realistic, to acknowledge this. The Christmas spirit is understandable enough, for instance, in a world of hardship and poverty, which is where Dickens most normally assumed it to be. If the poor do not enter into minor and occasional pleasures with gusto,

what hope have they for any pleasures at all? The gulf dividing
rich from poor is great and absolute; a Tom Pinch could no
more aspire to wealth or education than he could fly in the air.
Modern critics, oddly, often overlook this, and Tom undeniably
fails a test of 'maturity' when 'maturity' is Shakespeare and
D. H. Lawrence rolled into one. Yet Tom's virtue remains recognisable, and in its social setting admirable, a heart-warming
response to poverty in its way. To understand it we must
remember Dickens's continual delight in little gardens, little
amateur theatricals, little family parties, little castles – as long
as they were built firmly in Walworth like Wemmick's, and not
left, like William Dorrit's, in the air. Dickens liked to think of
the poor relaxing and feasting, even if they couldn't create
much, and losing themselves in the happiness of goodwill and
the will to goodwill. But he knew that this was real virtue and
not simple escapism; it wasn't easy to live with privation, to
make the best of things, to create small oases in a desert world.
Hence the sheer exuberance of small moments of happiness that
could be created: the intense warmth and security of a very
poor fireside, with a thought spared for the many worse-off,
and perhaps a moment's innocent patronage of the whole outside world. Anyone out of sympathy with this is out of sympathy
with Dickens. The child, in games where expensive toys are
discarded for an old golliwog, is nearer the mood of it. So are
the simple: and Dickens admired simplicity in a New Testament
way. Of course there were dangers of delusion for very simple
adults, and Tom Pinch's Pecksniff is an instance, but not more
danger than all kinds of virtue must run. And the danger is
balanced by something deeper than anything as yet done justice
to: when the poor in spirit or in circumstance see a flower-pot
or a sooty window-box as paradise, they may be seeing the
truth. Dickens was a romantic in this, if in no other respect,
that he believed in the transforming power of imagination, and
prized Reason, in Coleridge's sense, above the analytical mind.

Tom Pinch stands in a line which includes Kit Nubbles and
Joe Gargery, but which has affinities with other Dickens people
as well. He is a generally other-worldly person with a rich,
inner consciousness; Dickens conveys the power which music,

poetry, natural beauty have in his life. Though unable to create, he responds powerfully to creation; his openness is an indispensible prerequisite to criticism whether or not he has a critical mind. Dickens, though not himself unworldly, admired the quality; he shows Tom as a spiritual and even a mystical man. Tom is nearer to the childlike than he is to the childish. He belongs with the outstandingly virtuous – Little Nell and the far more intelligent Amy Dorrit – not with pseudo-children like Skimpole or with the many deplorable child-fathers like Mr Dolls. It is a triumph of Dickens's art that he could enter into a person so dissimilar to himself, and one whom he might himself have been inclined, by temperament, to despise. Even John Westlock admits at one point that Tom lacks a touch of the devil, and Dickens admired devils even while he scourged. Dickens was also right to see, surely, that virtue like Tom's requires the absence of certain kinds of energy – the energy of ambition and self-aggrandisement – as well as the absence of certain traits of the critical mind.

Our chief difficulty with Tom then, if we desert the prosecution and join defending counsel permanently, may be that Dickens has not yet seen what is to be done in his novels with such a character: Tom is likeable and moving, but has little organic connection with the plot. His life with his sister is interesting and half-idyllic, but also somewhat embarrassing, and not particularly useful to the novel as a whole. We are forced to conclude that Tom is very undersexed, or that Dickens must salve his conscience by pretending this; also, that Tom would not have been a plausible husband for Mary Graham even in an ideal world. Tom's failure to ponder the logic of this is a positive hindrance; surely he must have ideas and feelings which we would be interested to know? Later, Dickens was able to present sacrificial virtue much more powerfully in Amy Dorrit, who has precisely the kind of analytical intelligence denied to Tom Pinch. Amy's apparent unawareness for much of the time of the moral flaws of her father is nothing like obtuseness: given that William Dorrit could only be destroyed by self-knowledge, it is a most costly and heroic pretence. Amy Dorrit belongs, however, to a tragic novel, and Dickens was no

doubt right, with Tom Pinch, to stop short of questions too
sombre in tone. The mood of *Martin Chuzzlewit* is consistently
zestful, and Tom undeniably belongs to *this* book.

v

Martin Chuzzlewit is a moral fable, comprehensive in scope and
resourcefulness, where Mark Tapley has to learn the tinge of
selfishness in his own desire to earn credit by being jolly even
while he rejoices in the similar, but deeper, lesson that Martin
learns. Old Martin, again, is as much a victim of selfishness as
his nephew – though one is glad to find that his suspicion of his
fellow men, in itself unamiable, does not stop short of the one
person most calculated to bear it out.

The moral fable is one strand of *Martin Chuzzlewit* : another
is the darkly Dostoevskian vision of murder, which penetrates
deeper than (say) the Gothic insets in *Pickwick*, and yet seems
undeniably part of the novel and its success. *Martin Chuzzlewit*
is no idyllic comedy, just shaded with evil, like *Pickwick* : it is
comedy poised over a near-tragic abyss. The chapters following
Jonas's disintegration belong to the novel, but much as a
feverish illness might belong to normal life. The best criticism
about Jonas has been offered by Steven Marcus, who points out
that whereas most of the other active characters create themselves by flamboyant willpower, Jonas, who is sullen and uncreative, wholly fails to do this. He tumbles out of the comic
world into pure alienation, and thereby shows what lies just
beyond. Pecksniff nearly tumbles out when he goes one degree
too far with Mary Graham; Mrs Gamp runs the risk when she
tests Mrs 'Arris just a little too far. But Jonas oversteps completely, and descends into horror. The liberty he seeks, by
killing a father and marrying an enemy, is revealed as enslave-
ment and death.

Martin Chuzzlewit has been rightly acclaimed as an important
novel, and for some critics it is the first of Dickens's novels to be
really great. Dorothy Van Ghent, in her celebrated essay 'The
Dickens World : a view from Todgers's', points out that we see
throughout it inanimate things becoming animate, while men

turn into things. It is 'a world undergoing a gruesome spiritual
transformation', where the 'animation of inanimate objects' in
particular 'suggests both the quaint gaiety of a forbidden life and
an aggressiveness that has got out of control'. This is admirably said, though it should be remembered that Dickens's
own control over his invention was nearly always masterly. In
Barnaby Rudge, a richly animate universe is given to Barnaby
and placed as idiocy, precisely because no creative intelligence
keeps it in check. In Dickens's other novels, rioting fancy can be
a manifestation of fear, delusion, guilt, childish innocence, many
other things, and deliberate caprice can range from the innocence of Mr Dick's Memorial to the evil of Miss Havisham's
wedding feast. The peculiar place of rioting fancy in *Martin
Chuzzlewit* is, I am suggesting, central; exuberant, unbridled
fancy transforms the book.

An excellent chapter on *Martin Chuzzlewit* will be found in
J. Hillis Miller's *Charles Dickens: the world of his novels*, where
the moral theme of selfishness is shown to be reinforced by the
whole texture and tone. 'The arena of *Martin Chuzzlewit* is the
present, a present which is irrevocably cut off from the past and
in which society in the sense of an integrated community has
been replaced by a fragmented collection of isolated self-seeking
individuals.' After praising Dorothy Van Ghent, Mr Miller goes
on to say :

But the spectator on Todgers's roof discovers something more
disquieting. He discovers that the withdrawal of something from
the scene produces not simply a blank in his consciousness, a
blank which he cannot easily replace, with his own interior life,
but an unfillable gap. The exterior and visible void is 'ridicu-
lously disproportionate in its extent' because it proves to the
observer his own interior nothingness.

The effect is very close, in short, to that analysed by Sartre in
La Nausée, and the various characters pursue their quest for
identity against a cosmic void.

Miller's account of the novel is full of excellent perceptions
and is an excellent answer to readers who fail to see any organic
unity in it at all. But I think he goes astray by being too literal :
he fails to do justice to the transforming exuberance which is at

work. Tigg and Jonas are made to sound unnecessarily central, and the price is apparent in his dealings with Mark Tapley and Sairey Gamp. Mr Miller is fairly stern about both of them, and endorses old Martin's moral exposure of Sairey: 'in the end, Sairey fails, fails because she has never ceased to be alone, selfish. Her way is firmly rejected by Dickens when he includes her among the villains exposed in the denouement . . .' But the 'exposure' is surely a mere sop to the novel's residual social realism. Mrs Gamp remains, for us, exposure or no exposure, a pagan goddess, a triumph of resourcefulness, a triumph of life.

The novel, taken as a whole, has many of the characteristics of an ironic quest. America is the land of romantic promise, a green world, where Eden blooms again; but it turns out to be a waste land, a cruelly ironic hoax. Yet the hero is flawed, and his visit to America becomes a purgation of disabling pride. So one returns to the more normal, chaotic world of England from which one started, where people bump together and exploit one another in selfishness, but where life and resilience splendidly go on. The transformation I have been pointing to is in my view the true organising principle – a gaiety that Dickens realised could not be used in quite this same way ever again. The American transcendentalist lady delivers herself, it will be recalled, as follows: 'Howls the sublime, and softly sleeps the calm ideal, in the whispering chambers of Imagination. To hear it, sweet it is. But then, outlaughs the stern philosopher, and saith to the Grotesque, "What ho! Arrest for me that Agency. Go, bring it here!" And so the vision fadeth.' Whatever this means, it means *Martin Chuzzlewit* among Dickens's works.

5 *Dombey and Son*
cobwebs to sunlight

I N *Dombey and Son* Dickens writes with unabated vitality, but he now acknowledges his gift for ridicule as a danger. The new novel is planned to exclude the transforming gaiety of *Martin Chuzzlewit*. Its great proud characters remain cold as marble until their long-delayed awakening in disgrace and suffering. Dickens's moral purpose is more single-minded than it was in *Martin Chuzzlewit*. Pride is no longer a series of virtuoso demonstrations almost redeemed by panache. It is the high melodrama of Dombey, Edith, Carker, Alice, locked in hatred and despair. For Carker there is no moral awakening, only a nightmare humiliation followed by death. For the others there is redemption only when they are broken – Alice on her deathbed, Dombey during serious illness following bankruptcy, Edith when she realises that to all decent people she must be as if dead. The main action develops through tremendous scenes of passion and hatred, scenes too tremendous indeed for some tastes, though the anger rings bitterly true. Where should we look for melodrama if not in the family? Where is ham acting to be found if not in the home? Dickens captures the extravagance of violence between father and daughter, husband and wife, lover and mistress, its taste for soaring periods and sanctified clichés, its coarse and coarsening self-indulgence, its spiritual rape. When Dickens's rhetoric gets out of hand, this is not usually for any lack of realism, but because we suspect that the author is enjoying himself altogether too much. 'Awake, doomed man!' he shouts, bouncing into the story like one of his own Victorian nannies intent on frightening a baby into fits. This relish for melodrama is frequently associated, moreover, with his relish for Florence, a weakness in the novel to which I shall return.

But first the magnificence of Dickens's inventiveness must be glanced at, no less rich for all his pruning of comic passages in the proofs. Though the colour of the novel is 'iron grey autumnal', like the day of little Paul's christening, this is conveyed through passages of quite remarkable vitality : 'A rusty urn at each high corner, dug up from an ancient tomb, preached desolation and decay, as from two pulpits; and the chimney-glass, reflecting Mr Dombey and his portrait at one blow, seemed fraught with melancholy reflections.' Two rusty urns, preaching desolation and decay, and two Mr Dombeys, as static as the urns. The demonic life of the passage belongs, characteristically enough, to the mirror, which reflects 'at one blow' as if in derision, and transfers 'melancholy reflections' from the passive objects reflected to its active self. This liveliness of fancy is Dickens's, and not Mr Dombey's; none of it rubs off on *him*. But coldness is evoked with quite poetic intensity. We are reminded of the Clennam house and Miss Havisham's wedding feast in late Dickens, as well as the great cold places where Ibsen's heroes live and die.

A little later in this episode (little Paul's christening) Dickens creates his chill through direct humour :

He [Mr Chick] gave Mr Dombey his hand, as if he feared it might electrify him. Mr Dombey took it as if it were a fish, or seaweed, or some such clammy substance, and immediately returned it to him with exalted politeness.

'Perhaps, Louisa,' said Mr Dombey, slightly turning his head in his cravat, as if it were a socket, 'you would have preferred a fire ?'

'Oh, my dear Paul, no,' said Mrs Chick, who had much ado to keep her teeth from chattering, 'no, not me.'

The liveliness again plays round its victim without at all rubbing off on him; we remember Mr Dombey as a coldly humourless man. The controlling image of the chapter is cold – 'there was a toothache in everything' – and the proceedings are ominously more like a going-out of the world than a coming-in. Death seems to radiate from father to son in the passage : a suggestion nowhere explicit, nowhere clarified as symbol, but disturbingly diffused through the imagery and tone.

D

Dickens's rich fancifulness in this novel is often wholly serious, and akin to metaphysical wit: 'And there, with an aching void in his young heart, and all outside so cold, and bare, and strange, Paul sat as if he had taken life unfurnished, and the upholsterers were never coming.' And, sometimes, the fancifulness, as increasingly in Dickens's later novels, is a mode of observation, surprisingly original only because unarguably true :

Forty years at least had elapsed since the Peruvian mines had been the death of Mr Pipchin; but his relict still wore black bombazine, of such a lustreless, deep, dead, sombre shade, that gas itself couldn't light her up after dark, and her presence was a quencher to any number of candles . . .

The castle of this ogress and child-queller was in a steep by-street at Brighton; where the soil was more than usually chalky, flinty and sterile, and the houses were more than usually brittle and thin; where the small front gardens had the un-accountable property of producing nothing but marigolds, what-ever was sown in them; and where snails were constantly discovered holding on to the street-doors, and other public places they were not expected to ornament, with the tenacity of cupping-glasses. In the winter-time the air couldn't be got out of the castle, and in the summer-time it couldn't be got in. There was such a continual reverberation of wind in it, that it sounded like a great shell, which the inhabitants were obliged to hold to their ears night and day, whether they liked it or no. It was not naturally a fresh-smelling house; and in the window of the front-parlour, which was never opened, Mrs Pipchin kept a collection of plants in pots, which imparted an earthy flavour of their own to the establishment. However choice examples of their kind, too, these plants were of a kind peculiarly adapted to the embowerment of Mrs Pipchin. There were half-a-dozen specimens of the cactus, writhing round bits of lath, like hairy serpents; another specimen shooting out broad claws, like a green lobster; several creeping vegetables, possessed of sticky and adhesive leaves; and one uncomfortable flower-pot hanging to the ceiling, which appeared to have boiled over, and tickling people underneath with its long green ends, reminded them of spiders – in which Mrs Pipchin's dwelling was uncomfortably prolific, though perhaps it challenged competition still more proudly, in the season, in point of earwigs.

There are many details in this to remind us of *Martin Chuzzlewit* ('gas itself couldn't light her up after dark, and her presence was a quencher to any number of candles'), but the effect is more than ever disciplined by the actual world. Isn't Mrs Pipchin's collection of plants precisely the collection in every murky front-parlour? – the hanging one has tickled us all. Haven't we seen her marigolds in a hundred front gardens, and wondered *why* always marigolds and nothing else? Yet all of this in no way prejudices Mrs Pipchin's uniqueness. Indeed, uniqueness is required of her, since if she is not indisputably like anyone known to us, this is only because, like everyone at all resembling her who is known to us, she is so wholly herself. Which is not to say, again, that Dickens transcribes her directly from life, or (alternatively) that he simply creates her. The Dickensian illusion is more subtly poised between life and art.

Her place, with Mrs Gamp and a hundred other Dickens people, is mythic; and belongs very particularly to little Paul's imagination, where she is most distinctively and for once almost amiably herself. Like all imaginative and privileged children, Paul is both a match for her and a suitable complement; he is most perfectly adapted to setting her off:

Mrs Pipchin had an old black cat, who generally lay coiled upon the centre foot of the fender, purring egotistically and winking at the fire until the contracted pupils of his eyes were like two notes of admiration. The good old lady might have been – not to record it disrespectfully – a witch, and Paul and the cat her two familiars, as they all sat by the fire together. It would have been quite in keeping with the appearance of the party if they had all sprung up the chimney in a high wind one night, and never been heard of any more.

This is so timeless, so perpetual, that it must be mythic: yet Mrs Pipchin's foothold in the social world lends itself to satire as direct as this:

It being a part of Mrs Pipchin's system not to encourage a child's mind to develop and expand itself like a flower, but to open it with force like an oyster, the moral of these lessons was usually of a violent and stunning character; the hero – a naughty boy – seldom, in the mildest catastrophe, being finished off by anything less than a lion, or a bear.

While drawing attention to the vitality of *Dombey and Son*, and
before passing on to closer analysis, it is impossible not to
reflect upon the presence in it of Captain Cuttle and Joey Bagstock – those rumbustious polar opposites – of Mr Toots, Polly,
Susan Nipper, Mrs Skewton, Good Mrs Brown : a cast characteristically lavish in scale. In this novel we find more characters
than ever before who are to a high degree created through
unmistakable rhythms of speech. Though Dickens surpassed
himself at this particular miracle later (the palm belongs on my
reckoning to *Bleak House*, with the strongest competition from
David Copperfield and *Our Mutual Friend*), there are no fewer
than fourteen such characters here. I exclude from the fourteen
many characters like Dombey himself, Carker and Edith, whose
speech is always consistent and recognisable without being
wholly distinctive, and include only one really eccentric case
which could be ascribed to verbal trickery, Captain Bunsby.
The other thirteen are : little Paul, Susan, Mrs Pipchin, Joey
Bagstock, Captain Cuttle, Rob the Grinder, Good Mrs Brown,
Mrs Chick, Miss Tox, Mrs Skewton, Mrs MacStinger, Mr
Toots and Cousin Feenix. Dickens's power of noting or creating
exact speech surpasses that of all other novelists. No-one except
Shakespeare approaches him in this.

                                    II

Dombey and Son is among the most telling of Dickens's titles, in
that it reminds us continually of little Paul's status in life and
death. As son (small 's') he dies before the novel's real development has started, and is influential mainly as a poison in his
father's mind. As Son (capital 'S') he remains indissolubly
linked with the great firm until its downfall, the idea for which
life and humanity – his mother's and sister's, his own – are
spent. But the dichotomy is not simple. As Son, he is not only
the focus of all Mr Dombey's ambitions, but the recipient of
whatever love Mr Dombey has it in him to give. As son, he is the
flesh-and-blood boy whose preference for Florence is the post-
humous poison in Mr Dombey's soul.

There is also Son the abstraction, a position precariously

filled by Paul in his short lifetime, and a complex vacancy after his death. Captain Cuttle in his disastrous interview with Carker proposes Walter as replacement, Carker in secret counsels proposes himself. Carker fails in his assault upon Son, but through Edith's agency, not Dombey's, and only when he has fulfilled his carker-role in Dombey and Son. Captain Cuttle turns out to be right, but ironically beyond expectation; Walter *is* Mr Dombey's heir in more ways than one.

The reader in this novel is therefore aware of Paul in several capacities. He is the real boy, sensitive and doomed, drawn to the waves, and puzzled to think what they are always saying; and he is the boy born to be Son, a tragic destiny in life and death. The chapters depicting his childhood are among the most moving in Dickens, notably the long fourteenth chapter, where the dying boy's consciousness is presented in depth. It is an interesting prefiguring of Virginia Woolf's method of presenting consciousness, though Dickens never allows his readers or himself to become wholly submerged. Paul's feelings in this last illness are conveyed with an intensity bordering on hallucination as his vivid childhood world grows tenderer, happier, and starts to fade. Only at the end of chapter 17 does Dickens intervene directly, and at the very last moment spoil his effect.

III

Little Paul's life is a masterly inset in the novel, but our main interest is always directed elsewhere. At the centre, isolated and statuesque, is Mr Dombey, located where delusion seems natural, at the focus of pride. A man like Dombey, seeing, acknowledging, needing nothing outside his own grandeur, might well become more like Pride Incarnate than a man. The Dombey consciousness is a whole universe both in its completeness, and in its consequent lack of perspectives; it is a world frozen towards allegory, where Dombey exists, fittingly enough, as purest 'case'.

Dombey's pride is of the particular kind, however, which Dickens saw coming to birth as the 1840s progressed. For the first time in his novels, we sense evil as an impersonal force transcending its agents, and the novel comes close to being the tragedy of Mr Dombey himself. Who is Dombey? He is The City; he is Export/Import; he is Exchange; he is the Mystery of Equity; he is profit and thrift rolled into one. He is *laissez faire*, finding his level in the free market, somewhat above the level of most other men. He is, or appears to be (but appearances are deceptive), the embryonic hero of Samuel Smiles. He is also, to those more jaundiced, a portent of the collapse of civilised values from within. As slave-owner he perfectly exemplifies Disraeli's thesis in *Sybil* (1845) that the new rich are enemies and exploiters of the poor. He seems again (and appearances are again deceptive) to be a perfect blueprint for Matthew Arnold's Philistine, no sweetness or charm, no graces, much energy and drive.

But whatever evils we find in Mr Dombey, his integrity is apparent; there is no touch of hypocrisy in such a man. He is totally honest and honourable in his worldly dealings; even in ruin, his chief thought is for the investors who have trusted themselves to his firm. He represents the mercantile powers who for two centuries or more have been making England prosperous and are now in the ascendant – a perfect contrast to poor old Sol Gills, with his shop that no-one any longer comes to, and his melancholy sense of a world that has passed him by. Naturally Mr Dombey has no need for props or creeds to sustain him, when his grandeur is so properly and generally acknowledged by society at large.

There, then, is Mr Dombey, as he sees himself, and as his dependants and flatterers affect to see him for nine-tenths of the book. As we see him, under Dickens's guidance, he is somewhat different, more statue or Gorgon than flesh and blood. At the core of the depiction is savage satire, unqualified by the high spirits bubbling along on top. Dombey's sin is that of worshipping the false god Mammon; indeed, of revering himself as incarnation of the god. Hence the blasphemy of little Paul's questions in the very temple: 'What is money?' – 'what's money after all?' – 'what can it do?' Money, replies Mr Dombey sternly, can do 'anything'. No, not anything, argues Paul; it couldn't save his mother from death. Well 'anything – almost' amends Mr Dombey. If money couldn't save Mrs Dombey, at least it could provide Dr Parker Peps for her, the next best thing in Mr Dombey's view. As little Paul is soon to discover, money can also provide other experts when the occasion calls for them, Mrs Pipchin and the Blimbers in all matters relating to education, rough and tough old Joey B. in affairs of the heart. What else can money do? It can bring Walter Gay as a suppliant and beggar, with powers of binding or loosing – powers educatively delegated, on this notable occasion, to Son. 'I like Walter,' says Paul afterwards, sensing the sweets of patronage (but Paul is innocent enough to recognise responsibilities too, as his dying request for Walter shows). Money also brings independence, flattery, self-sufficiency, and emancipation from the needs and solaces of love.

No-one is richer than Dombey because he takes care to mix with no-one richer, and recognises no order of privilege or excellence superior to his own. In a striking manner this bears out Disraeli's perception that the capitalist ascendancy is more careless of its dependants than the old feudal society, more heartless in the kind of society it creates. There is no bond between master and servant any longer, only naked exploitation of the poor by the rich. Dickens did not share Disraeli's vision of a lost feudal harmony, yet he was to show a much more human – if no less doomed – relationship in *Bleak House* between the aristocratic Sir Leicester Dedlock and his dependants and retainers at Chesney Wold. Clearly Mr Dombey would fit excellently into the Young England casebook, as he would also into the more explosive casebook of Engels and Marx. In the year when *Dombey and Son* was being written (1848), the *Communist Manifesto* came into its at first obscure existence, an analysis of capitalism hardly bleaker than Dickens's in its force. Dickens, like nearly all of his contemporaries, did not know the *Manifesto*, but many aspects of it would have interested him – not least, the analysis of the new railways as a revolutionary force. Railways bring the two worlds of rich and poor face to face with one another (Mr Dombey's ride to Leamington), and offer new possibilities of mobilisation for the poor. It is of

particular interest to note how the darkness in Mr Dombey's
mind is projected on to the railway through the very rhythms in
which Dickens creates his journey, so that the landscape of
squalor which he responds to almost as a personal insult seems
to be spun also (as indeed it is) out of himself. There is a
profound fitness in the perception that the nightmare fancies of
Mr Dombey's diseased consciousness are also nightmare
realities in his capitalist world :

Louder and louder yet, it shrieks and cries as it comes tearing
on resistless to its goal; and now its way, still like the way of
Death, is strewn with ashes thickly. Everything around is
blackened. There are dark pools of water, muddy lanes, and
miserable habitations far below. There are jagged walls and
falling houses close at hand, and through the battered roofs
and broken windows wretched rooms are seen, where want and
fever hide themselves in many wretched shapes, while smoke and
crowded gables, and distorted chimneys, and deformity of brick
and mortar penning up deformity of mind and body, choke the
murky distance. As Mr Dombey looks out of his carriage window, it is never in his thoughts that the monster who has brought
him there has let the light of day in on these things : not made or
caused them. It was the journey's fitting end, and might have
been the end of everything; it was so ruinous and dreary.

The railway is a destroyer elsewhere in *Dombey and Son*. It
tears down Stagg's Gardens, and it kills Carker – after turning
to nightmare in his guilty thoughts. Yet in other places its role
is creative. The reactionary M.P. is satirised for his doubts
about its triumph, and there is exhilaration as well as violence in
Dickens's account.

Dickens is close to Marx and Engels in his analysis of
England's social situation, but he is far from sharing their views
of its root causes or its political cure. Though nineteenth-
century economic developments put a new edge on the debate
about money, the debate itself was not new. 'The love of money',
said St Paul, 'is the root of all evil', and Dickens is much closer
to St Paul than he is to Marx. For the communists, exploitation
is part and parcel of capitalism; for St Paul it is the inborn curse
of human nature since the fall. St Paul finds the root of all evil
not in money itself but in the love of money, and Dickens surely

concurs with this. There is no hint in his work that changing the political and economic system will spiritually improve things; indeed, in *A Tale of Two Cities* Dickens's analysis of political revolution is surprisingly close to George Orwell's in *Animal Farm*. He accepted the social world as a tragic scene – though not a hopeless one – and characteristically looked for alleviations chiefly in the enlightened private charity of an Esther Summerson, and in his own protracted battle for a welfare state.

In *Dombey and Son* everything turns on the personal awakening of Mr Dombey and the love of Florence, and Dickens quite remarkably does not envisage a political nemesis for Dombey through trade unions, political conspiracies or rebellious men. The firm of Dombey and Son is not even studied closely. We remain vague about its exact enterprises, and if we even consider the scale of the operations presented to us they are apt to seem unexpectedly small. Dombey's downfall comes about moreover through very untypical people – his trusted business manager who betrays him, his second wife, whose pride happens to match, and oppose, his own.

At the same time Dombey is no capitalist bloated with over-indulgence and brutally committed to grinding the poor. He is austere in his life and by intention a benefactor, with no conscious love of suffering or pain. Dombey and Son is the salvation of the lower orders of society, and its proprietor's only demand in return for this is that the lower orders should not inflict themselves, whether in anger or gratitude, upon himself. In personal life he prefers serenity to brawling. His choice of Carker as an intermediary between himself and Edith is not only a plan to humiliate her, but an attempt to avert unpleasant scenes in the home. He even treats Florence kindly, given his rooted aversion; she is not ordered about, beaten, deprived of money, forbidden her friends or her dog. Walter, of course, is a different problem, an upstart of unbelievable presumption who must be put in his place. But Mr Dombey retains an uneasy conscience about Walter, and broods unhappily, no doubt because his dying son's wish has not been obeyed. Polly and Susan Nipper on the other hand conspire their own downfall, the first by neglect of duty (real enough, whatever the excuses), the second by daring to insult her employer to his face.

Mr Dombey's hatred is kept well in check until it is tried unbearably, and he is slower to anger than we might expect. Moral indignation afflicts him, but not hatred; he broods inwardly and unhappily about imaginary threats from Florence while real threats grow around him unperceived. His own instincts are temperate and obscurely puritan; and fittingly symbolised, like Mrs Clennam's, in a dank, gloomy house.

Dombey is neither actively wicked nor in any sense dishonourable; he is merely lacking in all qualities of warmth and love. The other side of this lack is his extreme vulnerability, an aspect hidden from himself but apparent to us. There is no more natural victim in the book than Mr Dombey, not the impulsive Captain Cuttle even, or the lovelorn Toots. Dombey's very empire is one with neither wisdom nor stability; wealth is anything *but* the unshakeable hereditary rule that he seems to suppose. There is no proper medicine available to him and no proper education (defects of course very general in his society), and he is unable to assess even such resources as there are. He does not know how to obtain a nurse for his motherless baby, and is thrown back on the recommendation of his sister's dim, and dimly perceived friend, poor Miss Tox. He has no ideas of his own about little Paul's education, and in the age of Dr Arnold little Paul is thrown back on another Toxian candidate, her own old instructress the respectable Pipchin, with the Blimbers waiting fittingly in the wings. In 1848 (it is worth recalling) Lancing College was being founded within a few miles of Mrs Pipchin and the Blimbers, but it seems unlikely that Paul's education would ever have reached up to there.

Mr Dombey's ignorance goes even deeper, and affects the most elementary aspects of ordinary life. He does not know how to choose a friend, a wife, or a business manager; his lack of insight into Major Bagstock, the two Skewtons, and Carker, is complete. He has no erudition, no wit, no hobbies or enthusiasms, no gossip or small-talk; he is ignorant of piquet, chess and all other games. Bagstock is surprised to find his new friend's business manager so proficient in matters where his new friend is lacking; but as Carker explains, a humble man *needs* certain arts and talents to see him through life.

We readily see that Dombey's ignorance is the price of his grandeur, 'Mr Dombey, who had been so long shut up within himself, and who had rarely, at any time, overstepped the enchanted circle within which the operations of Dombey and Son were conducted.' The hollowness of Dombey and Son complements its completeness, for had Mr Dombey taken one step outside the enchantment, what a larger, more frightening world he would have seen! But he remains inside, a prisoner of greatness, and the logic inexorably unfolds. He has arrived at high eminence by inheritance, not by ability, and his personal contribution to Dombey and Son is its collapse. The actual management has been forfeited to Carker, who alone understands and manipulates the books. Carker, it turns out, hates Dombey, and is a reckless gambler, two disabilities for a position of trust that anyone less self-absorbed than Dombey might have sensed. Dombey's ignorance extends, then, even to business. He is the last man required for the glory of Dombey and Son.

The final irony, as often in Dickens, is not overemphasised. It is left to speak for itself. We merely hear at the end that Walter Gay is now part of a new business venture, which with time and fortune might rival the fallen house of Dombey and Son. Money is not after all a stable empire, like the old aristocracy, but an empire with continual laws of growth and decline. The last shall be first and the first last by laws of self-help and industry, good luck and enterprise, not by accidents of birth. It is Walter who has the requisite qualities, the flair for business by which he will win, not only Florence, but such reality as the Son of Dombey and Son ever had. The novel infuses therefore into the fairytale ending much hoped for by Captain Cuttle, social criticism of a particularly astringent kind.

It is important to note that this denouement is profoundly non-Marxist, even to the extent of having Sol Gills' worthless old shares start to pay off. There is no suggestion that the fall of Dombey and Son has improved or even altered the world it seemed central to, or that human nature itself has been improved. Perhaps Walter *will* redeem money by a wise and human stewardship, but this remains for the future to show. Mammon will no doubt stay in business, as these chief actors fulfil their destinies, and bow themselves from the stage.

We notice also that though some of the worst evils of poverty are depicted in Good Mrs Brown and Alice, these are not represented as especially typical of the capitalist world. Under any system Good Mrs Brown and her daughter would be vagrants. They are not victims as Jo is victim in *Bleak House*. And Florence herself is never put to the test of real poverty. Captain Cuttle's teaspoons, sugar-tongs, silver watch and ready money, though offered frequently and generously, never finally stand between the heroine and her fate.

IV

The intended moral of *Dombey and Son* is simple. It is the redeeming power of sacrificial love. This has been so often discussed that little demonstration is needed. An excellent account of Florence's role is offered by Kathleen Tillotson in her *Novels of the Eighteen-Forties*. However we feel about Florence, the fairytale depiction of her, stranded in a darkened house like the Lady of Shalott or Sleeping Beauty, achieves the authentic flavour of myth.

The moral is that our human lot is cast in a darkened world, where love may still conquer, but only sacrificially, and within limits clearly defined. In its wider implications the novel is far from hopeful. It is not to be supposed that Captain Cuttle can irradiate, or Florence redeem, Exchange or City, those immensely complex and oppressive worlds. But in personal matters love does conquer. Though Florence is persistently and in the end savagely rejected by her father, she perseveres until, broken and defeated, he responds to her love. Salvation by love extends also to Edith (again through Florence) and to Alice (chiefly through Harriet Carker), but once more only when they are defeated by life and their habitual hate and anger are almost extinct. After all the rage, guilt, revenge and near murder encompassed in the action, *Dombey and Son* moves to a happy end.

In all this – and I am speaking of what I believe to be Dickens's clear intention – the novel is conceived as a Christian work. As in *Bleak House,* and the far more sombre *Little Dorrit,* love is a force working small personal miracles in an alien world. The tragedy of life is apparent to even the meanest intelligences – to poor Mr Toots in his clouded universe, and to Cousin Feenix: 'In regard to the changes of human life', he tells Walter, 'and the extraordinary manner in which we are perpetually conducting ourselves, all I can say is, with my friend Shakespeare – man who wasn't for an age but for all time, and with whom my friend Gay is no doubt acquainted – that it's like the shadow of a dream.' There is an undercurrent of the vanity of human wishes as much in *Dombey and Son* as in *Vanity Fair,* which Thackeray was publishing alongside it.

Nevertheless the novel ends happily, in marked contrast to (say) *Hard Times* later. The hero and heroine marry and live happily ever after, with the heroine's broken old father doting on them, and Sol Gills's last bottle of old Madeira coming into its own. There it has lain, in the cobwebs of the cellar, through most of the action, waiting for Walter's homecoming and success in life. Must it lie there for ever? – until the great wine turns imperceptibly to vinegar, and some later generation, coming unexpectedly upon it, finds its meaning, like its flavour, eroded by time? Almost, we think, this must be the fate of it; yet in chapter 62, called 'Final', the hour of the old Madeira arrives:

A bottle that has long been excluded from the light of day, and is hoary with dust and cobwebs, has been brought into the sunshine; and the golden wine within it sheds a lustre on the table.
    It is the last bottle of the old Madeira.
    'You are quite right, Mr Gills,' says Mr Dombey. 'This is a very rare and most delicious wine.'
    The Captain, who is of the party, beams with joy. There is a very halo of delight round his glowing forehead.
    'We always promised ourselves, sir,' observes Mr Gills, 'Ned and myself, I mean . . .'
    Mr Dombey nods at the Captain, who shines more and more with speechless gratification.
    ' . . . that we would drink this, one day or other, to Walter

safe at home, though such a home we never thought of. If you
don't object to our old whim, sir, let us devote this first glass to
Walter and his wife.'

'To Walter and his wife!' says Mr Dombey. 'Florence, my
child' – and turns to kiss her.

There it is : not Dickens at his best, but typical Dickens, and
the culmination of *Dombey and Son*. The Captain speechless
with joy, Sol safe home, Dombey happy, Walter prospering,
Florence loved : the restored microcosm, storms blown over,
lessons learned. And, of course, life can turn out like this : if we
feel uneasy about it, something stronger than simple realism
must be at stake. As we know, things might have been very
different even in Dickens's handling; the fate of the old Madeira
was never completely sure. Walter might have come to a bad
end. At one stage Dickens pondered the possibility of having
him depraved and ruined by experience, in accordance with Mr
Carker the Junior's most ominous fears. Mr Dombey himself
might have ended very differently. If Carker had not stumbled
under a train, Mr Dombey would almost certainly have killed
him. As Alice reminds us, from the moment when Edith leaves
Dombey to the moment when Carker dies in front of him, we
are watching the genesis of murder in his heart. Sol Gills might
have died sad and disillusioned, a man really frustrated and
passed by. Captain Cuttle, even, might have met the deplorable
fate at the hands of Mrs MacStinger reserved in the end for his
oracular friend, Captain Bunsby. All of these circumstances
would have come well within Dickens's normal perception of
probability and the scope of his genius, but *Dombey and Son*
moves to a happier end. Things turn out, in fact, much as they do
in *A Christmas Carol* – though the corruption of money is studied
with far greater insight, and Dombey is altogether subtler than
Scrooge. Florence's role is closely akin to that of a Christ-figure,
despised and rejected, but in the end redemptive through love.

v

Why, then, should a reader feel profoundly uneasy about the
ending ? – and about the whole structure of the novel, in so far

as the ending casts long shadows before? The presentation of Florence is to my mind a serious weakness, at the very core of the book. Dickens seems determined to wear blinkers when creating her, perhaps because of twinges of unease in himself. 'The study of a loving heart': we hear a good deal of this; but what is 'love' as Florence exemplifies it? We find nothing approaching the psychological insight which Dickens brings to bear upon hate.

On Mr Dombey's feelings for Florence, he is altogether more incisive, and it is interesting to examine these first. Dombey's aversion is traced from its origin in his deep sense of a daughter's irrelevance, to his pain and fear as she emerges as a rival to himself. His resentment grows during little Paul's lifetime, and deepens after Son's untimely death. From indifference to unease, from unease to dislike tinged with paranoia, the process authentically unfolds. How can Dombey share his son, his second wife later, with anyone? Florence's affectionate relationships are a deliberate affront, especially since he only dimly perceives their nature and their hold. His aversion increases as he senses her affectionate assault upon himself, a development wholly opposed to his will. Dickens's exploration of Dombey is conducted with a sureness of touch more familiar to our post-Freudian world than it was to his own. Consider Mr Dombey's slip in the inscription intended for little Paul's tomb: 'Beloved and only child.' He is gently corrected: 'It should be "son", I think, sir?' and replies: 'You are right. Of course. Make the correction.'

'Of course': yes. But what a marvellous stroke! Mr Dombey cannot confront the word 'son' in this most painful crisis, so the word 'child' presents itself to him instead. 'Son' is little Paul, the boy Dombey loved in his fashion; 'Son' is also the great house in all its future prospects, now horribly frustrated by death. But how can the word 'child' come so easily to Mr Dombey as a synonym? Only because Florence has temporarily slipped his mind in her specific reality as his child. This is nothing like normal forgetting, and is certainly not a forgetting of Florence: *she* remains, as rival and enemy, too much in his mind. It is what we would now call a psychological block, a temporary amnesia to intolerable fact. 'No child of mine . . .'

the moment's amnesia penetrates beyond verbal rhetoric to the
inner resonance of such a phrase. If Dombey remembered
Florence as child at this moment, it would surely be to hate her,
for daring to live on when her brother is dead. With the coffin
before him, who knows how she would be present to him, if his
mind could clearly confront her? Better that she should, for this
instant, be 'no child'.

The implications of Dombey's slip are profoundly understandable, if not forgivable, and Dickens is free to probe to the
depths. Dombey's feelings are 'unnatural', and therefore labyrinthine, in the self-destroying manner acknowledged of Vice.
Florence's love, in contrast, is 'natural', and must be exemplified
through the joyful or painful simplicities deemed more appropriate to moral health. Dickens has a twofold obligation to set
Florence right with his readers. They would instinctively pour
out their sympathies to her as a pure, suffering heroine; and
they would require her Virtue, happily unqualified, for the
novel's happy and salutary end. Florence is to remain unchanged
until she can at last prove redemptive : a role simple, important,
and only slightly embarrassing (more perhaps to the author
than to his readers) in that it leaves her, for such long stretches,
with so little to do.

It is clearly impossible for Dickens to initiate any criticism
of his heroine, or to be aware, even, when such criticism might
legitimately arise. His remarkable eye for bizarre behaviour
and complex undercurrents must be kept turned on Mr Dombey,
Joey Bagstock, the Skewtons, Carker – on anyone rather than
Florence herself. Yet the undercurrents are there, whatever he
does to avoid them. Her desolating childish perception of her
father : 'O no, no! He don't want me' is her first, and last, clear
moment of truth. Terrible, indeed, this aversion of a father for
his daughter, and Florence is clearly pitiable : but a fact, and
not easily to be wished away. But Florence cannot or will not
accept the fact of her father's aversion, because it conflicts with
her obsessive need to be loved. She prefers the delusion that Mr
Dombey's love has been forfeited by reason of some specific
fault in herself, and decides that if she studies other children
with happy homes and loving fathers she will at last find the

way to his heart. The delusion is highly understandable, and undeniably moving, as a child's unmerited suffering must always be. But it is too inward-looking, too obsessive, to be pure love with healing properties. It would be better interpreted, on the evidence which Dickens himself presents to us, as the damage done to a sensitive child by an unhappy home.

For what does Florence's 'love' amount to? Compared with Mr Dombey's aversion, it is hardly examined as a complex psychological display. The occasional comparison between Mr Dombey's neglect of Florence and the love of a 'Heavenly Father who does not neglect his children's love' is a patent evasion, as Dickens in his own dubiously successful role as father would later have known. What Florence does is to invent her own rules for parental love, in total ignorance of Mr Dombey as a person, and in defiance of every fact of her life as it must really appear. She never begins to know her father, or indeed to show any respect for him as the person who, for better or worse, he really is. Dickens grimly endorses her with an occasional melodramatic gesture, 'Let him remember, years to come' and so on, but this hardly alchemises Florence into an ideal. Naturally Dombey's neglect is a sin, which he will bitterly regret if he later repents it, but Florence's consciousness is something apart from this. Her need for love blossoms through late childhood and early adolescence into a possessive obsession, which is fulfilled only when Mr Dombey's manhood is broken in the game of life. This persistence, surprising in itself when it is offered as Virtue, is also surprising in the general context of Dickens's world. When so many of his young heroines are saddled with child-fathers or child-grandfathers who are a cross to be crucified on, it seems strange that Florence should fight and fight to have one of her own. When Dombey is financially ruined and recovering from serious illness, her persistence is rewarded, as she announces in a final tremendous meeting with her ruined stepmother:

'Did you tell me,' asked Edith, 'that you were very dear to him?'
'Yes!' said Florence in a thrilling voice.

No doubt Dickens's heroines need someone to love sacrificially, but Florence remains a very peculiar case. Although she is most explicitly cast in a role demanding virtue, she is resolutely self-centred and driven chiefly by need. Her feeling that she is deprived of love is not strictly justified, though it is true that she is left to brood far too much on her own. She enjoys, indeed, an excess of devotion, though always, unhappily, at the margin of her normal life. Her brother (while he lives), Walter (in London or shipwrecked at sea), Susan Nipper (paid or unpaid), Mr Toots (requited or unrequited), Edith (after her fashion), Captain Cuttle (after his), and the splendidly paranoid Diogenes, all dote on her. None of this proves enough – and one senses the strain of it: yet Susan Nipper and Diogenes *are* in constant attendance, even though removed from real equality with herself. The fact of a father's dislike becomes central to her consciousness, souring the springs of her life.

My criticism is not of the realism of this, which seems unanswerable; and it is not, essentially, of Florence herself. A sensitive child's need for parental tenderness and reassurance may be great, and the lack of it can indeed be a tragic force. I would urge, however, that in the light of the situation presented, and the nature of Florence as Dickens depicts her, she would have been better presented as a victim than as an ideal. Had she been so presented, her many excellent qualities would then have been far more endearing – the sensitive affection which attracts so many people to her, her generosity to the lovelorn Toots. But the framework of the novel and its morality push her towards allegory, and towards a role she is far too realistically presented to bear.

The force of this becomes more evident if we compare her with some of Dickens's other heroines. The much maligned Little Nell is vastly her superior, as she lives and dies for her senile and treacherous old grandfather with no thought for herself. Amy Dorrit is altogether superior, in her sacrifice to a father whose whole life mocks a sensitivity such as hers. And in Esther Summerson Dickens achieves perhaps his greatest study of virtue, a girl uniquely endowed with courage, poise, selflessness, humour and goodwill. In such company Florence's inward-looking obsessions show up somewhat badly – a fact aggravated by the static role forced upon her by the plot.

There are other characters in *Dombey and Son* who suffer from its closeness to allegory. Mrs Skewton suffers considerably, for instance, from her continual collision with Florence's real virtues – Heart, Nature, Love – and her perpetual reduction of this sacrosanct trinity to farce. Dickens can as little forgive her this as he can forgive her the make-up. So we are forced away from Cousin Feenix's charitable, slightly uneasy verdict 'a devilishly lively woman' towards the much severer judgements of everyone else. Caught between a disapproving daughter and a disapproving author, Mrs Skewton is indeed unfortunate; yet Edith's view of her mother is surely harsher and odder than Dickens makes it seem. Mrs Skewton is pursued to a horrid death, with the waves again 'always saying', as if her author had taken on the Mephistophelian humours of Joey B. Which would complement the fact that in his dealings with Florence, Dickens is all Cuttle : as if he really could be thought to share either the high innocence or the diminished intelligence of that radiant soul.

VI

If a dislocation is allowed in the novel of the kind I have suggested, it will be seen how very easily we could have watched Mr Dombey's tragedy instead of his daughter's triumph. From the start he is a victim; and if we feel that this is chiefly due to the system he represents, his sufferings remain poignantly real. But Dombey's misfortunes are at least partly due to circumstances going against him, from the moment when his first wife dies in childbirth and his son turns out to be doomed. He is unfortunate in Carker, a man of exceptional evil, who may serve Dombey right in the way of poetic justice, but who would have been a carker in any position of trust. He is still more unfortunate in Edith. Although his second wife does not offer herself to him with enthusiasm, neither does she warn him openly of her hatred and scorn. On his side, he offers a marriage of convenience, the joining of her beauty and aristocratic connection with his wealth, and he has every reason to believe that in marriage her pride will be in alliance with, not opposed to, his own. It indicates, perhaps, how far Dickens was committed to the Victorian cult of romantic love, that a marriage of convenience should be made to seem so obviously wrong. The result is that we accept more or less on its own terms Edith's disgust for her mother, and her plan to make her marriage an occasion of revenge and humiliation, as though this, too, were the most inevitable thing in the world.

In fact Mrs Skewton's plan to make a 'good marriage' for her daughter is not unusual, and money features in her calculations as a matter of course. Such a woman would always, of necessity, appear vulgar (it would be enlightening to have had Jane Austen's account of her), but her schemes need not have been represented as unprecedented in quite this way. Most daughters, again, would either have accepted the arrangement – as Edith tacitly does by marrying not one but two husbands at her mother's instigation – or rejected it out of hand. Edith is not bound to her mother by necessity. Mrs Skewton is not a real invalid but a tough old woman, and Edith in her role as widow has it in her power to seek some congenial marriage (she is attractive enough) on her own. To a man who loved Edith, Mrs Skewton would no doubt have seemed a joke, but not a total impediment. In fact, Edith's sense of some deep wrong that has been done to her is left as something of a mystery, and by allowing us to accept her own version – all Mrs Skewton's fault – Dickens takes an easy way out. She would have been better seen no doubt as a potential Miss Wade or Miss Havisham, a woman reacting proudly and indeed insanely to a blow of fate not in itself impossible to meet. As with Florence, however, Dickens prefers to let an unexamined view of natural love operate, so that we are left to infer that arranged marriages without love must, or ought to, turn out this badly, and that we are watching not Mr Dombey's misfortune but his nemesis for pride.

The assumption appears to be that all successful marriages must be romantic, all personal relationships melting and fond. The reality, as Dickens had cause to know, was sometimes otherwise. Indeed, if Mr Dombey had been luckier (given his own

cold temperament) in wife and daughter, he might have settled
down as a very ordinary Victorian *pater familias*, preoccupied
with his business and his place in society, domestically responsible but an undeniable tyrant, well-meaning but lacking in
domestic warmth or affection – in all these respects except the
final one not wholly unlike Dickens himself. As it is, Dombey
is thwarted by Edith, and in his plans to subdue her all his
latent evil is released. But Edith, who married him with open
eyes, has no reason to be surprised. She provokes him, after all,
beyond endurance, in her strange plot, which destroys Carker as
well.

VII

My feeling about *Dombey and Son*, it will be seen, is that it
contains many magnificent things, but that it is flawed; the
most flawed, perhaps, of all Dickens's major novels. One way
of describing this flaw is to say that Dickens pushes most of his
leading characters too close to allegory. Usually the texture of
his novels is remarkably open, not only to great diversities of
incident and embroidery (as here), but also to great diversities
of human behaviour. The morality of the novels is linked with
insights into human oddity and irrationality that are altogether
too subtle for the lucid frigidities of Type. Here, however –
perhaps because he wished to pose a very direct confrontation
between cold materialism and Christian love – he pins down
Dombey as Pride, Florence as Love, and makes the other
characters fit. This places a constraint on him which leads to
actual falsifications, of the kind which we sense not by some
outside yardstick, but as the undoubted concomitant of his own
success. Dombey's psychology *can* be fully probed, because he
is evil, and nothing therefore needs to be concealed. But
Florence and Edith certainly, and Mrs Skewton arguably, all
have to be simplified into their moral roles, so that Dickens for
once is writing in chains. And this, in turn, may be due to his
attempt to construct a theoretical idea for marriage, fatherhood
and family life which he tried out, also, in his Christmas books,
but not, as a rule, in his major works. Or it may be due to

the fact that among his readers he was writing very particularly for the approval of Carlyle, as he did in *The Chimes* and, later, in *Hard Times*.

If my criticisms are allowed, the novel remains among the masterpieces of Victorian fiction. The penetrating study of the malaise springing from the love of money is in no sense invalidated, and Florence remains a fascinating portrait of a neglected child. The chapters about little Paul remain comparable with the chapters about young David Copperfield, while Florence's adventure as a child with Good Mrs Brown remains unsurpassed as an occasion of pure childish terror. Dickens also lavishes upon us Captain Cuttle and Joey Bagstock, who belong with Pecksniff and Mrs Gamp among his 'immortals'.

6 *David Copperfield*
the favourite child

BEFORE his birth, David is Betsey Trotwood Copperfield, and Miss Betsey's god-daughter. His name presents problems from the start. When he turns out to be the wrong sex, and his strange aunt rises up and vanishes into legend, he is christened 'David' after his father. But he is seldom called by this name. Almost everyone rechristens him, some affectionately, some contemptuously, some for odder or more elaborate reasons. Dickens's people are constantly renaming their friends and enemies, but none is more subject to renaming than David. Perhaps this suggests something flexible in him : is he the potter or the clay? David does not have a name for himself, it will be noticed. He takes his names as they come.

To his mother he is 'Davy', a natural and affectionate diminutive, but spoilt when the Murdstones arrive. After her second marriage, his mother's 'Davy' is almost always edged with reproach or fear. To Peggotty he is 'Master Davy', to Mr Peggotty and Ham 'Mast'r Davy', a blending of affection and respect with a kind of added breeziness in the masculine version which suggests the very reverse of deference. At the same time, it is a continual reminder that David is a 'gentleman', that birthright so important to him in his boyhood shame. Em'ly stresses their class difference when they play together as children. ' "Besides", said Em'ly, as she looked about for shells and pebbles, "your father was a gentleman and your mother a lady; and my father was a fisherman and my mother was a fisherman's daughter, and my uncle Dan is a fisherman." ' Em'ly herself wants to be a lady, and her capriciousness towards David from the moment she becomes aware of sex may be a reflection of this. Certainly it is one of the springs of her dissatisfaction with Ham (there are others, of course), and of her decision to

risk her lot with Steerforth despite the guilt. The fact that she
is not a lady may also help to explain why David never seriously
thinks after his childhood years of marrying her. Mr Omer's
remark that 'an ill-natured story got about, that Em'ly wanted
to be a lady' does not surprise or shame him, and he eagerly
accepts the suggested mitigation: ' . . . if she was a lady she
would like to do so-and-so for her uncle – don't you see? – and
buy him such-and-such fine things'. When Ham announces his
engagement to Em'ly, David's regret is very slight. His own
wives are social superiors both times.

David is as aware of being a gentleman as he is of being
talented, and his violation by the Murdstones has this twin
aspect. What is Mealy Potatoes to him? I shall be returning
later to this matter, but want to emphasise that David's reaction
to the Murdstone and Grinby's warehouse seems to me to be
nothing like snobbery, except in our most simplified modern
sense. In essence it is fear; the fear of being wasted, which
Dickens remembered, so bitterly, from the blacking factory. We
have to remember not only the nature of the Victorian social
system, but its total lack of safety-nets: no educational ladders,
no welfare services, no second chances. Either David swims or
he sinks. This is the main reason why he runs off to his unknown
and enigmatic aunt in Dover instead of seeking refuge with the
known and dependable Peggotty. Naturally he is also thinking
of Peggotty, who is far too poor to take him on. But he obviously
knows that if any prospects of a decent education still remain for
him, it is not to Peggotty that he can turn.

The degradations David suffers while poor are not allowed
to spoil his life; he is a fighter. He flees to Dover, more terrified
of commonness and failure than he is of death, and retains his
birthright as 'Master Davy' and 'Mast'r Davy'. The Murdstone
and Grinby period becomes a sealed-off period of his life. The
only person who ever brings it up against him and casts doubts
on his right to be a gentleman is Uriah, when the horrible mask
at last comes off.

To return to David's names: the only person who normally
calls him 'David' is Mr Murdstone, a sinister use, measured and
cruel, and intended to degrade him like a dog. Mr Murdstone

makes some half-hearted attempt, however, to tamper with his surname. When David stops at an inn on the way to Salem House he finds that lunch is prepared for 'Murdstone', not for 'Copperfield'. But at school, David reverts to 'Copperfield' and the Murdstone name fails to stick – perhaps because Murdstone hates the thought of him far too much by now to persevere.

As a small boy David is much worried about being thought young. The apotheosis of this fear is Littimer, but in lesser forms it haunts him for half of the tale. Before his mother's second marriage, he was turned into 'Brooks of Sheffield' by Mr Murdstone (Mr Murdstone's one attempt at a joke). In a sense this is typical adult insensitivity; who does not recall bewilderment and resentment from far back in childhood at obscure grown-up jokes? But David is not only the butt of the joke, he is also its victim, and the episode sets up echoes through much of the tale. There are elements of ignorance about grown-up things in David long after he should have left them behind. Surely he is Brooks of Sheffield to Steerforth, during the whole period leading up to the elopement? 'Child, child', Miss Mowcher reproaches him afterwards, as she thinks back to her misreading of his behaviour at that time. It seems remarkable, indeed, that despite Murdstone and Grinby, which initiates David into experiences that make him feel almost unfit for Dr Strong's academy, he remains less versed in the world's ways than Steerforth. As usual, Dickens provides us with a company of innocents, Peggotty, Ham and Mr Peggotty – all close relations to Captain Cuttle – but surprisingly often David seems himself to belong with these. This is not only odd, but even suspicious, given that Dickens was set on some degree of self-portrait.

When David is a boy, he is called 'six-foot' by the waiter who eats most of his lunch for him – a typical piece of lower-class cheek – and 'sixpenn'orth of bad ha'pence' by the long-legged young man with the donkey-cart who robs him. This second episode is a frightening introduction to his status on the road: no gentlemen here; and he learns to fear the world of tinkers and trampers, with their vicious self-help. In the Murdstone and

Grinby warehouse, his nicknames had been even more wounding
– 'the little gent' and 'the young Suffolker'. The faint hint of
contempt, routine and without any particular ill-will, rubs in
David's isolation; the pit he has fallen into is equally perceived
on both sides. Just as 'little' and 'young' hit on a recurring fear
of David's, so 'gent' mocks his greatest loss. It seems all the
more commendable that later on in life he resists the very real
and pernicious snobbery of his beloved Steerforth, and continues
to regard Ham and Mr Peggotty as the salt of the earth –
nature's 'gentlemen' – even while his own destiny sets him
apart.

At school David is 'Copperfield' in the private school
tradition, kept up even at Creakle's; and this remains his chief
name for the world. He and Traddles remain on surname terms
with a tenacity that no degree of friendship can thaw. When
Sophy at last marries Traddles and calls him Tom, David is so
astonished that he dignifies the name with quotation marks :
'Tom'. Steerforth remains 'Steerforth' through love, loyalty,
betrayal and eventually death : 'No need, O Steerforth, to have
said, when we last spoke together, in that hour which I so little
deemed to be our parting-hour – no need to have said, "Think
of me at my best!" I had done that ever; and could I change
now, looking on this sight!' But Steerforth invents for David
the pet name of 'Daisy' – not when they are at school together,
during the whole of which time David remains 'Copperfield',
but when they meet again later as young men. Steerforth coins
this nickname because David is as fresh as a daisy (his peachlike
face and clean good-looks), but the girlishness of Daisy seems
double-edged. At school Steerforth wished that David had a
sister (a narrow escape for Betsey Trotwood Copperfield), and
he always knows how to exploit David's love. David's freshness
is a naïveté which Steerforth at once admires and violates, so
'Daisy' must have a touch of contempt.

David is also 'Copperfield' to Mr Micawber, whose preposterous resilience is a great tonic for the young boy. David is
fond of Micawber, and enjoys meeting him again (with only a
twinge of unease about the Heeps being there), but he never
fully acknowledges his debt to Micawber's zest. Micawber, for

his part, exempts David from the otherwise standard procedure with I.O.U.s, a proof of affection if anything could be.
Mrs Micawber calls David 'Master Copperfield' affectionately,
though vaguely, since she has only a misty idea who he is;
Uriah Heep assimilates 'Master Copperfield' to his own
poisoned deference, keeping to 'Master' long after David is too
old for it, with occasional slithers towards and away from
'Mister'. Uriah's 'umbleness is pure revenge, and even more
venomous than his mother's, though Mrs Heep sometimes wins
on points. Her gambits against David on his first visit are
masterly: ' "If I could have wished father to remain among us
for any reason", said Mrs Heep, "it would have been, that he
might have known his company this afternoon." '

With Betsey Trotwood we come into a more extensive area
of naming and renaming; it is an aspect of her formidably
strong will. In adopting David she generously adapts herself to
his sex, but still renames him 'Trotwood', which she then
shortens almost immediately to an affectionate 'Trot'. It
becomes notable that 'Trotwood' is the name we then most
often hear from Agnes, who calls him Trotwood up to and
including his belated proposal: 'I am so blessed, Trotwood.'
Betsey's renamings reflect her habitual determination, and
remind us that her virtue is won at a price. After her disappointment in marriage, she has retreated from the world and declared
war on men. Her personal maid was taken up expressly to 'be
educated in a renouncement of mankind', and her plans for Clara
Copperfield's daughter even prefigure Miss Havisham's plans
for Estella: ' "There must be no mistakes in life with *this*
Betsey Trotwood. There must be no trifling with *her* affections,
poor dear. She must be well brought up, and well guarded from
reposing any foolish confidences where they are not deserved.
I must make that *my* care." ' Yet Betsey's plans for revenge go
splendidly wrong. Her spotless yet charming little house at
Dover is a universe away from Satis House. Betsey even
continues to support her husband for the sake of old happiness,
and when David falls in love she overcomes her forebodings for
Dora's sake. After the marriage, she treats David's child-wife
with a tenderness that she had withheld from his mother, and

preaches to herself the one lesson that eccentric, strong-willed
Victorian ladies most needed, that she must not interfere for
any reason in another home. Betsey's renamings are, after all,
kindly. The name 'Peggotty' she can't forgive (though fortunately 'Barkis' is better, so Peggotty's marriage removes the
only barrier between them), but Miss Murdstone's name she
will have nothing to do with at all. Miss Murdstone becomes
'that murdering woman of a sister' – 'on whom', says David, 'I
think no pain or penalty would have induced my aunt to bestow
any Christian or proper name, or any other designation'.
Betsey also respects the whims of others about names. She
warns David against ever calling Mr Dick 'Richard Babley',
since he has suffered too much from his family and cannot bear
it. In short (as Micawber would say) she is the very kindest of
the novel's non-innocents, and a most fitting complement to Mr
Dick (who, it will be noted, takes very kindly to the designation
'Mr Dixon' when Traddles confers it upon him by accident
during the unmasking of Heep).

There are other episodes involving or turning on David's
name. Mrs Crupp is a slovenly creature who always calls him
'Mr Copperfull', this familiar concept being the nearest conces-
sion to his identity she can make. For her, David is 'Lodger',
and when she has discovered how far she can go in exploiting
him – a long way – no other interest remains. From the other
end of the social scale, David's identity suffers a rebuff from Mrs
Steerforth. When David is first introduced to her in Highgate,
she tells him graciously (referring to her son): 'Indeed, I
recollect his speaking, at that time, of a pupil younger than
himself who had taken his fancy there; but your name, as you
may suppose, has not lived in my memory.' There is nothing
factually wrong with this; names do not live in our memories;
but the tone tells its tale. If nothing hurtful is intended in that
'as you may suppose', this is simply because its implications are
altogether too natural for Mrs Steerforth to see. Like her son,
she knows that lower-class people do not feel or notice nuances,
so no problem of tact need arise. The Steerforths indeed are free
to charm and despise their acquaintances without calculation,
since they take care to avoid any real superiors in the social

scale. It is made clear that Steerforth went to Creakle's school just for this purpose; the bargain was simply that Steerforth should be king. At school the other boys sensed the feudal ambience, and responded with as little calculation as Steerforth's own. David handed his money and property to Steerforth quite naturally, for Steerforth to redistribute as he found fit. Steerforth's powers of life and death extended to staff as well as to fellow students, and Mr Mell was judged guilty of treason and condemned. In all this, charm, good-looks, natural grace and dignity were all utilised; 'there was a charm in his manner,' David recalls later, 'a gay and light manner it was, but not swaggering – which I still believe to have borne a kind of enchantment with it. I still believe him, in virtue of his carriage, his animal spirits, his delightful voice, his handsome face and figure, and, for aught I know, of some inborn power of attraction besides (which I think a few people possess), to have carried a spell with him to which it was natural weakness to yield, and which not many persons could withstand.'

But Mr Mell could withstand the spell, and Steerforth sensed this, together with the possibility that David might be influenced against himself. So Steerforth destroyed Mr Mell in the most effective manner possible, taunting him as a beggar and betraying David's confidence at the same time. Later he told the boys that Mr Mell was too common to feel real pain or humiliation, pressing his own sincere and habitual assumptions into play. Mrs Steerforth sums up almost all of this when she reminisces to David about her son's schooldays: 'He would have risen against all constraint; but he found himself the monarch of the place, and he haughtily determined to be worthy of his station. It was like himself.'

When Steerforth meets Mr Peggotty, Ham and little Em'ly, he entertains the same contempt towards them that he previously felt for Mr Mell. This is laughingly expressed to David, who as usual disbelieves it; David is so sure that Steerforth is his twin soul in all spiritual matters that any real gulf on such a topic seems absurd. Besides, David cannot believe that Steerforth could charm the Peggottys as he does without meaning it: David has no more learned to believe in acting and duplicity

than he has learned to believe in sex. His whole experience of
life, including Murdstone and Grinby, Creakle's, Miss Shepherd,
Miss Larkins, and even Dora has left him fully as innocent as
when he set out. So he deludes himself that Steerforth does not
mean what he says and is a fellow innocent, and when he comes
upon Steerforth in dark mood – a wonderful passage – he has
no idea what it can mean. Steerforth's contempt for David
naturally blossoms, until it reaches a stage when he can risk
introducing him to Miss Mowcher and enjoying the tight-rope
walk of *double entendre*. Yet David's blindness is somehow
accounted to him as righteousness. Better be blind, like Dr
Strong, than alive to sex.

The other thing David fails to see about the Steerforths is
that they have, after all, to compromise, since they are not
wholly the real thing. They gravitate by instinct either towards
the ignorant and helpless, or towards creatures like Creakle
whom their money can buy. Steerforth goes to a deplorable
school which even his mother knows is not good enough for
him, since a better school would have rival monarchs to do him
down. Mrs Steerforth's companion is a woman with little other
choice in life open to her, who is as much Steerforth's victim as
Em'ly later becomes. Steerforth chooses for his mistress an
illiterate girl, wide open to his upper-class glamour, and extremely likely – though he miscalculates here – to bend to his
will. Even David is 'Daisy'; to this nickname one nearly always
returns.

Before I leave this matter of David's names, it is impossible
not to mention 'Doady' – Dora's pet name for him, as affectionate as 'Daisy' and far more innocent: a beautiful instance, in the
tone surrounding it, of Dora's love, trust, tenderness and
unfitness for life.

II

David's names and styles are one among many instances of the
homogeneity of the book. We could follow a score of such
details, each reinforcing our vivid sense of the people and
incidents. Speech rhythms take pride of place as usual. A reader
has only to listen to Rosa Dartle, Mr Micawber, Uriah Heep,

Betsey Trotwood to find himself mimicking them; producing them in the mind's theatre; looking up, and seeing them out of a window or just crossing the street. Their life is not primarily in analysis, though analysis is interesting; it is primarily in the unfailing illusion of truth. If anyone should accuse Micawber of non-existence, how could we refute it? Speak him; act him; listen to his views on almost any subject: there he is. And like all vivid people, he has depths and mysteries; a different kind of life, almost, from the puppets that many writers create.

If we wished, we could pursue sea images through *David Copperfield*, noting similarities and dissimilarities between the sea here and the sea in *Dombey and Son*, and gradually apprehending the subtle nuances Dickens creates just underneath the exuberant obviousness of certain dramatic effects. Or we might pick up snake images, with the continual and resolute linking of two characters apparently wholly different from each other, Uriah Heep and Rosa Dartle. Uriah's speech mimes his physical writhings, which are caught up in his very name. Slimy, as well as devious: nothing like the genial obliquities of a Micawber. Rosa Dartle is a different kind of serpent. *Her* name suggests a forked tongue, flickering and darting like the passionate scar across her lips. In speech she is all brittle indirection finding direction out – devious, compelling, unignorable, with the occasional lash of pure venom. It is perhaps with a touch of surprise that we first notice *her* professions of humility :

'Oh, but, really? Do tell me. Are they, though?' she said.
'Are they what? And are who what?' said Steerforth.
'That sort of people. – Are they really animals and clods, and beings of another order? I want to know *so* much.'
'Why, there's a pretty wide separation between them and us,' said Steerforth, with indifference. . . .
'Really!' said Miss Dartle. 'Well, I don't know, now, when I have been better pleased to hear that. It's so consoling! It's such a delight to know that, when they suffer, they don't feel! Sometimes I have been quite uneasy for that sort of people; but now I shall just dismiss the idea of them, altogether. Live and learn. I had my doubts, I confess, but now they're cleared up.

I didn't know, and now I do know, and that shows the advantage of asking – don't it ?'

The bitterness is just sufficiently controlled not to declare itself, at least to the Steerforths; but it radiates deadly unease. Though Dickens would have endorsed the irony as social comment, he conveys its destructive poison in Rosa's mouth. Steerforth's house will have built up in Rosa a not dissimilar bitterness to that created in Uriah at his charity school, and her habitual style is at least as intelligent as his. Both Rosa and Uriah create continual unease under the cloak of deference, finding some outlet in speech for their chafed souls. Both hate David and wish him harm, and we always know this, despite Uriah's professions and the fierce complicity of Rosa's moods. David is, after all, their rival, Uriah's rival for Agnes, Rosa's rival for Steerforth; and *they* know it well enough, whatever he does.

The linking of two characters through serpentine images and suggestions in no way makes them seem alike. Like all Dickens people who are thematically linked they remain as totally unlike one another as such people no doubt would be in life. The other snake-like character in *David Copperfield* is Littimer, a different serpent again and more like Milton's, urbane, subtle and coarse. *His* affinity with Heep is finally apparent only when we see them in prison together. Hitherto, they have seemed to have little enough in common in speech or thought.

III

Critics who delight in Dickens chiefly for his health and sanity often think of *David Copperfield* as his finest work. C. B. Cox has expressed this view in recent articles; and it is implied strongly, I think, in G. K. Chesterton's brilliant little book. Chesterton has several fine things to say about the novel, one of which I should like to quote :

The point of the book is that, unlike all the other books of Dickens, it is concerned with quite common actualities . . . It is not only both realistic and romantic; it is realistic because it is romantic. It is human nature described with the human exaggeration. We all know the actual types in the book . . . They are not purely poetic creations like Mr Kenwigs or Mr Bunsby. We all know that they exist. We all know the stiff-necked and humorous old-fashioned nurse, so conventional and yet so original, so dependent and yet so independent. We all know the intrusive step-father, the abstract strange male, coarse, handsome, sulky, successful, a breaker-up of homes. We all know the erect and sardonic spinster, the spinster who is so mad in small things and so sane in great ones. We all know the cock of the school; we all know Steerforth, the creature whom the gods love and even the servants respect. We know his poor and aristocratic mother, so proud, so gratified, so desolate. We know the Rosa Dartle type, the lonely woman in whom affection itself has stagnated into a sort of poison.

But while these are real characters they are real characters lit up by the colours of youth and passion. They are real people romantically felt; that is to say, they are real people felt as real people feel them. They are exaggerated, like all Dickens's figures : but they are not exaggerated as personalities are exaggerated by an artist; they are exaggerated as personalities are exaggerated by their own friends and enemies. The strong souls are seen through the glorious haze of the emotions that strong souls really create. We have Murdstone as he would be to a boy who hated him; and rightly, for a boy would hate him. We have Steerforth as he would be to a boy who adored him; and rightly, for a boy would adore him. It may be that if these persons had a mere terrestrial existence, they appeared to other eyes more insignificant. It may be that Murdstone in common life was only a heavy business man with a human side that David was too sulky to find. It may be that Steerforth was only an inch or two taller than David, and only a shade or two above him in the lower middle classes; but this does not make the book less true. In cataloguing the facts of life the author must not omit the massive fact, illusion.

This is admirably put; and in endorsing the main drift of it (not all the details), I would very much want to enrol Uriah Heep, Traddles, Dora Spenlow, Mr and Mrs Micawber, Creakle, Dr Strong, the Old Soldier – indeed, most of the cast – among the people whom we 'all know'. We all know them – it is impossible to keep for long from this perception – because without Dickens we should have known none of them;

E

they would never have been. Many real people are by comparison unreal and shadowy; if they had never lived, there would
have been other people so very like them, that no gap in nature
would be felt. But imagine the human race without Mr Micawber
or Betsey Trotwood! It cannot be done. Their very uniqueness is
their universality; it is precisely because they are unlike anyone
else that their quintessence seems spread through so many
people we know. Dickens's characters tend in fact to pale most
real people, and they do this precisely by their inescapable truth
to life. The vitality is a triumph of art: and perhaps its corollary
is that almost every real person, however shadowy, might be
interesting if Dickens recreated him (even Mrs Gradgrind
becomes almost real and substantial in his hands). Dickens's
characterisation achieves its vividness by the convergence of
techniques I have already hinted at: the speech rhythms; the
underlying archetypes (Betsey as fairy-godmother, Uriah as
serpent in Agnes's Eden); the images. It is to be found in every
detail surrounding his people: their mode of naming one
another; their physical appearances; the rooms they live in;
their tone. If there was ever a grand error in criticism it was
surely E. M. Forster's, when he called these people 'flat'. They
are, rather, in Forster's own terminology, 'round'; as in-
exhaustible as life. Dickens has made them, presented them,
given them to us, and they really are among the people we never
forget. Such characters can be called 'types' only as a second
line of asserting their reality. Before they are types they are
atypical; they are like no-one else in the history or fiction of man.

The wholesomeness of *David Copperfield* is in some of its
characters; it is also in touches of sentiment finer than Dickens
ever achieved elsewhere. There are marvellous moments in the
novel, many of them foreshadowing or celebrating death.
Chesterton said of *David Copperfield* that 'parts of it seem like
fragments of our forgotten infancy', and almost everything to
do with David's mother bears this out. There is the marvellously
Chekhovian music of the first chapter, as Clara and Betsey
Trotwood sit waiting for David's birth:

The evening wind made such a disturbance just now, among

some tall old elm-trees at the bottom of the garden, that neither my mother nor Miss Betsey could forbear glancing that way. As the elms bent to one another, like giants who were whispering secrets, and after a few seconds of such repose, fell into a violent flurry, tossing their wild arms about, as if their late confidences were really too wicked for their peace of mind, some weatherbeaten ragged old rooks'-nests, burdening their higher branches, swung like wrecks upon a stormy sea.

'Where are the birds?' asked Miss Betsey.

'The —?' My mother had been thinking of something else.

'The rooks – what has become of them?' asked Miss Betsey.

'There have not been any since we lived here,' said my mother.

'We thought – Mr Copperfield thought – it was quite a large rookery; but the nests were very old ones, and the birds have deserted them a long while.'

There is David's last sight of his mother:

I was in the carrier's cart when I heard her calling me. I looked out, and she stood at the garden-gate alone, holding her baby up in her arms for me to see. It was cold still weather; and not a hair of her head, nor a fold of her dress, was stirred, as she looked intently at me, holding up her child.

So I lost her. So I saw her afterwards, in my sleep at school, – a silent presence near my bed – looking at me with the same intent face – holding up her baby in her arms.

We recall also Peggotty's account of the death of David's mother, and three other moving accounts of death, all of them different – Barkis, Dora and Steerforth. And, more cheerfully, *David Copperfield* has at least one moment of splendid release which everyone remembers: the moment when Betsey Trotwood confronts the Murdstones in David's presence, and at last fully reveals herself: 'You can go when you like; I'll take my chance with the boy. If he's all you say he is, at least I can do as much for him then, as you have done. But I don't believe a word of it!' The Victorian sublime.

All this side of *David Copperfield* is warm, like its famous phrases: 'Barkis is willing' – that superbly simple declaration; 'waiting for something to turn up' – it does at last; 'I will never desert Mr Micawber' – nor does she; 'Janet! Donkeys!' –

Betsey at her militant worst. None of this needs underlining, it is so splendidly obvious; but it is not all there is. Indeed, a startling aspect of the book, given so much warm humanity, is the very unconventional nature of its cast. In his usual manner Dickens has assembled forty or so highly individual people, for whom the laws of normality, whatever they are, scarcely apply. It is interesting to recall that until David's marriage to Agnes there is only one marriage in the book that could remotely be considered normal – if by 'normal' we mean a marriage where the husband is the dominant partner, the wife a friend and helpmate through good and bad, and the relationship loyal, affectionate and comparatively stable. This of course is the Micawber marriage – threatened once, by Uriah Heep, but even then not seriously; a marriage of extreme individualists, with the man an unreliable breadwinner, but the general pattern one which might be found going on, only a shade less histrionically, in a good many streets. Mrs Micawber's loyalty to her husband is most apparent in her unconscious echoes of his style. In her somewhat faded way, under the oppression of childbearing and housekeeping, she shares his resilient optimism, his certainty that something will turn up. She shares his love of melodrama, and his ability to wrest stylistic triumphs from chaos; and his enjoyment (when these do turn up) of the good things of life. She also shares, in the same slightly faded way, his rhetoric – that final hallmark of a settled married life. There are moments of public oration when she is worthy of her husband, and moments when she almost surpasses him. Her letter to Traddles is a quite masterly pastiche of the full Micawber style.

I can add here, perhaps, that for my own part I find no difficulty at all in believing that this marvellous family makes good in Australia, and that its place in Port Middlebay Harbour society is just as splendid as the *Port Middlebay Times* records. Micawber is a hard worker who would have made good in Canterbury, if it had not been for the ghastly Heep. The colonial second chance was made for a man of his calibre. A Micawber dynasty surely flourishes in Port Middlebay Harbour to this day.

It remains odd, however, that the Micawbers are sole representatives, for the length of the book, of a normal family. When
we turn our back on them (but there they are behind our back)
in search of other happy relationships, we next find two
highly irregular establishments crying aloud, one might think,
for gossip – except that, unlike poor Annie Strong, the participants are too robust to bother about gossip, and therefore far
less vulnerable to its power. Mr Peggotty's boat-house, with
Mrs Gummidge in residence, a 'lone, lorn creetur' who is
treated much more tenderly than most such women would be by
husbands; and Miss Betsey's cottage at Dover, with Mr Dick
in residence, writing his Memorial, flying his kite, and proclaiming Betsey a wonderful woman just as she proclaims him
the wisest of men. In both these establishments there is an
exquisite instance of human love and mutual support; and if it
is unthinkable that sex has anything to do with either of them,
there is something triumphantly Victorian about our instant
recognition of the fact. Dickens conveys the truth that the help
and comfort given by these stranded people to one another is
far above sex. It is love of a kind which certainly exists in the
best marriages, as in the best friendships, and which may be
expressed sexually, but in essence it is purer and far more enduring than sex. Such insight is a positive contribution of
Victorianism to human understanding, and the other side of
whatever was wrong or limited in their views about sex. If the
excessive fuss about Em'ly and Steerforth strikes many modern
readers, for instance, as distasteful or ludicrous, there is the
powerful counterbalance provided by these still more important
human truths. It seems to me no exaggeration to say that if the
novel were written now the beauty of Mr Peggotty and Betsey
Trotwood would be violated in the search for sexuality, while
David would almost certainly come out as a tormented queer.
But on this matter Dickens was right and we are wrong. *David
Copperfield* confronts our modern sexual sanctities with the in-
sight that love greatly transcends sex and is far more enduring.
If it did no more than this, it would be a most salutary book.

I shall be returning to this when discussing David and
Em'ly, but it can fittingly be touched on here. The novel is

surely right to show that although Em'ly and Martha are
doomed to unhappiness in illicit love, and not solely because of
society's disapproval, great tenderness and love outside marriage can still be achieved. Such relationships are deeper than
sex, and would be spoilt by it; sex would complicate and
debase, as it usually does. It is worth noting that Betsey's
independence of public opinion is an aspect of rectitude; hers is
that strong and very typically Victorian independence which
flourishes purely on strength of will and self-respect.

The actual marriages in *David Copperfield* are less satis-
factory, and most of them seem to go astray. Mr Murdstone
marries first Clara Copperfield and later another unfortunate
lady, and each time Miss Murdstone moves in. Brother and
sister then establish themselves as jailers, parading their firmness and breaking the wife's heart. The undercurrents are
certainly sinister. Their sour natures, sour religion, sour inhumanity hint at sadism, if not at deeper disorders; certainly the
two Murdstones are nearer to each other in their complicity of
pain (the young David catches a wink between them as Mr
Murdstone is using him to torment Clara) than Mr Murdstone
appears to be to either of his wives. Miss Murdstone is a
'metallic lady' with the 'numerous little steel fetters and rivets'
that adorn her setting her tone. It is a truly Dickensian touch
that when David grows up to be an educated and independent
young man and falls in love with his future bride Dora, he finds
Miss Murdstone – still firm, still metallic, still his enemy – in
charge. The effect on David is astringent and demoralising, but
for readers there are more implications than David sees. The
reappearance of the ogress turns a spotlight on telling similarities between Dora and David's mother – both tender and
impractical, both loving and needing love, both terribly ill-
equipped for life. David's love for Dora may indeed be regress
in search of lost childhood. He has told us (much earlier) that
from the moment he lost his mother 'I remembered her . . . only
as the young mother of my earliest impressions, who had been
used to wind her bright curls round and round her finger, and to
dance with me at twilight in the parlour.'

Miss Murdstone in her new role as Dora's companion spies

on David, and brings about the shattering confrontation with
Mr Spenlow. There is courtroom language from Miss Murdstone, 'I have frequently endeavoured to find decisive corrobor-
ation of those suspicions' and so on, and David is forced to blush
for his silly, tender love. This attempt to convict David of
duplicity embodies all Miss Murdstone's old use of a dark
religion in the service of cruelty, and now that he loves he is
more than ever her game. In adapting her often-professed
belief in David's depravity to a class matter – David's attempt
to ensnare a social superior in marriage – she manages to play
on his dread of losing his birthright as a gentleman, as he so
very nearly did at her own hands and those of her brother, as
well as upon adolescent uncertainties and fears. Understandably
David appears at a disadvantage, and his fears and embarrassments closely resemble guilt. At this point of the tale David
foreshadows Dickens's two future partial self-portraits, Arthur
Clennam and Pip, both of whom are very seriously crippled by
a sense of guilt deliberately implanted in them when they were
young.

Three other marriages in *David Copperfield* are happy, though
not precisely typical. The marriage of Peggotty and Barkis
must be the least romantic in literature; Barkis is not only
inarticulate, but mean, and they are both too old to rear a family.
But it is a very happy marriage all the same. Barkis and Peggotty have no illusions, no problems, and they suit each other.
Dickens lets its happiness be quietly felt, and it is wholly
characteristic of him that the music of mortality plays so memorably about its end. Dr Strong's marriage to Annie is also
happy, though spoiled by misunderstanding and gossip, and by
the difference in ages which may after all be too great. The
other happy marriage is that of Traddles. After his terrible
courtship he marries Sophy, and very happy they seem, though
with too many in-laws; will even the best-natured fellow in the
world be kissed and exploited for the rest of his life?

It is interesting that David's two wives have in common
fathers who are left widowers and who spoil them and who are not
as successful in business as they seem. Mr Wickfield's love for
his daughter becomes in fact unnatural (his word for it), since

when his wife dies all his love turns to his daughter and away from the world. The result is that his business suffers, and Agnes herself nearly ends as Mrs Heep. It seems clear that Agnes's excessive self-restraint (also unnatural?) develops through her need to survive her father, and that she is to be numbered among the many victimised heroines in the Dickens world.

If marriage can be poison, so can spinsterhood; in addition to the gentle delusions of the two Miss Spenlows, Dickens shows Rosa Dartle's frustrations taking passionate and virulent forms.

IV

Dickens's people are always tried, and David's terrifying adventures on the road to Dover – the boy who robs him, the trampers, the Goroo man – are a paradigm of the human lot. The Murdstones might have been the end of David as a person, but he is lucky enough to have excellent friends. His old nurse Peggotty and his eccentric great-aunt Betsey Trotwood surround him with strong loyalty, and provide something of the stability that a normal family might have had. There is also his good angel Agnes and his eventual marriage to her, which creates that institution rare enough in Dickens, a settled family, where children are loved and cared for, which is not at the same time either very grotesque or very poor.

Many of the characters, uprooted and fending for themselves, are defined by obsessions, as always in Dickens's tales. In the very first paragraph we are introduced, merely as an *en passant* felicity, to the robust old lady who buys David's caul to keep herself from drowning, retires well away from the sea as an added precaution, and spends her old age warning people against meandering. 'Let us have no meandering' is *her* motif; and it scarcely exaggerates to say that though she never appears outside a single paragraph, we know her better than many a major character in other tales. Mr Dick is obsessive because he is 'simple', and his 'King Charles's Head', now proverbial, is a clinical symptom. The same cannot quite be said of Betsey's donkeys, though these inhabit that area where elderly Victorian ladies tended to be a little peculiar without really being mad.

Betsey harasses donkeys in defence of property and in pursuance of independence, but how far the habit controls her or she controls it is hard to say. Many other characters adopt roles or attitudes – Miss Murdstone's 'firmness', Barkis's willingness, Micawber's optimism – and these range from *personae* required in the first instance for survival such as Uriah's 'umbleness, Rosa Dartle's sharpness, Mrs Micawber's loyalty, Miss Mowcher's volatility, through that indeterminate range of anxieties or eccentricities which include Betsey's donkeys, Mrs Gummidge's 'lone, lorn creetur', Barkis's wooing, Dr Strong's dictionary, Traddles's skeletons, the delusions of the Spenlow sisters, to such deeper disorders as poor Mr Dick's Memorial and the wild Goroos of the Goroo man. Dickens reminds us that minor madnesses can coincide with great sanities. Betsey teaches David the great Victorian virtues of courage, reliability, independence, hard work, and it is clear that behind such eccentricities as the donkeys there is a firmness of purpose as fine and good as the superficially similar firmness of Miss Murdstone is soiled. Mr Dick, again, is the epitome of gentleness, and though he never produces quite the pearls of wisdom which Betsey expects of him, she is surely right to keep him free to sport in the day.

These obsessions are hallmarks – not the only ones – of Dickens's characters, and in their essential insight they look forward rather than back. Though there are literary precedents in the comedy of humours and in eighteenth-century ideas of ruling passion, Dickens's concern is with the irrational qualities of the human mind. He anticipates many clinical findings of modern psychiatry. The obsessions of his people are always congruent with the many other detailed perceptions through which he creates them, and contribute to our sense of depth and roundness behind the stylised façade.

v

David Copperfield is a 'favourite child' for many of its readers as well as for its author, and anyone unfamiliar with Dickens should certainly start here. But it has its problems for modern

E2

readers and, as I have already hinted, we ought to scrutinise the treatment of sex with particular care. It must be admitted that there are aspects of this quite peculiarly likely to repel modern readers, and that modern readers will not invariably be wrong. Yet the problems are not simple, and cannot be shed on any too comfortable hypothesis that Dickens was merely more hypocritical or less well informed than ourselves. My attempt now will be to disentangle one or two aspects of the problem, as they arise in a critical reading of the tale.

At least one scene might have been specially designed to rebuff present-day readers in most of their assumptions – the one where Annie Strong exonerates her reputation before an admiring and tearful crowd. Emotionally, it is certainly over-heated; yet the phrase which sticks in David's mind and teases him cannot simply be dismissed as cant: 'There can be no disparity in marriage like unsuitability of mind and purpose.' Another rebuff for modern readers is Martha, who excites less horror and compassion now than she was obviously supposed to, but perhaps because the social and economic realities of prostitution in Victorian London are overlooked. No way back from prostitution to other forms of employment; no tenderness or help from clients, or the general run of them; no penicillin; no sophisticated technique for evading guilt.

The novel's other heroines, on the other hand, do not greatly help matters; in their different ways, Dora, Em'ly and Agnes all fail to excite. Dora, I think, is a special problem, and dislike of her seldom goes deep. My own reading experience wholly accords with that of Trevor Blount, who says in his Introduction to the Penguin edition of the novel that 'Dora, sweet and empty-headed, grows more exasperatingly lovable at each reading'. But Agnes remains forbidding, like all Dickens's 'angel' women, while Em'ly is too hidden behind the three men she injures, Mr Peggotty, Ham and not least David, to be clearly visible in her own right.

All these difficulties centre on sex, that matter where we feel instinctively superior to the Victorians, simply because the subject is not taboo for us as it was for them. Yet sex is a constant for all centuries, however they deal with it, and no

great writer is a child. Would Dickens have been surprised by
Freud, and our new kinds of frankness? All the evidence to be
found in his writings suggests he would not. He seems amply
aware of most varieties of sexuality, including sexual inversion,
and has wider sympathies than were current in his age. His
insight transcends labels and blanket judgements, since he is
much more interested in particular relationships than in abstract
names. He has remarkable insights into all kinds of human
cruelty, including the kinds we should now group as sexual, and
while he usually disapproves of them, his reasons transcend the
sexual *mores* of any one age. He was also, of course, a Victorian,
and there were certain kinds of sentimentality and cruelty in his
view of sex which modern readers rightly mistrust. There are
blemishes damaging to the artistry which cannot be evaded, yet
compensating insights can be found, I have suggested, on the
other side. There may be some things to be said in his favour
even in the crucial matter of little Em'ly. It might help to
create an initial sympathy if David's main quest is noticed as a
quest for lost childhood – a profoundly haunting theme, which
underlies the whole treatment of Em'ly, Annie Strong and
Martha, and indeed of both David's marriages as they are
presented in the book.

David is a great idealist, whose childish love for Em'ly turns
into the image of purity cherished during his youth. It is not
too much to suggest that Em'ly is unintentionally assimilated
by David to his private development, and that her prolonged
disgrace and suffering somewhere just out of our direct line of
vision is a sacrifice to David's childhood. It is the price she pays
for the marvellous memories David has of his mother, and the
tenacity with which David seeks his lost mother throughout the
world.

The fall of Em'ly has two aspects, one social and one romantic,
and these two are not one. The romantic, unhappily for her,
looms largest, since she becomes entangled with the happiness
of those rare innocents Ham and Mr Peggotty, and of course
David, and she cannot escape their part in her fate. But socially
(to start with the easier aspect) she ruins herself to a classic
formula, and it must be remembered that Victorian young girls

of her class who went off with good-looking rakes to be turned
into ladies did tend to come to bad ends. Dickens is right to
show the contempt expressed for her by her sister women, and
to demonstrate that while this might be balanced in Minnie by
something capable of secret kindness, in Rosa it breaks out in
verbal murder and persecuting hate. It is Littimer who propounds the worldly version of Em'ly's predicament, after her
eventual break with Steerforth: '. . . still matters were patched
up here, and made good there, over and over again; and altogether lasted, I am sure, for a longer time than anybody could
ever have expected'. But it is one of the oddities of the book
that instead of sounding here a typical worldly sophisticate,
Littimer remains his usual depraved self. David's unusually
innocent view of the situation is therefore endorsed, and the
realistic perspective is somehow swept out of sight.

Em'ly's social prospects after this are not bright. Given her
temperament, she would almost certainly have sunk to being a
prostitute like Martha. With no wealth, no skills, no social
character, she has precious little other choice. At best she
would have been taken back by Mr Peggotty, as in fact happens,
to live a chastened and wounded life. It would require the energy,
wit, resilience, charm of a Becky Sharp to survive in the sexual
jungle, becoming a mistress to important people or otherwise
brazening things out. Em'ly has none of these talents, and is
far too scrupulous; her virtues as well as her vices are all wrong.
There can be no doubt either that following in Martha's footsteps she would have felt suicidal like Martha. Prostitutes who
hated their lot did end in the river; and while the Martha
chapters are written with a baited-breath quality that is off-
putting (some hidden relish, surely), Dickens cannot be said to
be exaggerating the social facts.

But at this point a rather odd factor intervenes; is Em'ly
worse, or more unforgivable than Martha, or not? It is stressed
that Martha has fallen much lower in actual practice, since while
taking a lover is bad enough and more than half-way to ruin,
joining the profession must presumably be worse. But Martha
redeems herself by reuniting Em'ly with Mr Peggotty just in
time to save her, while Em'ly finds no sufficient outlet for her

sense of guilt. For Martha, then, there is forgiveness; and Dickens does full justice to the explicitly Christian view that reformed prostitutes are not irredeemably lost. She is allowed to go to Australia – though only through Mr Peggotty's exceptional private charity – and once there is even allowed to marry a vigorous young Australian, after her past has been revealed to him and he has accepted it. With luck, she lived happily ever after, though Dickens stops prudently short of saying this. All we know is that the two of them live four hundred miles away from 'any voices but their own and the singing birds': which might be pastoral and idyllic, or might mean that Martha still can't risk full contact with respectable folk. Anyway she has the Australian and hears the birds singing, and if readers think this happiness, who can say 'no'? But Em'ly comes off worse than Martha; and here the social realism and indeed the Christian charity become coloured by other concerns. David stops well short of the possibility that he might still marry the reformed Em'ly – or of the possibility that he might even look at her. Em'ly goes off to Australia along with Martha, but renounces sex and marriage despite all vigorous Australian offers – 'that's gone for ever', she tells Mr Peggotty – and lives on as a subdued spinster.

Has she done worse than Martha after all, then? It is true that she had greater potential, and has therefore fallen farther, and violated more than Martha did. But what exactly has she violated? – Ham's love, Mr Peggotty's love, and David. For better or worse, she has become entangled with all these; and though their love for her has its positive riches, and will naturally grieve for her, an over-hectic reaction takes place. It is significant, I fancy, that Dickens does not give Em'ly any great natural attributes. She is beautiful, but not exceptionally beautiful; otherwise she is a very ordinary child. There is no great social success that she might have won in default of Steerforth, no great creative contribution that goes to waste. The adolescent David does not seriously think of marrying her even before her fall, but cherishes her rather for the memory of what she was. And Ham, though a good man, is a very ordinary fisherman. Em'ly's life with him would have been blessed only, presumably, if she had responded to his love.

But this she does not: and one cannot help feeling that the punishment she suffers for being unable to return his love, much though she likes and respects him, is savage. Is the real truth that she should have recognised his fitness for her station, and married him to make everyone else happy? This isn't precisely said, and it would be in contradiction to Dickens's enthusiastic belief in romantic love as a proper basis for marriage, but it seems to be implied. There can be little doubt that poor Ham was partly to blame for what later happened by proposing to Em'ly without sufficient encouragement, and this is a reproach which he himself comes to feel. The unease of Em'ly's false position makes her very unhappy, and Steerforth's seduction is made all the easier by it. The virtue of Ham, though splendid, is coals of fire for Em'ly. When she goes off, he behaves like a man deeply and irrevocably wronged; and of course he suffers, as any man who loved her would. But the bare bones of the situation include the fact that an engagement entered into in error has been broken off before it turned into the greater disaster of an unhappy marriage. Ham's decision not to marry anyone else is still more coals of fire for Em'ly, even before he dies in the storm trying to save Steerforth. (After recognising him? This possibility is left open, as a counterpoint to David's previous fear that Ham would be Steerforth's death.) My point is not, of course, that Ham does not suffer greatly and behave nobly, but that his engagement to Em'ly turns out disastrously for *her*.

But Em'ly is also part of another vision, Mr Peggotty's; and Mr Peggotty's long career as a kind of virtuous wandering Jew in search of her naturally perpetuates and increases her guilt. It seems paradoxically true that if he does catch up with her he will save her, but his wanderings and sufferings must then be one more of the things she must bear. In strictly realistic terms Mr Peggotty's wanderings seem rather futile; he moves about more or less at random, and when news does reach him it is as likely to be through David or through Martha as anything else. The force of the wanderings is mythic: devotion and love become as stylised as a liturgy: 'Everything seemed, to my imagination,' David recalls, 'to be hushed in reverence for him, as he resumed his solitary journeying through the snow.' But despite the good that comes of it, the rescue of Mrs Gummidge from the morose state she had sunk into and later Em'ly's rescue, the main suggestion is that Em'ly has made a desolation of Mr Peggotty's life.

As, of course, she has: Dickens is not wrong to show the extreme sorrow which the shame of a beloved child can bring. This is imaged most memorably in the destruction of the boat-house. That place which for David in his childhood had been an 'Aladdin's cave' turns into the dismantled vision which Peggotty leaves for his wanderings and finally turns his back upon before setting off to Australia for good:

In truth, the wind, though it was low, had a solemn sound, and crept around the deserted house with a whispered wailing that was very mournful. Everything was gone, down to the little mirror with the oyster-shell frame. I thought of myself, lying here, when that first great change was being wrought at home. I thought of the blue-eyed child who had enchanted me. I thought of Steerforth: and a foolish, fearful fancy came upon me of his being near at hand, and liable to be met at any turn.

And here, of course, David comes in, and our suspicion that somewhere at the back of everything Em'ly is having to pay for her part in his life. When they were children, he had recorded: 'I am sure my fancy raised up something round that blue-eyed mite of a child, which etherealised and made an angel of her.' But Em'ly is not an angel after all: that is Agnes. Em'ly is a fallen angel, belonging with the 'bad angel' of David's life, Steerforth, as Agnes has identified him in a previous scene. And, like Steerforth, Em'ly becomes absolutely banished from David's life. David forgives Steerforth and thinks well of him, but never again sees him alive. And in a similar manner, though more mysteriously, he feels he ought never to see Em'ly again. The banishing of Steerforth is readily understandable. Steer-forth has been introduced to the boat-house by David and has then used David's innocence as a cloak for seduction; and he has done this knowing the passionate love and loyalty of David to himself. None of this could be readily forgotten or set right, and a meeting of the two would have been a rather terrible event.

But what has Em'ly done to make her banishment so complete?
– something she is less aware of, or perhaps not aware of at all.

I cannot feel that David is merely being 'Victorian' in a
conventional sense, or that his avoidance of Em'ly is wholly
explicable in terms of her social guilt. When Em'ly is rescued
by Mr Peggotty and is therefore accessible, he feels that a
face-to-face confrontation would be too much for *her*. He even
prefers to let her suffer the outrageous insults of Rosa Dartle
rather than intervene and show himself; so presumably the
sight of David would be more distressing for Em'ly than
indefinite exposure to Rosa's tirade. Mr Peggotty continues to
keep Em'ly out of sight until the last minute; and then, when
she is embarked for Australia and finally out of his way, just for
a moment – an epiphany almost – she is revealed to David as
the ship sails away :

As the sails rose to the wind, and the ship began to move, there
broke from all the boats three resounding cheers, which those
on board took up, and echoed back, and which were echoed and
re-echoed. My heart burst out when I heard the sound, and
beheld the waving of the hats and handkerchiefs – and then I
saw her!
   Then, I saw her, at her uncle's side, and trembling on his
shoulder.

After this, David hears of her only once, thirteen years later,
from Mr Peggotty :

'A slight figure,' said Mr Peggotty, looking at the fire. 'Kiender
worn; soft, sorrowful, blue eyes; a delicate face; a pritty head,
leaning a little down; a quiet voice and way – timid a'most.
That's Em'ly!'

Even after Em'ly's rescue, but before her departure to Australia,
there had been a strong sense that she was already dead.
Peggotty tells David that Ham would talk about Em'ly sometimes in the evening in the old boat-house as a child, but 'he
never mentioned her as a woman'. When Ham speaks of her to
David, he says : 'I loved her – and I love the mem'ry of her.'
Em'ly's final letter to David endorses the equation of her life
with her childhood, and her womanhood as it has turned out to
be with death : 'Good-bye for ever. Now, my dear, my friend,

good-bye for ever in this world. In another world, if I am forgiven, I may wake a child and come to you. All thanks and blessings.' This is quite as dreadful as any sentimental child's death-bed scene I can remember, with the dismaying difference that Em'ly is not actually dying and is not actually a child. It is also odd that she plans to 'come to' David when they are children again. Even when they were children, she preserved a teasing distance from him, except in the very first visit; and since childhood he has shown no disposition to want her to come to him as a bride, or a close friend. What must be said perhaps is that while we cannot doubt the truthfulness of this letter, or the truthfulness of everything that concerns the unhappy Em'ly, it is a pity that Dickens so entirely endorsed, through David, her tortured sentiments.

David's place in Em'ly's story and Em'ly's in David's are linked; and from the first David's sexual development, where the link is forged, is profoundly odd. His nature as we see it is always passionate. There was the childhood love for Em'ly, the juvenile crushes on Miss Shepherd and Miss Larkins, the adolescent hero-worship, strong and enduring, of Steerforth. When David falls in love with Dora he is head-over-heels immediately, and becomes totally saturated in love. It is enchanting, and idyllic, and beautifully observed and depicted; yet Dora is a toy to everyone, and everyone seems to have doubts about David's love for her, including poor Dora herself. What is doubted is not so much whether his love is a good thing as whether it is real. 'Blind, blind, blind,' sighs Betsey, obviously convinced that David is really in love – or should be – with Agnes; and David himself records : 'Heaven knows, folly as it all was, it would have been a happy fate to have been struck immortal with those foolish feelings, and to have stayed among the trees for ever!' But *is* David in love with Agnes, unbeknown to himself? Agnes is necessary, it seems, to set off Dora : ' . . . and round the little fairy-figure [Agnes] shed some glimpses of her own pure light, and made it yet more precious and more innocent to me!' It is easy enough to sense the truth of this, but also its naïveté; if it *is* an innocent feeling, this can only be because David is too entirely lacking in self-knowledge

to sully it. From earliest days Agnes is associated for him with
a kind of purity and idealism which he hasn't yet identified as
'love':

I love little Em'ly, but I don't love Agnes – no, not at all in
that way – but I feel that there are goodness, peace, and truth,
wherever Agnes is; and that the soft light of the coloured
window in the church, seen long ago, falls on her always, and
on me when I am near her, and on everything round.

David always feels at home with Agnes, so much so that his
family circle with Dora is far more complete when Agnes is
also there. But he continues not to 'love' Agnes 'in that way' –
a form of torture for the poor girl, given his continual decla-
rations of an absolute need for her, which he seems unaware of
throughout. He has identified the feeling she inspires in him as
belonging to a sister, and assumes that brotherly affection
complements it on the other side.

The motivations of David's love are indeed complex; he has
loved Em'ly childishly, but when she goes off with Steerforth
his deepest pang is for his friend: 'Never more, oh God forgive
you, Steerforth! to touch that passive hand in love and friendship.
Never, never more.' The accents here are those with which
Tennyson's readers would have been familiar – the thought and
feeling of 'Break, break, break', the verbal echo from 'Oenone',
and the affinity with *In Memoriam*, that elegy for the dead
Hallam which Tennyson published in the same year as *David
Copperfield*. It reminds us again that Em'ly is as much a rival to
David as she is to Rosa Dartle, when she runs off with the person
he most loves. The truth is that Dickens is depicting the
emotional life of David with a fidelity which rings true to his
period, and in a wider sense rings true to human feelings we all
recognise, yet he is weighting his *analysis* towards a naïveté
which does not quite convince. We might pinpoint this by
suggesting that although various aspects of love and passion
are being explored, the meaning of 'love' is somehow restricted
to David's gropings around the word. David is indeed in the
dark on many things; but what degree of illumination is
expected of us?

At this point we must recall the importance to David of the

affairs of Annie Strong. When David first becomes aware of the possibility that Annie might be unfaithful to the Doctor, he records the moment in this way:

I cannot say what an impression this made upon me, or how impossible I found it, when I thought of her afterwards, to separate her from this look, and remember her face in its innocent loveliness again. It haunted me when I got home. I seemed to have left the Doctor's roof with a dark cloud lowering on it. The reverence that I had for his grey head, was mingled with commiseration for his faith in those who were treacherous to him, and with resentment against those who injured him. The impending shadow of a great affliction, and a great disgrace that had no form in it yet, fell like a stain upon the quiet place where I had worked and played as a boy, and did it a cruel wrong. I had no pleasure in thinking, any more, of the grave old broad-leaved aloe-trees, which remained shut up in themselves a hundred years together, and of the trim smooth grass-plot, and the stone urns, and the Doctor's walk, and the congenial sound of the Cathedral bell hovering above them all. It was as if the tranquil sanctuary of my boyhood had been sacked before my face, and its peace and honour given to the winds.

This is very soon after David leaves his schooldays behind, and before his first dissipation; it is also before Dora, but after Miss Shepherd and Miss Larkins have impinged on his life. The sense of lost innocence is pervasive, and what adolescent has not known such a moment as this? The sanctuary of David's boyhood is violated and seems already lost to him, a paradise guarded against re-entry by angels with swords. David has seen an enigmatic look on Annie's face, which he misinterprets, though he knows it is on the other side of a threshold now to be crossed. Naturally David fears the crossing and tries to hold back; less naturally, he expects little but disaster on the other side. Is the disturbance of sexual knowledge pure violation? – and does David ever fully emerge from the disturbance that troubles him here? It seems significant that David honours Doctor Strong for his total ignorance of his wife's possible infidelity even when to David himself the guilt appears proved. This moment comes much later in the book, with Uriah's disclosures, when the dim foreboding David feels about Annie is given a name. Doctor Strong's virtue in David's eyes seems all along to have been not so much that he believes in his wife's innocence against false evidence (though this is the truth of the matter, and he is in fact vindicated), but that he exists in a world too high and pure for the knowledge of sex. David enlists him as a total innocent in the garden of boyhood, and Annie becomes the person who brings forbidden knowledge to that place.

Later, Annie exonerates herself, and everyone is happy; but Doctor Strong's own doubts about whether he was right to propose to her are left unresolved. David's chief concern is with the restoration of innocence, and with certain aspects of this as they concern himself. (Dickens returned to the situation in *Bleak House*, with Jarndyce's proposal to Esther, and there treated it more penetratingly on its own terms.) David once again shows his choice of innocence against adult sexual experience, with the added insight that a disciplined heart alone can keep passion at bay. This choice seems certainly to have governed his depiction of little Em'ly's story; and now it leads him to feel that his love for Dora was after all youthful folly: the true love must always have been Agnes, pointing upwards, like that distant memory of a stained-glass saint.

The part played by Uriah Heep seems another aspect of this, since Uriah's love for Agnes is represented throughout as the attempted rape of good by evil. Uriah of course is sexually as well as morally repellent; in his repellent qualities he is all of a piece. But this is partly because, being repellent, he ought not to be sexual; or failing this, he should decently pretend he is not. In Dickens's novels it seems true to say that the characters who are physically grotesque or ungainly but also virtuous keep their sexual impulses well under control. They can adore the heroine, and protect and cherish her, but they no more really expect to marry her than they do to fly. From Kit Nubbles, through Tom Pinch to Mr Grewgious, various examples of this pattern can be found. Either they cherish inward sentiments but settle for chastity, or they are rewarded with a virtuous but sexually ineligible bride.

The characters who are grotesque or ungainly but evil are another matter. In them physical ugliness is usually a manifestation of baseness, and when they aspire to marry the heroine – Quilp with Nell, Uriah with Agnes – a kind of horror envelops the idea. This is realistic enough – Dickens is always a realist in such matters – but it underlines the high demands that society is likely to make. David, at any rate, is horrified and affronted; yet even this tormenting thought of Uriah marrying Agnes does not alert him to tender feelings of his own. And this *is* odd : Uriah sees David clearly enough as a rival, after all. If David still does not see it, then how does he love Agnes? Still not in the 'way' he had loved little Em'ly in childhood? Or Dora? In what way then?

In the end David marries Agnes, but the processes continue to be odd. When Betsey Trotwood hints that Agnes is herself in love with an unknown suitor, he doesn't understand, though he has now persuaded himself that he loves *her*. Even now, his love isn't passionate; indeed, the passionate love he has had for Steerforth and for Dora have both failed him, and joined those earlier passions for Miss Shepherd and Miss Larkins in the folly of youth. It is, rather, a full knowledge at last that he cannot live without Agnes; that she is good for him; that her presence heals him; that his home without her is not complete. And perhaps this *is* the best basis for marriage; it makes for a happy and settled family, where David can work, prosper, grow and have peace of mind. It is what nearly everyone but himself has always expected. Events prove it to be right.

Before this, he has thought of Agnes as 'sister', but it now appears that 'sister' is not what she is. But whatever she is, she is not another Dora, not another Steerforth. So passion is renounced – the passion which has taken foolish forms in David, dark forms in Em'ly and Martha and Rosa Dartle – and David sails into the light. In memory, poor Dora has to be downgraded, and her pathetic dying insight endorsed. 'Oh, Doady, after more years, you never could have loved your child-wife better than you do; and, after more years, she would so have tried and disappointed you, that you might not have been able to love her half so well! I know I was too young and foolish. It

is much better as it is!' This is moving not because it is sentimental, but because it is ruthless. David comes to accept it as
true. Dickens endorses him. No doubt it is true. But how
sad!

If any simple moral can be abstracted, it may be that the best
marriages are between two deep yet not passionately tormented
friends of opposite sexes – David and Agnes, Traddles and
Sophy, Dr Strong and Annie, Mr and Mrs Micawber – and
that certain other sexually innocent relationships partake of
these qualities: Betsey and Mr Dick, Mr Peggotty and Mrs
Gummidge. If this seems unattractive, one reason may be
artistic; there is far too much of Agnes pointing upwards, more
an ideal than a wife, and not an alluring ideal. David has specifically learned to subdue his 'undisciplined' heart before he
marries her. It is an organ we hear of increasingly as unhappiness gathers round him, as though the tragic elements in
David's relationships with Steerforth and Dora were indeed a
purely moral matter, which some inner stoic adjustment could
make come right.

We cannot help sensing that all the life and gaiety of the
book belong away from Agnes: and that Dickens now seems to
see virtue, in women particularly, as a draining out of energy
and passion in favour of will and sacrifice. Agnes has had a good
training in discipline herself at David's hands, and indeed she
has never complained. In later novels, she is followed in her
austere path by Amy Dorrit, Lucie Manette, Biddy, Lizzie
Hexam – all women who can give and give, if need be unrewarded, and who with luck might be blessed with happiness in
marriage as a reward. It is a noble ideal, but a somewhat
daunting one, since it carries none of the dynamic spartan or
puritan rewards. All these women are victims, and to some
degree crushed by the circumstances which test their virtue;
and it seems that increasingly Dickens saw virtue at bay in a
tragic world.

A further flaw may exist in our suspicion that David is
himself devitalised by his second marriage; that in escaping the
wheel of passion and suffering, he is too gratefully putting off
youth for middle age.

VI

The ideal of marriage celebrated in *David Copperfield* deserves respect, and perhaps it is the formula for lasting happiness, as the novel suggests. One continuing strand in the book is the thought that love can be independent of sex and is greater than sex; this strikes me as true, a genuine insight acknowledged in most ages, and unaccountably mislaid by our own to its very great loss. The most stark statement of the theme is no doubt Martha's, when from her degradation she sees a total gulf between love and sex. 'Oh,' she tells Mr Peggotty, 'don't think that all the power I had of loving anything, is quite worn out.' She shows her love by rescuing Em'ly from prostitution and restoring her to a life where she can live without sex. This is an extreme instance; but in many places we find the conviction that whereas sex can be either absent or a very junior partner in any truly fine relationship, on its own it is often crippling, obsessive, tormenting – a force of death. The truth of this again seems indisputable; and whatever crudities mar the treatment of Annie Strong or Martha are best seen as a price paid for insights of such a positive kind.

This is controversial: but what is less controversial is that almost everything to do with David's sex life differentiates him from his author; there is not much direct self-portrait here. We know that the pieces from his own life which Dickens adapted for this novel developed in a very different way. Maria Beadnell, the tormented love of Dickens's adolescence, rejected him, yet remained in his memory as a potent ghost. Like the blacking factory, she belonged to a sealed-off area of experience, among secrets too delicate for the world to know. It is possible that in having David marry Dora, but then succumb to subtle unhappiness, Dickens was doing his best to exorcise Maria Beadnell (though it was not until the lady herself turned up, ripe for translation into Flora Finching, that the therapy was complete). Agnes, on the other hand, is one of the women remotely indebted to his sister-in-law Mary Hogarth, whom he had loved with a great intensity and whose death while he was still a young author was a tragic sorrow to him. David's second

marriage, to Agnes, and his ten years of happiness might well
be wishful thinking. Dickens's own marriage to Kate was already
deteriorating, and in the 1850s he became increasingly tormented by the sense of one great love missing from his life. It
would appear, however, that the missing love was passionate
rather than tranquil, so Agnes might have been invented in an
attempt to sober himself to a vision of some real happiness that
could also be serene.

Dickens was altogether more moody and demoniac than
David, and less susceptible to the lure of a disciplined heart.
Not long after writing this book, he took the young Ellen
Ternan as his mistress. This does not convict him of hypocrisy.
There is no reason to think that Dickens was not wholly sincere
both in his admiration for Agnes and in his grief at the ruin of
little Em'ly. But it certainly suggests that David was nothing
like a vehicle for the whole of Dickens: or, rather, that David's
innocence was too readily allowed to operate throughout the
moral and emotional development, while whatever was more
worldly or sophisticated in Dickens himself was exiled to the
outer darkness inhabited by Littimer, Heep, Steerforth, the
violators of innocence in the book. Presumably Dickens did not
feel a few years later that he was exposing Ellen Ternan to the
irrevocable ruin suffered by Em'ly; or that he was breaking the
innocent hearts of a Ham or Mr Peggotty; or that he was
violating his own childhood or anyone else's childhood in an
unbearable way. And why should he? Art is not life; never
trust the teller, trust the tale. Yet more than most books *David
Copperfield* was supposed to be autobiographical, and we may
legitimately feel that in so far as it includes solemn warnings
against the horrors of passion, seduction and undisciplined
hearts, then its author, at least, was not finally convinced. At
any rate its author didn't live up to it; and possibly realised that
too great a sacrifice of his own energy might be involved if he
did.

But of course David is very little like Dickens, even though a
number of traumatic episodes from Dickens's life are bestowed
upon him and he is passed off as a novelist of rising fame.
What Dickens stresses very much is the vulnerability of his

hero – David's fear of being thought young and inexperienced, his sensitivity to the degradation of Murdstone and Grinby, his loneliness on the Dover Road, his loneliness in love. The next Dickens character with an element of self-portrait was Arthur Clennam, a man so drained of energy and reconciled to sadness that he has ceased to look for happiness in life. After this we have Pip in *Great Expectations*, a character more reconciled to life than Arthur Clennam and more vigorous, but also crippled by a burden of unresolved guilt.

None of these characters is in any complete sense The Inimitable : certainly not Arthur and Pip, equally certainly not David. David embodies marvellously sensitive memories of childhood and of young love, but for all his renamings he has no personal nickname, and if he looked for one, The Inimitable clearly wouldn't do. Too many aspects of the author are left out of the picture : the fierce energy and showmanship; the enthusiasm; the passionate commitment to social causes; the tremendous willpower and exuberance; the acting, the hypnotism, the public readings; the walks around London, the triumphal progresses through Europe and America; the arrogance of genius; the ultimate resilience and indestructibility; all this is missing. Perhaps Dickens felt it expedient to tone himself down for the occasion; there might have been less appeal for early Victorian readers in his uncensored self. Perhaps he was merely being an artist, and adapting himself as he had adapted so many other people to the delicate requirements of a fictional tale. I have suggested elsewhere that if we want other aspects of Dickens we might have to turn to characters less openly acknowledged as part of him : Dick Swiveller and Quilp; Mr Pecksniff even; John Jasper perhaps. In my final chapter I shall argue that to identify Dickens naïvely with his more evil characters would be at least as big an error as it would be to identify him with David. But we should remember that he contained their possibilities and understood them, better than David Copperfield would have understood. David is presented to us as an author. But I cannot imagine *Edwin Drood* or, indeed, *David Copperfield* among his works.

7 *Bleak House*
Esther better not born?

'In *Bleak House* I have purposely dwelt upon the romantic side of familiar things.' So Dickens tells us in his 1853 Preface. The wording recalls Wordsworth's ambitions for his part in *Lyrical Ballads*, but *Bleak House* is 'romantic' in an older sense. Its heroine, cheerfully sane and domestic, and much loved by those nearest to her, is surrounded by unsolved riddles concerning her birth. Who is she? How important are the gloomy words remembered so sadly from childhood: 'It would have been far better, little Esther, that you had had no birthday; that you had never been born!'? Lady Dedlock, proud, haughty, riding high above the great world of fashion five miles around, is strangely threatened: by a legal document, whose handwriting disturbs her; by footfalls on the Ghost's Walk at her place in Lincolnshire; by a portrait, fascinating to the young man of the name of Guppy; by a family solicitor, whom she increasingly fears. We stumble on other characters no less mysterious, tucked away in back streets or in legal chambers, or looming suddenly through the fog. Who is Krook, the sinister illiterate nicknamed Lord Chancellor? Who is Krook's mysterious lodger, Nemo? Who are Mr George and his friend Phil? – Tulkinghorn and Bucket? Who is Jo? – our worry as well as Mrs Snagsby's, Dickens assures us. There are further mysteries in *Bleak House* of 'why?' Why is Esther disapproved of, Jo hounded, Sir Leicester deferred to? Why does Tulkinghorn behave so – well, unprofessionally? What professional ethic does Bucket observe? No-one in the novel has a safe or stable place in society, not Jo, who is very well aware of this, not Sir Leicester, to whom the discovery will come as a shock. Several of the characters spend their lives rummaging among dust and debris for secrets; Tulkinghorn in his chambers,

Krook in his shop; Grandfather Smallweed in 'a rather ill-
favoured and ill-savoured neighbourhood', the Lord Chancellor
in his High Court of Chancery among the great of the land.
Nearly everyone is searching for meanings not easy to come by.
Bleak House is pervaded from its magnificent opening chapter
by the London Particular, as we watch ghostly suitors suing for
justice in a world of ghosts.

A romantic setting, and a romantic plot; the plot is particularly important to *Bleak House*. Dickens's new friend, the
young Wilkie Collins, must have been fascinated by this fore-
runner of his own genre. With its shameful secret, its beautiful
victim, its implacable blackmailer and its vintage detective,
Bleak House is a tale of detection and crime. We are obliged
therefore to pay the closest attention to Dickens's tone and
structure in the novel, as well as to his intentionally transparent
hints. This is truer indeed of *Bleak House* than it is of any of
the other novels, with the obvious and tantalising exception of
Edwin Drood. Dickens's early plots from *Pickwick* to *Chuzzlewit*
are mainly picaresque in character, and guided by the fortunes
of their hero or heroine towards aesthetic shape. The plot of
Barnaby Rudge, of course, is more complex, but still essentially
linear and, like *A Tale of Two Cities* later, controlled by actual
historical events. *Dombey and Son*, though no longer picaresque,
proceeds chronologically through a fairly straightforward story,
with its mysteries clustering around the affairs of Good Mrs
Brown. *David Copperfield* is in the form of pseudo-autobiography,
and regresses, in plot technique, to the earlier mode.

The plot of *Little Dorrit*, in contrast, is of very great complexity, but is so far from being at the heart of the novel's
greatness that even Dickens was hard put to it to unravel the
strands. Much the same could be said of *Our Mutual Friend*,
where complexities of plot and symbolism are closely wedded,
but the plot counts for little on its own. *Bleak House* stands out
from all these in having a plot which is so central and fundamental that if the reader loses his way with it in this novel, he is
lost indeed. He is left, in fact, in bewildered fellowship with the
unfortunate Snagsby, making very Kafkaesque going of the
entire affair.

The reader who attends closely is less totally fogbound, in that he engages in the first place not with a metaphysical riddle but with a mystery story, a romance. A mystery story, however, with metaphysical overtones; the formula of *Bleak House* has its truest progeny neither in *The Castle* and *The Trial*, nor in the modern detective story, influential though it was in both these directions, but in such intriguing if comparatively minor masterpieces as Rex Warner's *The Aerodrome* and Graham Greene's *The Ministry of Fear*. A seeming nightmare is created and then in the end resolved by plot logic, but certain unresolved suggestions tease the mind. The plot has explained much, but it has not explained everything; and the novel's power is some-where in the gap. The word 'identity' is useful as a pointer to the gap in this particular instance. Esther's identity is a mystery raised, and then solved, at plot level, but profounder mysteries of identity pervade the whole.

'. . . the romantic side of familiar things'. The formula draws attention to Dickens's insertion of grim social realities and soaring moral challenges into a story which would have pleased the old writers of romance. But should the 'romantic side' of Chancery, or Tom-All-Alone's, or Lady Dedlock's guilt be so familiar? – the words are not innocent of an ironic twist. Yet 'romantic' hints, nonetheless, a promise, that unless the reader is to be wholly misled the author's treatment, or his conclusion, will not be unremittingly grim. Many accounts of *Bleak House* make it sound as sombre as its immediate sequel, *Hard Times*, but this is far from being true. On the contrary, I would even call this an optimistic novel, given the nature of its material and its themes. The optimism may be felt in a certain expansiveness and humour – mainly Esther's – but more particularly in moments of explicitly religious hope. Jo dies with the unfamiliar words of the Lord's Prayer on his lips, Richard Carstone starts a new world which sets this world to rights. The optimism of such passages is too clear to be doubted, unless we miss the 'strangers and pilgrims' theme so omnipresent in Dickens and absentmindedly ascribe all his religious passages to cant. At the same time *Bleak House* develops the encouraging symbolism of its title. For one Bleak House blighted by Chancery

and fully deserving its name we receive two Bleak Houses, both
created by Jarndyce and irradiated by Esther, both calm and
fruitful, with 'delightful irregularities' enhancing order and
charm.

Bleak House is, moreover, a novel with an astonishing number
of virtuous characters, far more than Dickens presented in such
numbers elsewhere. To the roll-call of Jarndyce, Esther and Ada
we must add Miss Flite, Allan Woodcourt, Charley, Mrs
Rouncewell, Mr Boythorn, George and Phil, Mr Snagsby, Mr
and Mrs Bagnet, Caddy Jellyby, Rosa and Walter, and, in their
hopeless ways, Guster, Jenny and her friend, Mrs Blinder –
the poor who are 'so much to the poor'. These characters
achieve by their concerted goodness an effect of radiance akin
to Esther's serene good humour in 'her' prose. There are also
many characters, from Sir Leicester and Lady Dedlock down
through Richard, Jo, Prince, even to Guppy, who on balance,
with whatever admixture of weakness or absurdity, strike us
as more good than evil at heart. If we turn to the evil characters,
they include several in whom Dickens's transforming zest is
richly at work. Skimpole and Old Mr Turveydrop create themselves in the manner of Pecksniff and Micawber, not only
atrocious but atrociously attractive, while Mrs Jellyby and Mrs
Pardiggle are softened, for all their awfulness, by Esther's eye.
The really vile characters are by Dickens's standards few :
Krook, Vholes, Grandfather Smallweed, Hortense, Mrs Snagsby
(perhaps) and of course Tulkinghorn. There is also the fascinating enigma of Mr Bucket – surely good at heart ? – yet more
like Tulkinghorn than we might expect.

II

But, it will be urged, is this not precisely the dividing line in
Dickens's work between 'evil' which is associated chiefly with
evil men, and 'evil' which invades the texture of society itself?
If the characters in *Bleak House* are often demonstrably virtuous,
why is there more actual suffering here than ever before ? In
place of great individual villains like Ralph Nickleby, Fagin
and Quilp, we now have Chancery, Tom-All-Alone's and a

darkened world. 'The system! I am told on all hands it's the
system!' Mr Gridley shouts, in his passionate and futile rage.

This account of Dickens's development is now highly familiar,
but more dubious than familiarity might suggest. Like all other
attempts to simplify him, it is highly selective. *Barnaby Rudge*
and *Dombey and Son* are disregarded, and there is some degree
of distortion everywhere else. In early Dickens, for instance,
we frequently sense a world in the grip of nightmare, where
terrible faces peer out at us, Fagin over Oliver's shoulder,
Quilp over Little Nell's, more like exhalations of evil than its
original cause. At the same time it is plainly untrue to say that
Bleak House lacks spectacular villains : Tulkinghorn is among
the two or three most sinister figures that Dickens ever drew.
Can we overlook, for that matter, Grandfather Smallweed and
his horrible family, or the vampire lawyer Vholes who drinks
Richard's blood?

It is important then to stress continuities as well as dis-
continuities, yet one must allow some definite change in
Dickens in the late 1840s and early 1850s, towards a more
pervasive sense of evils rooted in impersonal things. The
sinister villains are joined now by such urbane and kindly souls
as the Lord Chancellor, and by the just and honourable Sir
Leicester and the whole of his class. It can be argued that
Dickens became more conscious in the Great Exhibition era
than he had been even at the time of *Dombey* that his society was
nearer to the jungle, in its daily realities, than to Christian
ideals. Richard is killed, so are Jo, Nemo and the man from
Shropshire; so, with the assistance of Tulkinghorn's strange
vendetta, is Lady Dedlock. Miss Flite has become deranged by
suffering before we meet her, and shares honours with Krook as
choric commentator on the Lord Chancellor's Court. Jenny and
her friend exist in fear and squalor, and their babies live or die
as though nineteen hundred years of Christianity had never
been : ' "Why, what age do you call that little creature?" says
Bucket. "It looks as if it was born yesterday." He is not at all
rough about it; and as he turns his light gently upon the infant,
Mr Snagsby is strangely reminded of another infant, encircled
with light, that he has seen in pictures.' Even Jarndyce and

Esther withdraw from any large involvement with their society in favour of the domestic but still threatened sphere of private life. Meanwhile the poor rot in Tom-All-Alone's and men die in Chancery; systems seem indeed more powerful than men. Is it not apparent that traditional privilege and the new capitalism between them are breaking the human spirit and breeding despair?

Some such implications were detected, certainly, and no less certainly resented, by Trollope and other Victorians of Dickens's time. They resented the gloom and savagery of Dickens's social picture, when *laissez faire* and the Great Exhibition seemed to promise so much. (It was a different story when Trollope came to write *The Way We Live Now* in the mid 1870s, but economic optimism by then was starting to ebb.) Modern critics have agreed with Dickens's contemporaries in noting the gloom of his picture; yet the gloom is balanced by powerful forces on the other side. Just as Jo and Richard die with religious hope surrounding them, so Jarndyce proves that Miss Flite's theory of mystical *compulsion* in the Chancellor's mace is not true. Esther dispels the notion that the bastard child of an aristocratic lady need necessarily be warped by her misfortunes or grow up to lament her dubious identity and her uncertain fate. She survives illegitimacy, unrequited love, smallpox and the terrible knowledge that her very existence is her mother's nightmare, to exist triumphantly in a world of good. The depressing perversions of private charity witnessed by Mrs Jellyby and Mrs Pardiggle are more than counterbalanced by the constructive charity of Jarndyce, Esther, Mr Snagsby, George, Mr and Mrs Bagnet, Mrs Blinder and Guster. At the same time, *Bleak House* is itself a factor in *Bleak House*, a sufficient reminder that the author, at least, had not succumbed to impotent despair. He went on fighting, in fiction and elsewhere, for that ideal of social responsibility later embodied in the welfare state. In the twentieth century no-one lives in Tom-All-Alone's in utter hopelessness, dies like Jo in the London streets, suffers the law's delay quite as Jarndyce did. Other evils, yes, and Dickens would have expected them, but these particular evils have been removed.

Nonetheless *Bleak House* presents evils in abundance, as modern
critics rightly underline. If Dame Durden is there to 'sweep the
cobwebs out of the sky' there is ample work for her broom.
Nowhere else does Dickens survey society so comprehensively
and on the whole so gloomily, from the heights of Chesney
Wold down to the burying yard to which Lady Dedlock descends. The brickmakers, Nemo, Coavinses and his children,
Guster and Jo belong to the world of extreme poverty, driven
by the absolute neglect of society towards their death. From
this abyss, we rise through the genteel poverty of Miss Flite,
the honest, hard-working poverty of George and Phil, the self-
respecting near poverty of Mr and Mrs Bagnet, to the proudly
independent poverty (perhaps this is no longer the word,
however) of Mrs Rouncewell, loyal to her employers, and in
many true ways really one of the family at Chesney Wold.
Then, rising again in worldly prospects, though not in attrac-
tiveness, we pass through the lower-middle-class world of the
Snagsbys (genteel vulgarity pointing forward to Mrs Wilfer's
tragic stage in Holloway), the eye-to-the-main-chance opportunism of Guppy and Tony Jobling, the stomach-turning
self-imposed squalor of the Smallweeds, the shabby-elegant
ménage of Skimpole, the extraordinary manifestations of old
Mr Turveydrop's Deportment, the deplorable Jellyby home.
Above these scenes, we emerge into the world of the prosperous middle classes – Boythorn and Jarndyce prosperous on
inherited wealth, the Iron Gentleman on the wealth of self-made
business success – and upwards, again, to the splendours of
Chesney Wold. (Where, however, even amid the splendour,
poor Volumnia broods in the nightwatches on what is to become
of her if her rich relations die, or become bored with her, or
simply forget that she is there.)

In most places and in various patterns and combinations
Dickens sees money as a curse. At the top of the hierarchy it is
unproductive. Sir Leicester despises people who earn money,
and ascribes his own pre-eminence to immutable laws. Lady
Dedlock is bored to death, chiefly because her exaltation above

society leaves her with nothing to do. Rather worse, money at the top of the hierarchy is irresponsible. Sir Leicester may attend to his devotions at Chesney Wold with all sincerity, but neither the spirit nor even the letter reaches Jo. In Chancery, inherited wealth is the pretext for large-scale and horrible parasitism, which Dickens characteristically embodies in bizarre images: the vampire lawyer Vholes who drinks Richard's blood, Miss Flite's fantastic roll-call of birds. There is also the parasitism of the Smallweed family, and the parasitism of Skimpole, whose pretence to know nothing about money is yet one more mode of its vicious misuse.

Where else is money influential? In the North Country, of course, where the Iron Gentleman produces wealth for himself and for his country (yet his factory has sacrificed beauty and cleanliness, and Dickens had never taken kindly to industrial towns). Meanwhile Guster has her fits in the Snagsby establishment; and Jenny is beaten by her drunken husband; and Nemo dies by inches in Krook's chambers. And Jo is moved on, and on, and on in the London streets, until his mind darkens with bewilderment and his body falls prey to fever; and, after offering a few small gems of insight – about Mr Chadband, and about life; and after communicating his plague unknowingly and much to his sorrow to Esther; and after destroying or helping to destroy, unknowingly, Lady Dedlock; he comes to the end predicted for him all along: 'Dead, your Majesty. Dead, my lords and gentlemen. Dead, right reverends and wrong reverends of every order. Dead, men and women, born with heavenly compassion in your hearts. And dying thus around us every day.'

Money is entwined with most of these evils as it was in *Dombey and Son*, but is money their root? 'Dead, men and women, born with heavenly compassion in your hearts.' The savagery of this famous stroke of irony is that Dickens believed it to be the truth. In all the perversions of society around him he saw greed, apathy, cruelty, often (and here was a role for literature) simple failure of imagination, but these were familiar consequences of the Fall. 'The good that I would I do not, the evil that I would not that I do.' Behind man's fallen nature

F

another nature survived, if only fitfully, the original heavenly
compassion in his heart. It is from *this* conviction that Dickens's
creative energy drew so much inspiration that even *Bleak House*
could be infused with hope. Other evils he would have expected
to arise in human history, and these too would need hope in their
turn. But the here-and-now evils could be exposed, despite all
obstacles – despite Parliament even, dedicated as it seemed to an
evil *status quo*.

Perhaps it is to reinforce these insights that Tulkinghorn is so
important in the novel : Tulkinghorn, an extreme but by that
token exceptional example of the human malaise. A man of
power, infinitely malign and corrupt yet in no direct sense
motivated by money, he is the presiding genius of evil in *Bleak
House*. There are two great cobwebs in the novel, woven by no
directing intelligence yet entangling their victims – Chancery,
where Richard, the man from Shropshire and Miss Flite
flounder, and Tom-All-Alone's, where Jo and Nemo come to
their deaths. The two webs meet – Tom-All-Alone's is in
Chancery – but no malign creature has fashioned the threads.
But in the centre of *Bleak House* there is another web, woven by
Tulkinghorn, to catch and destroy one person whom he hates.
Hates ? – his motive indeed remains hidden, but the end is never
in doubt. Like Iago, Tulkinghorn admires and is fascinated by
his victim; like Iago, he relishes his power to entangle to
destruction, until there seems creative satisfaction, almost, in
what he does. Some critics have complained that Tulkinghorn
behaves unlike a normal solicitor – an insight that Dickens's
ironic heart would surely have enjoyed. We may safely concede
that Tulkinghorn's behaviour is surprising, and unprofessional,
and that whatever its outcome he could hardly have survived as
the trusted solicitor of the great. Whether acknowledged or not,
self-destruction seems part of his plotting : it is when Dickens is
reminding us that Tulkinghorn, the guardian of mysteries, is
himself a mystery, that we learn of the one bachelor friend he
has had : '. . . a man of the same mould and a lawyer too, who
lived the same kind of life until he was seventy-five years old,
and then suddenly conceiving (as it is supposed) an impression
that it was too monotonous, gave his gold watch to his hair-

dresser one summer evening and walked leisurely home to the Temple and hanged himself'. In Tulkinghorn, Dickens is presenting a study of highly abnormal psychology, yet not too remote for flashes of recognition to light the scene. He is familiar in the peculiarly frightening way that Iago is familiar, not as daily phenomenon, but as something glimpsed, inwards and downwards, in some private abyss. He is like Iago in that he becomes an ultimate image, at one of those extreme points where the ultimate may sometimes take flesh. Does he probe his motives also, like Iago, trying explanations, plausible though shifting, which never fully explain? We feel something wrong in him from his first appearance in Chesney Wold – musty, respectable, almost 'retainer-like' to Sir Leicester's admiring perception (far removed indeed from the Wat-Tylerish image of doom in the baronet's mind). What does he feel about the aristocrats and other exalted beings who depend on his services? His thoughts on these matters are not revealed. Yet Dickens conveys that Tulkinghorn in his respected old age walks a tight-rope; it needs something to snap merely, some long habit of restraint to be relinquished, some tug, resisted possibly for a lifetime, to be given its way. Some men break when a rational appraisal of them might least anticipate this, and Dickens records many such moments in his work. In *Dombey and Son* it happens to Carker. After a career of careful and successful fraud he risks everything on a reckless elopement, doomed from the start. It happens to Bradley Headstone in *Our Mutual Friend* when, after a painful and unnatural climb to respectability, he succumbs to a madness always waiting close, it seems, behind his back. It happens surely – though the full implications remain permanently inaccessible – to John Jasper, the respected choir-master of Cloisterham. Tulkinghorn fits into the abnormal yet frighteningly understandable pattern of a man – old or young, it might be either – giving his most destructive compulsions their head. At a certain moment he abandons himself to evil. By choice? We no more discern this clearly than he does himself. But he begins to weave a web which will be fatal to Lady Dedlock, and fatal in one manner or another to himself. When does he finally decide to destroy his victim? We find him

speculating that 'she cannot be spared'. He wonders resentfully
how she can show mercy to her maid Rosa, when no mercy is to
be shown to her. Clearly he has to goad her almost beyond
endurance, puzzled and elated by the courage she shows. Must
she break before his eyes for some metaphysical reason – to
prove, perhaps, that even an aristocrat is mortal and evil, like
himself? Or is it nourishment he seeks on a victim's fearfulness,
all the richer for a season of courage and peculiar restraint?
Whatever his motives, the result is nightmare, and gives its
distinctive colour to the book. The webs of Chancery and Tom-
All-Alone's become imbued with his evil: yet clearly *he* is no
ordinary blackmailer motivated by money, and there is no
heavenly compassion in *his* heart. Some impulse to power,
irrational and murderous, is incarnate in Tulkinghorn. Its
mystery reaches deep in *Bleak House*.

IV

Bleak House is a novel then of romantic themes and highly
disparate characters whose destiny is reconciled in the symbol
of a web. As John Harvey has noted, the novel introduces us to
groups of characters who at first seem wholly divorced from
each other. It is when we begin to perceive links in their destiny
that the web comes to be felt.

It is important to notice, however, that the web is not wholly
evil; there are threads of brotherhood and sanity, too, in the
book. Charley and Esther both contract smallpox as the price
of compassion, of their acknowledged responsibilities towards
each other and towards Jo. Lady Dedlock lies frozen to death
outside the foul graveyard where her lover rots, but she is
drawn by nature, as well as pursued, to this place. It is highly
appropriate that Guster should be the last person to encounter
Lady Dedlock before her death, and that the lady from Chesney
Wold should offer her dying blessing to one so wholly removed,
in all social intercourse, from herself. It is characteristic and
fitting, again, that though Lady Dedlock dies and the tragedy
moves to the sombre irony of her final tableau – the great lady
become, in fact, the pauper whose dress she wears – this final

meeting with Guster, and Sir Leicester's forgiveness, should strike us as a marvellous victory for good. 'Am I my brother's keeper?' Those who answer 'yes' in *Bleak House* suffer, but they are not crushed. 'And so I took it from her', says Guster, of Lady Dedlock's last letter, 'and she said she had nothing to give me, and I said I was poor myself and consequently wanted nothing. And so she said God bless you, and went.' Sir Leicester, who functions for much of the novel as a butt for very searching social satire, emerges in tragic affliction as a truly good man.

It is also appropriate that coincidence should play a very large part in this work. Throughout Dickens's novels, coincidences are frequent, usually in the measure that we recognise as 'realistic' for drama on so vast a scale. By which I mean that Dickens's usual coincidences have the hallmark of coincidences in normal life: they are unpredictable in that they happen by accident, but hindsight imbues them with suggestions of poetic justice, or unmerited grace. Such suggestions may be arbitrary and in defiance of logic, but there is ample repository for them in the reservoir of our wishes and fears. Given the circumstances (we say) things *might* have happened so; even *should* have happened so?: even *would* have happened so?: given Providence or Justice, or a lucky, or an unlucky, star. The mind broods hopefully or tormentingly in the night-watches, and a novelist defies no canons of realism in depicting such thoughts.

In *Bleak House*, however, coincidence plays a somewhat larger part than we might anticipate, yet this is congruous with our sense of men and women caught in a web. The coincidences turn out, after all, to be not unqualified, in that chains of probability, however tenuous, may be perceived. This is nothing like the experience of coincidence in (for instance) Hardy's later novels, where we sense extraneous pressures – the author's temperamental pessimism, his debt to Greek Tragedy – behind the scenes. And certainly it is not like the coincidences of lesser novelists, who might resort to such measures at desperate junctures of their plot. Dickens, by mingling good and evil in his coincidences, keeps close to one of the delicate yet elusive mysteries of human destiny, our sense of irrational aspects haunting the most 'ordinary' life. Consider, for instance,

Lady Dedlock's recognition of her former lover's handwriting: unexpected, yes, but not unprecedented; and the Tulkinghorns of life look for and build on such things. Guppy visits Chesney Wold and is reminded, by Lady Dedlock's picture, of Esther; but Guppy has dealings both with Esther and with Lady Dedlock through the Jarndyce connection; and who has not been teased by family likenesses in old pictures and prints? Esther and Lady Dedlock meet in church because Esther's host, Mr Boythorn, is a near neighbour of the Dedlocks; but Boythorn is Jarndyce's friend, we may infer, through the Chancery web. Mrs Rachel turns up again as Mrs Chadband and re-enters Esther's history; but she is one of the few people who really knows about Esther, and she and her husband are not without a holy eye to the main chance. Mr Allan Woodcourt lands at Deal just as Esther arrives there to reason with Richard. This is 'pure' coincidence, yet people do meet at odd and unexpected times. Charley is maid to the Smallweeds before her rescue by Esther: but her father's profession would have brought him in touch with people like the Smallweeds just as it brings him in touch with Skimpole, and so with Esther herself. Richard borrows money from Grandfather Smallweed and chooses Mr George's establishment for his military training: but Grandfather Smallweed is not unknown in the Chancery circles Richard chooses to move in, and Mr George has his own good reasons for haunting Lincoln's Inn. Mr Bucket's lodger turns out to be Hortense; but, as Bucket supposes, this is Hortense's deliberate attempt to bamboozle him.

What else have we in the way of coincidence? George was the one confidant of Captain Hawdon as well as being the long-lost son of Chesney Wold's housekeeper; the two people who are 'wery good' to Jo are Esther's unknown father and Esther herself. Jo, in turn, becomes involved both with Esther, whom he unwittingly infects with smallpox, and with Lady Dedlock, whom he unwittingly helps to destroy. These are perhaps again 'pure' coincidences, though they are not without associative threads. It is because Nemo is very good to him that Jo gets dragged into the Inkwich, and it is because he gets dragged into it that Lady Dedlock seeks him out. At the same time the community of Nemo and Jo in poverty is sufficiently probable, given Nemo's fellow-feeling for one worse off than himself.

The claim to be made about these coincidences is hard to formulate, but it ought, to my mind, to be high. The notion that coincidences should not be permitted in a novel belongs presumably to a theory that characters in fiction should interact only through patterns of logic and fitness inherent in some artistic purpose or design. This is to push the novel away from realism towards pure artifice, where laws, whether of the artist's intention or of art itself, hold unchallenged sway. But if coincidences are possible in life there should be a place for them in fiction, however this requires to be subsumed to aesthetic tact. Certain negative laws of tact, indeed, immediately suggest themselves. We should not feel that the author is using coincidence to manipulate our responses more than the whole action and concept sanction; we should not feel strains upon either the credibility of the subject-matter or the homogeneity of art. But such demands suggest a more positive test, which Dickens very readily passes : coincidences in fiction should be happily translated into the texture of art. In *Bleak House* the coincidences do not weight the novel towards any precise philosophy or genre commitment, yet they do not strike us merely as an easy way out. They release the characters into mutual interaction of the kind we sense as plausible, and artistically fitting; and they reinforce the manifold indications of a web. The manner in which the characters react to coincidences is invariably plausible, and the mingled good and evil which run through the coincidences accords with the sense of reality operative in the book. It may be, however, that Dickens is hinting at certain values inescapably binding people together in the social universe, beyond whatever nets Chancery, Tom-All-Alone's and Tulkinghorn may spread. Despite their diversity, the characters are all one with another : in the social dangers and challenges of disease and poverty; and in that intangible sphere where the bell tolls for us all.

One further facet of the novel's weblike quality may be pinpointed in the marvellous conjunction of Tulkinghorn and Bucket in a single book. Like Jaggers, Bucket poses problems which clearly teased Dickens. What are the ethics proper to a

detective? When (if ever) can lying and treachery serve higher
truth? How far need a man's profession commit him to guile?
Bucket is a man of natural friendliness and good nature who
uses these qualities most unscrupulously in his work. To all
appearance they become, therefore, their diabolical opposites,
a proof that warmth and good nature can never be 'known'.
Bucket is like Tulkinghorn in that he enjoys his power over the
people he probes, and is not above playing cat and mouse. Even
if George's arrest *is* justified by some higher expediency, can
we really accept Bucket's disingenuous account of the actual
arrest? Three of the novel's stalwart innocents are much
imposed upon; and Bucket is more or less sure (we learn later)
that George is not really his game. Bucket, again, is chiefly
responsible for Sir Leicester's stroke, by his method of breaking
his news. The mystifications which in a lesser detective tale
might be *frissons* intended solely and permissibly for the reader,
become psychological torture in a context as rich as this. Sir
Leicester cannot fail to think that a far worse accusation against
his much-loved wife is in the offing, and Bucket can scarcely
misjudge his victim's fears. Even before this denouement, we
note that Bucket enjoys his power over a noble family; there are
hints of some subtle if unpremeditated class revenge in the relish
with which he always calls Sir Leicester 'Sir Leicester Dedlock,
Bart'. The only alternative explanation would be in terms of
some mingling of innocence and ignorance such as we might find
in Mr Boffin; but Bucket is a shrewd and highly arrogant man.
At the best, Bucket seems too carried away by the pleasures of
detection to be reliably human; at the worst, his profession may
be a respectable occasion for insidious ends. There are moments
when it would seem as churlish to mistrust his frankness as it
would be to mistrust Pickwick. Yet he enjoys the pleasures of
establishing false trust, like Tulkinghorn; and he enjoys the
taste of a victim's fears.

   The enigma remains that Bucket may after all be what he
pretends to be; that a happy outcome, with justice done and
innocence vindicated, is all he desires. Put differently, one
might say that Bucket wants nothing better than to exist in
warm friendliness with his fellow humanity, and that the deceit

which prevents this is contributed by others, not by himself. If his friendliness seems both indisputably real and ineradicably devious, may it not be akin to the friendliness of a god? Yet there are seeds here of something profoundly sinister; more sinister it may even be than Dennis the Hangman in *Barnaby Rudge*. The technique of breaking down a victim by friendliness and imaginative empathy points to one of the most frightening roles in modern literature and life. The fact is that the friendliness and imaginative empathy *would* be real if the victim were not marked out to suffer; if the victim had not risked commitments which make him once and for all, and beyond all other appeals, fair game. From Dostoevsky's Grand Inquisitors, through O'Brien in *1984* to (say) Martin Eliot in C. P. Snow's *The New Men*, the pattern has become frighteningly familiar, and Bucket has his place in a line leading to these. He is splendidly uncommitted to anything except justice; and he has the Inquisitor's love, whether acknowledged or hidden, of power.

And yet Bucket is on the side of law, and resilience, in the healthiest form they can take. If anyone is fair game, is it not Hortense? Esther Summerson trusts Bucket, which is an important indication; and Dickens himself approved of the new detective force in actual life. So perhaps George's sufferings *are* inescapable, and Bucket's is the proper exercise of power. Yet Bucket and Tulkinghorn live and resonate in a single book.

v

I propose now to turn to the structure of *Bleak House*, and to the place of the heroine, in particular, in this. The structure of the novel, like that of *Wuthering Heights* (1848), is experimental, in that two narrations are intertwined. In *Wuthering Heights* the narration is shared between two minor characters, sharply contrasted in temperament and neither 'literary', who between them create, nonetheless, the uniquely elemental quality of that work. Dickens's procedure is sharply different. The narration of *Bleak House* is shared between an impersonal narrator – 'the author' if we choose to put it like that – and Esther Summerson, the most important character in the tale.

This arrangement has given birth to several critical over-simplifications, for which the term 'the author' – or even 'Dickens' – to describe the impersonal narrator must chiefly be blamed. 'Not to put too fine a point on it', as Mr Snagsby would say, the whole book is the author's, and the notion that Esther Summerson represents only a part of his genius, a deliberate impoverishment for reasons of 'realism', is oddly naïve. A number of famous novels are cast in the form of pseudo-autobiography and narrated by people who are not represented as novelists, let alone as novelists of genius, but usually we accept the convention readily enough. The author creates the required tone for his 'I' character, whether ordinary or extraordinary, and his success is a triumph, we realise, of creative tact. Far from being an impoverishment of natural gifts, indeed, this is their proper exercise, the adaptation of material to form and structure for particular ends. We are no more tempted to confuse the prose of Jane Eyre with that of a real governess than we are to confuse the painted scenery in a theatre with Venice or Rome. (It may be worth remarking, however, as a marginal irony, that while most readers seem to be able to accept Jane Eyre, Nelly Dean and the notorious Governess in *The Turn of the Screw* as authentic narrators, the complaint has sometimes been made that David Copperfield is not shown as being 'creative' enough to write.)

If ironies of any kind in this area seem largely spurious, this is presumably because the creativity or otherwise of such narrators is not a cause for concern. One way or another an exact equation between the pseudo-narrator and his book does not seem to be made, and there is no reason, given the irreducible artificiality of art, why it should. In the consideration of *Bleak House*, however, it has often been asserted that the issue comes alive for a particular reason: which is, that Esther's chapters are deliberately 'toned down' in order to contrast with the 'pure', virtuoso Dickens of the rest. Geoffrey Tillotson, in a charming epilogue to the Signet edition, has put this most forcibly:

One method used for the construction of *Bleak House* came near to imperiling Dickens's power of writing as a poet writes. He entrusted the telling of some part of the story to one of the participants in it – Esther Summerson. It is possible that he made a mistake here. In any event it was a self-denying arrangement, because it is a waste to have part of the story told by a comparatively simple person when it could have been told by a complex person such as Dickens himself.

This is courteously argued, but it seems to me mistaken, and to overlook the necessary requirements and varieties of form. W. J. Harvey argues a similar case in his admirable *Character and the Novel*, where he has excellent and highly sophisticated things to say about the structure, but includes in his defence of Dickens's method such admissions as this:

Esther's narrative is plain, matter-of-fact, conscientiously plodding. Only very rarely does her style slip and allow us to glimpse Dickens guiding her pen . . . Such moments apart, any stylistic vivacity or idiosyncrasy in Esther's prose comes from the oddities and foibles of other characters. Dickens imagines them; Esther merely reports them.

It is possible to see how such distinguished critics come to make this distinction between Esther and her author, but still to wonder whether it arises only when Esther is recalled in retrospect and not when the novel is actually being read. Esther *has* a tone certainly, very complex really for all its serenity, but what tone is not limiting to some degree? If we return to her chapters, we find in them many of the most characteristically Dickensian things we could ask. Chapter 5, for instance, is a marvel of symbolism. It describes the first visit of the wards in Jarndyce to Miss Flite's room, their first sight of her birds, their first meeting with Krook and Lady Jane. The web of circumstance which Esther does not know about already entangles her, in that she is now under her father's roof. The prose is richly poetic, and develops, as a subtexture to Esther's sane good humour, the themes and images of the chapters before. To describe this as 'matter of fact' or 'prosaic' can only be a compliment to Dickens, for preserving our sense of such qualities in Esther *despite* her style. Later, Esther's narrative contains scenes of vintage Dickens humour – the visit to the

Bayham Badgers, the announcement of Caddy's engagement to old Mr Turveydrop and then to Mrs Jellyby, the visitation of Mrs Guppy – where satire is beautifully controlled by Esther's humorous eye. In addition, a number of the most famous of all Dickens's characters are created wholly or almost wholly in Esther's chapters: Mrs Jellyby, John Jarndyce, Miss Flite, Harold Skimpole, Mr Turveydrop, Mrs Pardiggle, the Bayham Badgers, Richard Carstone, Allan Woodcourt and his mother, Mrs Guppy, Mrs Blinder, Mr Boythorn. She also has her fair share in the creation of still further unmistakably Dickensian characters: Krook, Vholes (the best descriptions are hers), Guppy and Bucket himself. To suggest that Dickens 'imagined' these characters and Esther merely 'reported' them must be an oversimplification since where, but in 'her' prose, do they exist? Her quality of observation, moreover, is essentially creative; Skimpole and Turveydrop would not have grown quite as they do without Esther's tone. All of this inventiveness not only stands up excellently to the inventiveness of the impersonal narrator (whose characters include the whole or most of Sir Leicester and Lady Dedlock, George and Phil, the Rouncewells, the Smallweeds, Mr Chadband, Mr and Mrs Bagnet, Mr and Mrs Snagsby, Jo, Guster, Tony Jobling, Volumnia, Bucket, and pre-eminently Tulkinghorn), but they stand up as belonging to the same structure and texture, the same novel. It is worth re-marking that the fifty or so main characters in *Bleak House* have, almost without exception, their distinctive speech habits, whether they belong to Esther's chapters or not. Esther also enjoys the Dickensian distinction of creating unforgettable characters with *en passant* felicity: witness Professor Dingo, whose famous last words mediated by his relict are all we have of him ('Where is Laura? Let Laura bring me my tea and toast'), and the novel's escalating children – Mrs Jellyby's, Mrs Pardiggle's, Coavinses's, Mr Skimpole's and Mr Vholes's.

Esther is able to create Dickensian characters and situations plausibly by virtue of a number of qualities, some obvious, some apparently less obvious, which she is given. She is highly observant (the one quality she readily admits to), and extremely intelligent, the most intelligent good woman that Dickens drew.

Her intelligence is chiefly moral and intuitive, a kind of common sense raised towards wisdom. She can 'smell out' people's moral natures by instinct (a characteristic which she shares with one or two other virtuous characters, such as Little Nell, but also with one or two morally ambivalent characters such as Susan Nipper and Jenny Wren, as well as with villains such as Carker and Jasper, in whom the clairvoyance takes a frightening form). She is also given a high degree of self-knowledge and unusual gifts of self-sacrifice, even though she lacks the experience of the world required to 'place' people of unusual types. Her instinctive sense that there is something seriously wrong with Mrs Jellyby and Mrs Pardiggle, with Harold Skimpole and old Mr Turveydrop, co-exists therefore with suspended judgement, and a willingness to let them speak for themselves. In all this Esther's tone is wholly without malice. Indeed her morally aware but unmalicious intelligence is sufficiently a rarity to make of it, in so far as it is really Dickens's, a virtuoso display. Against her growing insight into Skimpole and Turveydrop we have counterpointed her charitable tolerance and her unfailing eye for the 'funny side'. Our own awareness of these characters, sufficiently scathing, is mediated through this distinctive view. It is modified, indeed, by Esther's tone, as well as by the more normal Dickensian complexities attendant upon larger-than-life characters with a talent for creating themselves.

My claim is that Esther is that rare thing in the novel, a convincing depiction of moral goodness; and what I have to say on the structure of *Bleak House* depends on this claim. But why, if this is so, is she unpopular? – as she seems to be with many students today. The deeper causes are no doubt historical, and to these I shall return. Changes in attitude towards humility and gratitude, for instance, have followed the rise of welfare services and the emancipation of women, and Esther's world is already extinct. But a few obvious strands must first be disentangled, in the area where modern readers rush towards a 'personal' response. The two most usual criticisms of Esther centre on her 'false humility' and her 'cloying sentimentality', the first in her references to herself when she is recording other people's praise of her, the second chiefly in her relationship

with Ada Clare. Some readers appear to read all humility as
false humility, and to forget that Uriah Heep's creator might not
have shared this view. If humility can be real, how can it
express itself? – how, except in terms of a whole personality,
can we tell true from false? Esther does not use her humility to
work upon or to embarrass other people, and her tone is
eminently part of shared household ease. She does not really use
it to evade self-knowledge; the passages in which she comes to
accept her lost looks, for instance, are touchingly direct and
frank. It arises, rather, from her unwillingness to be more
central to the novel than she need be, or to see her affairs as in
any way competing, in our attention, with her tale. And this is
because she doesn't see herself as central; it is only we who
come to see this before the end. There is no reason, after all,
why Esther should think of herself as important, since she
shares no romantic obsessions with the 'self'. As an illegitimate
child with no particular gifts or prospects, she has been trained
to regard herself chiefly as a blight. We have to remember that
she is born an outcast, and that her childhood is overshadowed
by the gloomy view that her birth is a misfortune and a disgrace.
One of the most basic challenges in the novel is voiced by
Esther's godmother: *would* it have been better if Esther had
never been born? If the reader is confronted even today with
complexities in such a question, it is unlikely that Esther herself
would have emerged unscathed. Then, we must recall Esther's
debt to Jarndyce, without whom she would have been at best
a governess, at worst part of the floating wreckage of society
like Jo. Gratitude seems a natural as well as an appropriate
response to Jarndyce's selfless love of her (selfless even after
he has been led, by all too understandable weakness, to his one
big mistake). A Victorian girl could expect no rescue through
educational opportunities or welfare services, and there is no
reason why Esther should have shared the mistrust of gratitude
which a modern woman, attuned to education and welfare,
might feel. Anything like political engagement with women's
rights is wholly outside the range of her social position or,
indeed, her temperament. (When Borrioboola-Gha fails, Mrs
Jellyby turns her attention to 'the rights of women to sit in

Parliament'. Esther's gentle scorn merely mirrors the larger scorn of Dickens and, of course, Carlyle, whom Mrs Jellyby might have been specially designed to please.) Esther pre-dates, in effect, democracy as well as socialism, and is happy enough to make the best of her lot in a tragic world.

'Happy enough': but this may still be found offensive, even when the historical imagination has done its work. Would a more spirited woman not have anticipated our modern attitude, and reacted with rebellion or despair? Esther's virtues, whether of patient suffering or domestic affection, seem curi-ously alien to our present time. It may be all too easy then to overlook that her good humour and sanity are won at the price of great courage and self-discipline or, noticing this, to feel that the victory is not worth the price. A modern Esther might brood on the problem of her identity as of obligation, and feel a moral duty, almost, to go mad. Such a character would undeniably be interesting, and it is no accident that Dickens's most emotion-ally self-indulgent heroine, Florence Dombey, finds an easier path to modern hearts. Yet courage and sanity like Esther's are not despicable, and are never easily achieved in a tragic world. Esther has to confront an existence overshadowed with gloom and mystery, and beset, despite Jarndyce's kindness, with suffer-ing; she has to endure Richard's downfall (dragging Ada with him), her own unrequited (as she thinks) love, smallpox and the loss of her looks, her Guardian's proposal (a very subtle sadness), and, most terrible for one of her temperament, the knowledge that her very existence is a threat to her mother's life. All of this is not melodrama but simple reality; the notion of a 'ruined woman' was not cant in Victorian society, whatever it might be in ours. It is in this context that we have to assess Esther's habit of spreading sanity and healing in other people's misfortunes, and her rejoicing in Ada's friendship and love. Many modern readers find the tone of this relationship particu-larly upsetting, since tenderness and whimsy in private life are currently taboo. Esther's relationship would be 'interesting' if it were labelled lesbian and pursued into sordid fantasies or dismal obsessions, but it is somehow embarrassing as it stands. Yet Dickens preferred not to label human affections, but to

sense their individual qualities – in Miss Wade destructive and
rooted in hatred, in Esther constructive and rooted in love.
It is unlikely that Dickens would have been surprised by the
insights of modern psychology, but he would have been contemptuous of any tendency to harden human relationships
towards dogmatic norms. No doubt he would have detected
hypocrisy in our present-day cult of toughness, just as we detect
it in his occasional sympathy with gush.

There is one further criticism often made, of the chapter
where Jarndyce reveals the second Bleak House to Esther, and
this stands apart from the rest. The problem arose from
Dickens's original marriage of a romantic plot and tradition
with the *Bleak House* material, since the use of such surprise
denouements is the classic stuff of romance. A similar doubt
will be felt about *deus ex machina* figures such as the elder
Martin Chuzzlewit, and the testing of heroines, such as Bella's
two testings in *Our Mutual Friend*. It may be that these romantic devices do not, or should not, consort with psychological
realism – yet Dickens belongs with Shakespeare among those
who made the attempt.

I have been making a case for Esther, but I hope not forensi-
cally, since it is not a matter of trying to assert personal liking
for her against opposite views. The importance of the issue
penetrates to *Bleak House*'s structure, to which Esther is more
central than any other heroine (Amy Dorrit may be a possible
exception to this) that Dickens produced.

Before my remarks on this aspect can be completed, however,
a few observations about the impersonal narration require to be
made. This impersonal narration isn't 'just' Dickens, it is
Dickens more than usually split between roles. The impersonal
narrative does not attempt the illusion of a single character, but
includes everything Dickensian that is outside Esther's range.
Perhaps for this reason it gives the impression of being 'masculine', but this is the only generalised comment I would care to
make. The opening chapter, one of the most magnificent things
in English, starts as a stage direction, then moves, with the
introduction of main verbs in paragraph three, to a hauntingly
permanent sense of here and now :

The raw afternoon is rawest, and the dense fog is densest, and
the muddy streets are muddiest near the leaden-headed old
obstruction, appropriate ornament for the threshold of a leaden-
headed old corporation, Temple Bar. And hard by sits the Lord
High Chancellor in his High Court of Chancery.

On such an afternoon, if ever, the Lord High Chancellor
ought to be sitting here – as here he is – with a foggy glory
round his head, softly fenced in with crimson cloth and curtains,
addressed by a large advocate with great whiskers, a little voice,
and an interminable brief, and outwardly directing his contemplation to the lantern in the roof, where he can see nothing but
fog. On such an afternoon some score of members of the High
Court of Chancery bar ought to be – as here they are – mistily
engaged in one of the ten thousand stages of an endless cause . . .

and so on. At a stroke, Dickens has performed his usual miracle
of combining social realism with myth. Fog is in the imagery,
in the long sentences, as it is in the endless causes brought up in
Chancery, and in the Lord Chancellor's contemplation of the
roof. All these things are one London afternoon, some time in
early Victorian England; they are also now, when we read
them; and they are always, in the always of art. Perhaps Dickens
achieves this by that irresistible 'as here he is': we look up,
and yes indeed, here he *is*. The 'large advocate' is not unlike
the doorkeeper of the Law in Kafka's celebrated parable in *The
Trial*: both seem dreamlike, permanent, undoubtedly significant;
but what do they mean?

The impersonal narrative is available for poetically rich
evocations, but also for very much more. The tone in which
Dickens deals with the Dedlocks is tinged with irony, yet the
description of Chesney Wold in the rain is incipiently tragic,
and the more we see of the Dedlocks, the more satire, in its
pure form at least, is forced to yield ground. In a very different
vein, Dickens depicts the three clerks conspiring together in
chapter 20, where the exact nuances of their shared tone –
heavy jesting, shabby goodwill or pretended goodwill, incurable
vulgarity – does not conflict with equally exact discriminations :
Guppy's minimal decency, given his opportunism; Tony
Jobling's directionless amorality; Small's family meanness just
faintly tinged with amiability. There is, in addition, the side of

Dickens which celebrates the Bagnets, and the side which savagely indicts society on behalf of poor Jo; the side which creates an exuberant maverick such as Bucket, and the side which probes Tulkinghorn's evil and Vholes's deceit. And, not least, the impersonal narrator is available for the tremendous set-piece when Krook goes off in Spontaneous Combustion : the chapter in this novel, and most of his novels have one such chapter, where under the sanction of symbolism Dickens lets his most horrendous imaginings loose.

VI

Bleak House presents us with many features reminiscent of Kafka, but its final effect is not the same. Why not ? Partly – and this aspect requires particularly to be mentioned – because Dickens believes in the human will. His pessimism has been overstressed by those who mistake his satire; if he overstates for effectiveness, as all ironists must, he is not one who stumbles, in overstatement, on despair. He was highly disillusioned with particular people and particular institutions, but he still believed in the divinity of man. He did not finally despair of men working through their own corrupt institutions and just occasionally producing – from Parliament even – a triumph of enlightened common sense. By the same token, he did not despair of righting wrongs, however longstanding and intractable. If he were writing today about Negro ghettos in great American and British cities (and if he were alive today, who would stop him ?) it would be more in the tone of battered liberalism than of bitter hate. His vision of suffering is not absurdist but tragic, with the particular areas of hope allowed by this.

It follows that Dickens would have expected *Bleak House* to be effective, and that he would not have been surprised by its success. He would have agreed with leading articles in *The Times* of the same period that the abuses of Chancery were curable, and that society might be forced in the end to pay for sanitation, however unwillingly, by the twin spurs of residual idealism and personal fear. He would have expected that horrors such as Tom-All-Alone's might be demolished and

relegated to history; first in Britain (*pace* Mrs Jellyby), and
later perhaps throughout the world. His novel is no statement
of the inevitability of such evils, nor does it employ them as
symbols of metaphysical gloom. It is important to reflect that
the specific abuses pervading *Bleak House* have in fact all been
remedied or greatly alleviated, including one which Dickens
would almost certainly have regarded as beyond repair. Even
the fog has been banished from London, *and* by Act of Parliament. Since the Clean Air Act there are no London Particulars
any more.

The social evils depicted in *Bleak House* were curable, and
Dickens knew this in his bones. The law still has its delays, but
none like Chancery; there is still disease in the world, but
cholera is controlled and so is smallpox; there are still slums,
but children like Jo no longer die in the streets around us every
day. How could such things ever be in Christian England?
This was Dickens's challenge and one source of his energy;
could ordinary men, once really appraised of such things, allow
them? He was assisted by confidence in his own power as an
artist, and in the power of art generally to extend human
imagination and compassion in practical ways. Humphry House
did a certain amount of harm by pointing out that some of the
abuses which Dickens wrote about had already been alleviated
before he published the novel in which they appeared. This has
turned in some versions into the notion that Dickens attacked
abuses only when they were safely past. Perhaps no-one who
has ever engaged in social reform could fall into this particular
error. Even specific evils – such as the Marshalsea – carry
possibilities of resurrection, while other evils, such as the Poor
Laws, required to be exposed and attacked throughout the span
of Dickens's life. It is a liberal fallacy to imagine that social
progress proceeds inevitably, and that any victory can be
supposed safe when once it is won. Dickens's task was not to
remove specific evils – not that only – but to re-educate his
readers in their own day and age. Contemplating the proliferating evils of industrial England in a *laissez faire* climate,
he was winding up human understanding and compassion
towards the welfare state. This, in turn, he would have seen as

no more than applied Christianity, the translation of the simple tenets of faith into simple deeds. Do as you would be done by; we are all members one with another; ask not for whom the bell tolls, it tolls for thee. The universality of these tenets raised his art also above its immediate context, since they are precisely the moral elements fitted for all time.

In this side of his work Dickens was motivated by tremendous energy and hopefulness, which is why we cannot stress his affinities with Kafka to the exclusion of all else; in his own life and creation, he never succumbed to despair. Misunderstandings about this may be aggravated by one notable aspect of his technique. Though he tried to arouse all that was most compassionate in his readers, he did not neglect the other spur to action through their fears. Hence the stress upon slums as a breeding-ground of disease, crime and political subversion; of plagues that would reach from the foul courts of London right to the mansions of the great. The cholera struck London in 1848, and again when *Bleak House* was being written (it was almost unknown there until 1832, when its appearance was greeted by some opponents of Reform as a sign). By having his heroine infected with smallpox, however, Dickens recognises dangers inherent in virtue itself in our fallen world.

It seems clear to me that for these and other reasons Dickens's novels ought to remain anchored, for the critic, in their author's close relationship with his readers – both the Victorian audience, to whose influence he was highly sensitive, and by only a slight extension to his very different audience of today. Our own society, confronted with the ghettos of Harlem and Detroit, Brixton and Notting Hill, is not much better placed socially than the Victorians. We can no more afford surely than the original readers either to deny Tom-All-Alone's its social reality, or to turn it into a symbol of some supposedly incurable spiritual or intellectual malaise.

VII

Which returns me to Esther, and her part in the novel's success. Esther's subversive role in the novel is that of simply existing, and the whole structure of *Bleak House* turns on this. What would the novel be like if she did not exist in it as a central character, but simply as Lady Dedlock's tragic mistake? Her godmother's fears might seem wholly justified, in that she is her mother's curse in life and her mother's death. She is – even more strikingly – the thread used by Tulkinghorn in the spinning of his murderous web. The fear which Lady Dedlock succumbs to, and which Tulkinghorn feeds on, is Esther's existence in the world. Esther's existence is unfortunate not simply, therefore, in her godmother's gloomy religion, but in the social realities it creates. 'It would have been far better, little Esther, that you had had no birthday; that you had never been born!' The novel challenges its readers with this formulation. Do we agree with it for reasons of expediency, perhaps, or of psychological realism, if for no other cause?

If Esther were not actually present in the novel, the moral challenge would be present in a less striking way. But instead, it exists in and through her personal reality as a centre of courage, humour, healing and love. By her actions, she proves the continuing reality of private charity and compassion; she forms, in company with Jarndyce, Mr Snagsby, Allan Woodcourt, George, Mrs Blinder and the two Bagnets, a most powerful witness to good. Though Dickens believed that such charity was not sufficient to heal society, he would have seen it as leaven in the lump. Esther, who has so much to lament and fear, counts her blessings, and is a source of blessing to all whom she helps.

This is the wholly simple and wholly subversive centre of the novel's complexity, the wood we must at all costs see for the trees. To see it isn't easy, as Dickens no doubt realised, even before he read (if he did) his earliest reviews. Esther is fair game to the righteous as an inconvenient bastard, just as she is fair game to comfortable sophisticates as a bore. But her tone is a triumph of courage and sanity over many varieties of suffering, and its simplicity, in context, is serene. She keeps *Bleak House* sane and sparkling, for all its terror; for all the strong pulls against her, even, from Dickens himself. With *Hard Times* Dickens plunged into his gloomiest decade, but *Bleak House* contrives to remain, somehow, in the sun.

Esther is a gravitational pull against pessimism and defeatism, the harbinger of domestic virtue, happiness and peace. In the larger structure of the novel, Dickens is released by his experimental form into a delicate patterning, of Esther's tone against the rest. The impersonal narration starts in fog and rain, rises through dramatic evil and mystery to large climaxes, and then returns to darkness and rain. A sombre start, and a sombre conclusion – the fall of Sir Leicester Dedlock's wife, his house, the whole order, in many ways so admirable, for which he stands. Through this, the heroine's narrative runs like a healing thread. The central character in the web of mystery and evil, though she only gradually comes to know this, she continually transmutes evil into good. The last chapter of the novel, after the impersonal narrator has left us in twilight, is Esther's; she is still counting her blessings, and speaking now of happiness; seven richly rewarding years with the man she loves. For once, Dickens depicts virtue as active and happy; and plausibly, as well as suitably, rewarded from within. Later, his virtuous people become more withdrawn again, more assimilated, like Agnes already in *David Copperfield*, to shadow and gloom.

But the world of *Bleak House*, though not irredeemable, remains tragic; it is the tragic world of Christian belief. Esther Summerson is a stranger and pilgrim, and lives like one; here she has no abiding home. It is her doing chiefly (though Allan Woodcourt's more directly) that Jo dies with the unfamiliar words of the Lord's Prayer on his lips, and Richard Carstone starts a world which sets *this* world to rights. For Dickens this is the heart of the human mystery; as it has been for Christianity in every age until (perhaps) our own.

8 *Hard Times*
the robber fancy

I

Towards the end of *Bleak House*, George Rouncewell goes
north for a reunion with his brother Jack.

As he comes into the iron country further north, such fresh
green woods as those of Chesney Wold are left behind; the
coalpits and ashes, high chimneys and red bricks, blighted
verdure, scorching fires, and a heavy, never-lightening cloud of
smoke become the features of the scenery . . .

Jack Rouncewell has been a hard and solid worker, and has got
on in life. He lives in a fine house, and his children are being
educated for a higher station than his own. As factory owner he
is as humane and cleanly as the urban squalor permits. His hands
seem reasonably contented, if a little covered in iron. These
evidences of success so impress the ne'er-do-well George, that
he concocts the pseudonym 'Mr Steel' to enhance his identity,
and only barely plucks up courage to go in.

Earlier in *Bleak House*, when Jack has met Sir Leicester to
discuss his son's love for Lady Dedlock's maid Rosa, he has
come out well in the exchange. Sir Leicester is pure barbarian,
all sweetness (in Arnold's sense) and no light. His simmering
outrage at the 'iron gentleman's' effrontery and the general
opening of floodgates is both ludicrous, and at the same time
tragic, in that we see other, deadlier floodgates already open at
the baronet's back. Jack Rouncewell, in contrast, has all the
strength and independence of his industrial breed, a striking
contrast to the baronet's world. His gospel of self-help and hard
work rubs off on his work-people, to their own material advantage as well as his. It is notable that Jack has his own brand of
natural courtesy to match against Sir Leicester's, a kind of
buoyant yet disciplined self-respect.

The depiction of Jack is unusual in Dickens, and relates to the

peculiar needs of *Bleak House*. The downfall of Sir Leicester and
his class is shown as inevitable, and what satire Dickens admits
is chiefly at his expense. Ignorant of social evolution, he is blind
to the birth of a new England outside his knowledge and control.
Yet Chesney Wold still has its green fields, its pure air, its
feudal decencies; we can understand George's choice to remain
in the old world as its last retainer, rather than plunge un-
prepared into the new. Jack, of course, does not understand, but
he is tolerant enough to accept his brother's choice. In *Bleak
House* the northern industrialist is not without honour in his
grim country. But this is the exception in Dickens's works.

II

In the autumn of 1853, with *Bleak House* finished, Dickens's
personal life was in a restless phase. The staid Forster was
openly jealous of Dickens's new friends, some of them young
and disreputable, such as Wilkie Collins, and Dickens's
marriage to Kate was deteriorating all the time. His habitual
wander-lust reasserted itself, and he set out on a two-month
holiday in Switzerland with Wilkie Collins and Augustus Egg.
The journey had all the hallmarks of a Dickensian progress, up
mountains, through glaciers, with a hectic social life in between.
In Geneva, Dickens was reunited with Madame de la Rue, that
strange woman, haunted by phantoms, who had been the cause
of an earlier quarrel between himself and Kate. Dickens had
practised hypnotism upon Madame de la Rue at all hours of the
night to alleviate her delusions, and Kate had become bitter
with jealous distress. This new meeting was duly communicated
to Kate in letters, together with exhortations that she should
set herself right with Madame de la Rue by writing 'to say that
you have heard . . . of her sufferings and her cheerfulness'. On
his arrival back in England, Dickens plunged straight into
amateur theatricals, and gave in Birmingham Town Hall the
first of the public readings from his works which were to loom
so large in his later life. The Inimitable, in short, in high
working order, though with a new touch of strain.

Was this the period when some particular shadow fell upon

him, and certain hopes, kept alive in *Dombey and Son* and *Bleak House*, for all their tragedy, started to fade? The amazing transition from *Bleak House* to *Hard Times* would suggest as much, on any tentative deduction from art to life. It was early in 1854 that he decided to write a new novel, and then for two converging and highly characteristic reasons. *Household Words* was suffering in its profits and needed a boost, and Dickens concluded that a novel alone would suffice. At the same time a creative idea had laid hold of him 'by the throat in a very violent manner', and the nag of this gave him no rest. As early as *Nicholas Nickleby* he had sworn to 'strike the heaviest blow in my power' for the victims of industrial England, and the idea had stayed with him ever since – in Little Nell's wanderings through the industrial midlands, Mr Dombey's train journey to Leamington Spa, the economic sub-stratum of *A Christmas Carol* and *The Chimes*, and the life and death of Jo. Now, for no immediately discernible reason, though with great force, the theme seized him again with redoubled power. *Hard Times*, dedicated eventually to Thomas Carlyle, was the result.

III

Hard Times is set in a northern industrial town far grimmer than Jack Rouncewell's town in *Bleak House*. Coketown takes us back to the nightmare chapters on the Birmingham to Wolverhampton road in *The Old Curiosity Shop*, but now the horror is seen more analytically than through the eyes of a dying girl. The presiding sensibilities are those of Gradgrind and Bounderby, two gentlemen well calculated to keep fancy and imagination at bay. There is a new ruthlessness of observation on Dickens's part, as befits his setting. It is as if he extinguished his most distinctive gift for poetic resonance and suggestiveness in order to capture a world where the creative powers themselves are in exile. Or rather, as if he drove the resonances of his art inwards, until they acquired a muffled and deadly quality, like Mr Vholes's voice. While there are still evidences of symbolism in Coketown, and it would hardly be Dickens's city without this, the very symbols are oppressive to

our minds. Coketown's 'fairy palaces' seen by travellers on the
railway in early evening are pure illusion, its 'melancholy mad
elephants' conjure no jungle freedom to our eyes. Any enchantment in Coketown is claustrophobic and sickening, like the
witch's house in *Hansel and Gretel* or Mrs Clennam's Room.
Hard Times indeed is a symbol of the world without creativity,
where the 'robber Fancy' is left, depraved by neglect, to seek
revenge.

There are other factors, it is true, which contribute to the
distinctiveness of *Hard Times* among Dickens's novels, but
none as central as this. We should remember, of course, that
Dickens was submitting to the discipline of weekly publication,
a form he never liked. 'The difficulty of the space is CRUSHING',
he complained. 'Nobody can have an idea of it who has not had
an experience of patient fiction writing with some elbow-room
always.' Yet *The Old Curiosity Shop* and *Great Expectations*
were also published in weekly parts, and no lack of poetic
richness can be complained of there. Again, Dickens's life was
entering a dark phase as has been mentioned, yet *Little Dorrit*
which also belongs to this period is the most open and mysterious of books. The claustrophobia of *Hard Times* needs, I
think, a particular explanation, which relates to the unprecedented
aesthetic problem set by its theme. It is, if one can put it so, a
skeletal novel; the realistic plot and the careful ironies show
like bones through the flesh. The very humour is skull-like.
What could be funnier than the pairing of Bounderby and Mrs
Sparsit, two humbugs perfectly calculated to serve each other
right? Yet we manage little more than a graveyard grin.

The skeletal qualities establish themselves in the first chapter,
which peppers its reader with facts. Like other opening chapters
in Dickens's novels it broods over the action which follows it,
yet not in his accustomed way. We miss that poetic and somehow timeless richness, so much easier to recognise than to
describe. 'Facts, facts, facts . . .' : very different, this, from the
fog in *Bleak House*, the prison in *Little Dorrit*, the marshes in
Great Expectations, the London river in *Our Mutual Friend*.
These other openings may be ominous, but they are also
liberating, with the strong and undeniable promise of major art.

They seem to exist somewhere outside the novel after their creation, like moons waxing and waning in orbit over the whole. The symbolism is not of a kind to be easily abstracted or intellectualised. Fog, prison, marsh, river are present in the first chapters in quintessence, as they are more diffusely present through the subsequent growth. The first chapter of *Hard Times* differs chiefly from these others by *being* abstract, since abstraction is here the quintessence of the book. 'Facts, facts, facts . . .' Mr Gradgrind fires at the souls of his victims and we encounter Louisa, Tom, Bitzer, as the living dead. Bitzer indeed is almost a zombie, while Louisa drifts, a shade less palely, through her lonely despair.

This absence from *Hard Times* of Dickens's normal resonances, or their presence in a strangely muffled mutation, is possibly the greatest sacrifice of art to art that he ever made. But there was no way round it, given his subject. Coketown must be seen and felt as a town without art. All myths and fairytales, all imaginative writing and creation, all fancies strange or consoling, and all mediators of such wares, Dickens included, are exiled from the Gradgrind and Bounderby world. In their place we have Coketown, a Fact complete and sufficient in its streets and chapels, its suspended smoke serpents, its 'melancholy mad elephants', as in the enslaved and destroyed consciousness of its children, its confines where Stephen Blackpool will live and die.

In other novels Dickens can risk an artist's normal paradox, that form transmutes content to beauty, that Hamlet and Lear are gay. Only here can he afford no such demonstration, since it is precisely the power of art that is conjured away. The one thing that Dickens must achieve, imaginatively, is the preservation in all its deadliness of Fact. It would not do for him to *be* Dickens, fully, in Coketown, for the mills to turn in his art into real fairy palaces, for the smoke serpents to haunt with endless mysteries and intimations like the *Bleak House* fog.

Hard Times is a successful novel because it is a uniquely unDickensian novel – except in so far as the triumph of tone and texture is, after all, so Dickensian, while Coketown, by so totally excluding myth, becomes a myth.

The jail might have been the infirmary, the infirmary might have been the jail, the town-hall might have been either, or both, or anything else, for anything that appeared to the contrary in the graces of their construction. Fact, fact, fact, everywhere in the material aspect of the town; fact, fact, fact, everywhere in the immaterial.

A world without Fancy is reduced to this, yet can Fancy be wholly exiled? If it is locked and barred out in its normal enriching aspects, may it not creep in through back gates for revenge? *Hard Times* is very much a novel of the revenge of the robber Fancy as he infiltrates Coketown in devious ways. At first we are aware chiefly of vacuum, of a room swept clean of devils and temporarily bare. We recall Louisa gazing into the fire, desolate and derelict, her heart kept alive only by love for a worthless brother; and Stephen, shuffling back through the rainy streets after a day in the factory to his terrible visitor and the mockery of home. The author, prophetic but sombre, comments on such scenes with a general sense of ravages to come.

Utilitarian economists, skeletons of schoolmasters, Commis-sioners of Fact, genteel and used-up infidels, gabblers of many little dog's-eared creeds, the poor you will have always with you. Cultivate in them, while there is yet time, the utmost graces of the fancies and affections to adorn their lives so much in need of ornament; or, in the day of your triumph when romance is utterly driven out of their souls, and they and a bare existence stand face to face, Reality will take a wolfish turn and make an end of you.

'A wolfish turn . . .' for Reality, as for Fancy, since the two may, after all, be inseparably linked. The most astonishing, though not of course the most painful, manifestation of this theme in *Hard Times* concerns Bounderby and Mrs Sparsit in their domestic life. Bounderby, whose war to the death with Fancy is the ruination of the woman he chooses to marry, turns out to be a creature of Fancy himself. Of Fancy reduced and depraved by hypocrisy, however, to a travesty, funny enough to be horrible, of the creative life. His one flight of Fancy turns out to be the lie about his upbringing, and the curious game of inverted snobbery which he plays out with Mrs Sparsit's ironic help. Both live out a fantasy, mutually satisfying to their snobbery, and satisfying also – to Mrs Sparsit, anyway – to some darkly sardonic streak below. In *fact*, both of them come from almost precisely the same kind of background – middle to lower middle class – and their respective roles represent nothing so much as an exquisitely balanced marriage of untrue minds. The Powler who is a 'born lady' is a fitting trophy for the Bounderby who has risen from nowhere precisely because both are a sordid sham. It is this game, however, which justifies Bounderby's treatment of all his hands, including Stephen, and which under-lies his one habitual flight of verbal imagery: 'I know 'em all pretty well. I always tell that man, whoever he is, that I know what he means. He means turtle soup and venison, with a gold spoon, and that he wants to be set up with a coach and six.' The robber Fancy returns for revenge in his minimal and irreducible form of a brutal lie.

Even by brutal standards, moreover, Bounderby exemplifies egotism in its most coarsely paradoxical garb. We cannot help being struck (with hindsight) by the fact that the lies which he trumpets so egregiously about his upbringing come close to those actual truths about his creator's life which Dickens hardly dared whisper to himself. Bounderby even mentions blacking! 'No, by George! I don't forget that I am Josiah Bounderby of Coketown. For years upon years, the only pictures in my possession, or that I could have got into my possession by any means unless I stole 'em, were the engravings of a man shaving himself in a boot, on the blacking bottles that I was overjoyed to use in cleaning boots with, and that I sold when they were empty for a farthing apiece, and glad to get it!'

But Bounderby is only one of several examples of the robber Fancy's revenge. It is there in poor Mrs Gradgrind's perpetual fear of fancy as a dreaded intruder of which, whenever and however it manifests itself, she will never hear the last. It is there, much more devastatingly for Louisa, and for Tom, a nemesis no child of Gradgrind could escape. A key passage in

the novel comes when Louisa returns to visit her mother, and
is shown as she nears her home :

Neither, as she approached her old home now, did any of the
best influences of old home descend upon her. The dreams of
childhood – its airy fables, its graceful, beautiful, humane,
impossible adornments of the world beyond : so good to be
believed in once, so good to be remembered when outgrown,
for then the least among them rises to the stature of a great
Charity in the heart, suffering little children to come into the
midst of it, and to keep with their pure hands a garden in
the stony ways of this world, wherein it were better for all the
children of Adam that they should oftener sun themselves,
simple and trustful, and not worldly-wise – what had she to do
with these ? Remembrances of how she had journeyed to the
little that she knew, by the enchanted roads of what she and
millions of innocent creatures had hoped and imagined; of how,
first coming upon Reason through the tender light of Fancy, she
had seen it as a beneficent god, deferring to gods as great as
itself : not a grim Idol, cruel and cold, with its victims bound
hand to foot, and its big dumb shape set up with a sightless
stare, never to be moved by anything but so many calculated
tons of leverage – what had she to do with these ? Her remembrances of home and childhood were remembrances of the
drying up of every spring and fountain in her young heart as it
gushed out. The golden waters were not there. They were
flowing for the fertilisation of the land where grapes were
gathered from thorns, and figs from thistles.

The vacuum in Louisa's life comes to be filled by Harthouse,
who, produced by a background wholly unlike Coketown, has
nonetheless arrived at a philosophy of life congruent with hers.
Harthouse's careless hedonism, nurtured on leisure, boredom
and cynicism, is in one wholly surprising way the mirror-image
of Gradgrind's world. 'The Gradgrind party', we are told,
'wanted assistance in cutting the throat of the Graces. They
went about recruiting, and where could they enlist recruits
more hopefully than among the fine gentlemen who, having
found out everything to be worth nothing, were equally ready
for anything ?' Nothing could be more direct than this perception
that because want of fancy and want of humanity are such near

neighbours, Gradgrind has prepared for himself the curious tragedy of his daughter's near-seduction by a libertine. Gradgrind's own goodness of heart proves inadequate to foresee or forestall the situation, since it has been disciplined into total insensitivity by his rigid beliefs.

Harthouse is one of the most purely realistic characters in *Hard Times*, possibly because he exists only in relation to Louisa's fate. Dickens is not concerned with Harthouse's personal destiny, as he is with that of certain similar characters – Steerforth in *David Copperfield* for instance and Eugene Wrayburn in *Our Mutual Friend*. But it is also true that Dickens was particularly fascinated by the blend of cynicism and irresponsibility present in Harthouse, which may explain why the depiction is directly realistic, and without grotesqueries or mythic overtones of any kind. The line of good-looking, or at the very least darkly compelling, lechers in his novels stretches from Sir John Chester and Carker through Steerforth, Harthouse and Sydney Carton to Eugene Wrayburn (with certain altogether more ominous and gothic variants from Quilp, through Jonas Chuzzlewit to John Jasper, in a related line). There are continual variants in his depictions, since Dickens never repeated the same character, or the same particular moral dilemma. Chester and Carker may be alike in their cold destructiveness, but whereas Carker's sexuality is overtly brutal, Chester's is coloured by the urbane graces he affects. Steerforth of course is a case apart, the most complex and attractive of Dickens's seducers, both in his inherent reality as Byronic hero, and in the marvellous images with which he is surrounded – David's hero-worship as boy and man, Rosa Dartle's savage frustrations in the house on Highgate Hill. Sydney Carton is an interesting variant on this theme, a man driven by compulsive sensuality and weakness against his own better nature, and with much to remind us of Richard Carstone in *Bleak House*, though their particular weaknesses take different forms. And finally Eugene Wrayburn, tinged with a new colouring of *fin de siècle* decadence (as we can now diagnose it), turns out to be redeemable in a way not felt as possible for any earlier such figures – perhaps because he alone among them possesses both goodwill and strong willpower, and the capacity therefore to make the difficult choice against cynicism in favour of love.

Of all these characters Harthouse is the most assured and in his own way perfect, since his sole *raison d'être* is to seem to us, as to Louisa, what he chooses to seem. His torments if he has any are not relevant, and perhaps he really is as free from such weaknesses as he leads us to think. He comes into the novel to tempt Louisa, and it is enough that the temptation should be plausible and strong. Later, Dickens has merely to remove him from Coketown, and this again is easy; it is enough to allow the minimal good in his nature – helped along by the stirrings of humour, and the natural desire to be well rid of complications – to respond to Sissy's appeal. This is a great help to his credibility, and to the novel's progress at this tricky moment, since Sissy's rhetoric, however sincere, is hardly sophisticated, and Harthouse might have found it easy enough to resist at some other time. Dickens lets him move off to other scenes – he is lucky enough not to be imprisoned like the primary characters in Coketown – and we are merely told that his one virtuous action of leaving Louisa unmolested is, by a law among such men, the action he feels most ashamed of in after life. The main point, however, is that he comes as close as he does to seducing Louisa, whose father has created in her, poor man, an answering abyss. Another near marriage of untrue minds is arranged by the robber Fancy, intent once again, in the vacuum, on his revenge.

It becomes apparent that Louisa's spirit, as it matures in Coketown under its educative influences, finds its dismal reflection almost equally in Harthouse and in Stephen Blackpool: in Harthouse, whose libertinism is the fruit of a similar emptiness and boredom, and in Blackpool, whose crushed decency she can admire but not reach or connect with over barriers of class. All Louisa's relationships or attempted relationships develop a horrifying logic, bred in the desolation of her heart. Between herself and her father there is an insuperable barrier, which extends naturally enough to her relationship with Bounderby when she is delivered over to him as wife. She tries to help Blackpool, and succeeds in ruining him – through

the treachery of a worthless brother who is the recipient, nonetheless, of her only real love. Harthouse almost ruins her as
part of a normal libertine's strategy, yet she experiences with
him her only illusion of requited love. There is the further
desolating fact that she is unfitted for the one relationship of
ordinary friendship which could have helped her. Sissy's tenderness is repulsed because of a moment's pity and amazement,
which Louisa, understandably, cannot accept.

v

If *Hard Times* is a special novel in the canon, this is partly, at
least, because it is also the angriest. Like *Gulliver* before or
1984 after, it is conceived and sustained in anger. This is no
doubt why it exudes energy and even exaltation, despite the
muffling of Dickens's normal poetic effects. Its energy is
specifically satiric, with anger unleashed and driven to extremes.
Bounderby is an extreme example of a self-made man in the
tradition soon to receive a powerful further impetus from
Samuel Smiles (*Self-Help*, 1859) – witness the mutated 'Ecce
Homo' in 'behold your Bounderby', a blasphemy which nothing
but savage seriousness could sustain. Gradgrind is an extreme
instance of a kindly man, intending as a father nothing but good
(and of how many Dickens fathers could this be said?), but
wholly perverted by his deadly ideas. Blackpool is an extreme
example of a worker, honourable and even noble in nature,
pursued by relentless impersonal forces to his downfall and
death. Behind these three instances is a sick society, where
Gradgrind's children merely enact, in terrifyingly human terms,
the extreme logic prescribed by their world.
    Dickens's social analysis is of two nations still, the rich and
the poor. But Coketown is a prison for both now, the masters
as much as the men. It is a society based on slavery, where
Gradgrind, far from counteracting Bounderby's crude savagery
by his own natural kindliness, provides the intellectual sanctions
which such cruelty needs. Malthusian *laissez faire* becomes
a universe in the novel. We never get out of Coketown, and
our nearest approach to escape – the journeys to Bounderby's

G

house, and to the mineshaft where Stephen dies – merely emphasise the claustrophobia. The characters who in any sense
escape disappear from our view as readers until their return
(if they *do* return) : Mr Gradgrind to the national cinder heap
at Westminster, Stephen's wife to whatever limbo she survives
in between her visits, Harthouse to his own careless, rootless
life, Stephen to outcast wanderings between his departure from
Coketown and his ill-fated return. The twin influences of
Malthus and utilitarianism, caught up in the triumphant
laissez faire of the mid-1850s and unblushingly equated by many
Victorians with Christianity, have led to the Coketown world.
In other novels – *Sybil* (1845), *Mary Barton* (1848) – there are
similar analyses of the condition of England, and a growing
consensus on the nature of the evils to be dealt with though
widely divergent views on what should be done. *Hard Times*
differs chiefly by being a greater work of art : a novel where,
despite the calculated sacrifice of art to art already alluded to,
we sense the compulsive power of myth. And the myth *is*
Coketown, the imprisoning streets and stifling air, a total
image of the spiritual malaise engendered there. Dickens is able,
even though he has sacrificed his habitual resonance, to retain
and even concentrate that element in his work now widely
referred to as 'projective fiction' : the creation of a world where
the houses and streets, the urban environs, the very feel of the
air initiate us into the psychology of living and suffering people.
It is not through formal description or analysis of character,
but through every detail of Coketown that we see into the human
heart. Coketown is the innermost dereliction and despair of
Louisa and Stephen, the environment which has shaped them,
the prison where they will die. Despite the social realism it is
tinged with nightmare, akin to the delirium of a fever running
its course. Everything seems fated and unalterable. As we see
Mr Gradgrind's 'metallurgic Louisa' handed over in marriage
to Bounderby, a 'big, loud man, with a stare, and a metallic
laugh', it is as though the moment had always been predes-
tined. There is the same sense of profound irrationality and
evil that we find in Dickens's other, more characteristic, books.
At the same time the thematic imagery of *Hard Times* greatly

reinforces the effect of proliferating evil. Its angry insistence on organic images needs little comment. The novel is divided into three books, 'Sowing', Reaping' and 'Garnering', where these natural processes, sufficiently ironic in Coketown, chart the logic of stunted and withered lives.

But Dickens's anger works also through a grimness peculiar, in his canon, to this book; to a remarkable degree *Hard Times* violates hope. This is apparent in the slap in the face administered to the Happy Ending, which readers of *Dombey and Son*, or *Bleak House* even, might have thought themselves entitled to look forward to, in however modified a form. Somehow Dickens held on to his readers through this bleak period despite everything, but *Hard Times* seems a How Not To Do It formula for popular acclaim. Surely Sissy Jupe's father will turn up again as she hopes and expects so fervently, and Stephen Blackpool's life won't be "aw a muddle' right to the end? Surely Louisa will escape the ravages of her upbringing, with help from Sissy's love and her refashioned father, and find some happiness for her long-suppressed heart? The lines of such an ending are easy to envisage, and would not have taxed Dickens's art. We could imagine Stephen's reputation exonerated by Tom's bungling, and his dreadful wife dead from alcohol, perhaps in the streets. No stretching of probabilities would be required, and Stephen might settle down with his good angel Rachael for the rest of their lives. It would be easy to imagine Bounderby dying, perhaps from apoplexy induced by Mrs Sparsit, and even – though this is more taxing – Harthouse turned by Louisa, as Wrayburn was later to be by Lizzie Hexam, to a worthier life. *Hard Times* might have tempered its astringency with some concessions, or Dickens might have risked, as in *Dombey*, a full happy ending, with Bounderby and Mrs Sparsit cast out after exposure, Louisa and her father saved, Stephen married off to Rachael, and the joyful barking of a dog, grown old but not senile, heralding the return of a rich and prosperous Mr Jupe. Dickens would have been tremendous with such an ending and his faithful readers might not have liked him the less for it; but it would not have done in the Coketown world. What we have instead is the rejection of all hope with

calculated brutality, while the smoke serpents and the melancholy mad elephants go on.

The violation of hope is emphasised still further in that
defeat in life is meted out to the really good. At first this may
not seem unusual; is it not a more or less constant possibility
in Dickens's world? The persecution of pure young children is a
recurring theme, and some of the children had met their deaths.
Yet Oliver Twist, Florence Dombey and David Copperfield
survived their violation, Little Nell died triumphantly, and even
Jo was not without his friends. The novelty in *Hard Times* is
not in the sufferings of the victims or the wickedness of their
tormenters, but in the arid waste of their hearts and lives.
Louisa and Stephen are defeated in their attempt to do good (as
indeed is Rachael) and enjoy no inward peace arising from pure
intentions and duty done. Emptiness is embodied in Louisa's
speech habits, formal even when she is with her brother or her
lover, and in Stephen's laboured and stately rhetoric – which,
whether or not it is true to dialect, is true to the man. Louisa
says that she is 'tired of everything', Stephen says life is "aw a
muddle'. Both lose their chance of finding happiness in marriage,
and are doomed to live without the consolations or even the
duties of love. The novel comes close at one point to being a
tract for divorce reform, but this possibility is not, in the end,
pursued. Louisa and Stephen both lose their reputations,
Stephen when he is cast off by his fellow workers and then by his
employer for disloyalty, Louisa when she is returned by her
husband to a sterile life in her father's home. Their losses in this
world are irrevocable. Nineteenth-century society offered no
second chances either to discarded wives who had compromised
their husbands or to workers who had been disowned. Stephen
is later proclaimed a thief on the public placards, and his fellow
workers find this possible to believe. Louisa does not marry
again after Bounderby's death.

It is still more significant that Louisa and Stephen are shown
almost falling into evil, as if to fulfil some curse upon their
lives. The night when Stephen is racked by his terrible dream
of weddings and gallows, and wakes or half-wakes as his drunken
wife reaches towards the poison bottle, is the most nightmarish

stretch of the book. His wife is saved only by Rachael, to whom
Stephen confesses the murder in his heart. It seems, then,
that Stephen comes close to joining the ranks of murderers in
Dickens's works, who are usually depicted as either totally mad,
or wicked, or at the very least as driven distracted by lust or
pride. Might a virtuous man also be pushed over this threshold,
to take his place with Rudge and Jonas Chuzzlewit, Hortense
and Rigaud, Orlick and Bradley Headstone, among ultimate
wanderers in the dark? And Louisa nearly becomes an adulteress, thereby committing a sexual sin beyond that of even Edith
Dombey or Lady Dedlock. This is a sensitive spot in the Victorian novel, since writers had to treat adultery as a sin more
abominable than they probably really thought it, and no
fictional adulteress could expect forgiveness, or even survival,
after the act. Louisa marries Bounderby in a spirit of bitterness
equal almost to Edith Dombey's, and descends Mrs Sparsit's
staircase to the last but one step.

How, then, do Stephen and Louisa remain virtuous? As usual
in Dickens, it is a final mystery of good.

So many hundred Hands in this Mill; so many hundred horse
Steam Power. It is known, to the force of a single pound weight,
what the engine will do; but not all the calculators of the National
Debt can tell me the capacity for good or evil, for love or
hatred, for patriotism or discontent, for the decomposition of
virtue into vice, or the reverse, at any single moment in the soul
of one of these its quiet servants, with the composed faces and the
regulated actions. There is no mystery in it; there is an un-
fathomable mystery in the meanest of them, forever.

By 'it' – though the syntax is uncharacteristically clumsy – I
take Dickens to mean 'the engine', and his contrast to be between
things, which are proper material for science, and people, who
are not. The implication is that political economists, in reducing
men to machines, are making a dire error of analysis, from
which Coketown itself is but one consequence for ill. But this is
asserted in the same paragraph as an article of faith about man,
which Dickens includes even in his bleakest book. Stephen and
Louisa both avoid the path of Edith Dombey, Miss Wade,
Miss Havisham and so many other Dickens people, who nourish

bitterness in their hearts and embark on darkly destructive and
self-destructive paths of revenge. They both keep alive some
pure love, Louisa's for Tom, Stephen's for Rachael. They both
remain passive at moments when any conceivable self-assertion
could only do harm. In her extreme temptation, Louisa summons
up the will to flee to her father and seek protection. Stephen,
when he is cast out, takes to the road, with nothing but Rachael's
blessing to lighten his way. They both preserve some citadel
of good in the inner self, even with circumstances wholly
against them and no sustaining ease of conscience in their lives.
In every respect other than their education and literacy, they
belong among the spiritually deprived with Jo.

The other good characters in *Hard Times* share such an
unusual impotence that Dickens might almost be asserting the
powerlessness of good. Rachael is the good angel of Stephen's
life, but the oath which she makes him take for his protection
results in his downfall, and her solemn blessing on his exile does
not save his life. Like Dickens's other angel women, she suffers
from seeming somewhat shadowy, and her virtue is asserted
rather than shown. Sissy Jupe is calm and serene, and survives
the Gradgrind onslaught upon her vitality, but she too has very
little to do. Her pity alienates Louisa during the period when
she might have been most spiritually helpful, and she exerts no
redemptive influence over Tom. The other sister, it is true, is
helped by her, but the other sister does not really belong in the
book. Sissy points the irony, of course, of Gradgrind's system,
particularly when her answers on political economy, drawn
straight from the Sermon on the Mount, cover her with school-
room disgrace. Sissy is not consciously quoting from scripture –
the effect would be destroyed if one supposed this – and Dickens
shows that uncorrupted nature and the New Testament speak
with one voice. Later, Sissy routs Harthouse by her virtue, and
this is just about believable, given Harthouse's boredom, but
her rhetoric reflects a somewhat commonplace mind.

Do we find active and operative virtue in Sleary? He is an
engaging person, but neither his vaguely alcoholic goodwill
nor his childishly friendly troupe of performers present a real
escape from the Coketown spell. It is noteworthy indeed that

Dickens does not create a more positive role for the circus. Someone like Lord John Sanger* really could have stood out strongly and refreshingly against Coketown: but, then, Dickens probably did not know Sanger, who was anyway an exception and not the rule. The travelling showmen in Dickens's fiction from *Sketches by Boz* onwards tend to be amoral, and tinged with the grotesque.

Hard Times is a novel where a dark view of reality prevails, and virtue is driven, literally enough, out of this world. We can say, no doubt, that Sissy and Rachael bear witness to the reality of values which Coketown neither sees nor allows to operate in its affairs merely by existing, the one to the Sermon on the Mount as a force natural and ineradicable, the other to the tenacity of patient, unrewarded love. But Stephen dies and Louisa returns home to the life of an old maid, and there is not much comfort there. If happiness exists for them at all, it can only be in the world to which Stephen is drawn by his star. Dickens's art falters as usual on this central issue, because he wanted to make it as affecting as possible for his readers, and perhaps for himself. One must hope that the failure is one of art, and not of moral sincerity, since if Dickens did not believe in an afterlife there is a serious dishonesty in many other of his works (*Bleak House* notably) as well as in this. Without an afterlife, *Hard Times* would cut us off from hope completely, since even if its savage intensity remained a potent factor in mid-Victorian society, it would remain a denial of the final victory and supremacy of good.

VI

In this aspect of the novel, there is a very important passage which occurs when Sissy and Rachael meet, to discuss Stephen, in a darkened room. Appearances against Stephen are at their blackest, since Rachael has sent her letter informing him of the charges against him, but he has not, as she confidently predicted, returned.

* See the extremely readable and lively autobiography, recently reissued in paperback: 'Lord' John Sanger, *Seventy Years a Showman*.

'I misdoubt,' said Rachael, 'if there is as many as twenty left in all this place who have any trust in the poor dear lad now.'

She said it to Sissy as they sat in her lodging, lighted only by the lamp at the street-corner. Sissy had come there when it was already dark to await her return from work, and they had since sat at the window where Rachael had found her, wanting no brighter light to shine on their sorrowful talk.

'If it hadn't been mercifully brought about that I was to have you to speak to,' pursued Rachael, 'times are when I think my mind would not have kept right. But I get hope and strength through you; and you believe that though appearances may rise against him, he will be proved clear?'

'I do believe so,' returned Sissy, 'with my whole heart. I feel so certain, Rachael, that the confidence you hold in yours against all discouragement is not like to be wrong, that I have no more doubt of him than if I had known him through as many years of trial as you have.'

'And I, my dear,' said Rachael, with a tremble in her voice, 'have known him through them all to be, according to his quiet ways, so faithful to everything honest and good that if he was never to be heard of more, and I was to live to be a hundred years old, I could say with my last breath, God knows my heart, I have never once left trusting Stephen Blackpool!'

These two are drawn together like twin souls, and sit in semi-darkness waiting; it is a symbolic role for virtue to play. They sustain each other, using their strong inner convictions against circumstances. Rachael says that without Sissy's companionship and faith in Stephen she might even have gone mad. But why does Sissy believe in Stephen? Not because she knows Stephen, but because she knows Rachael, and has formed an absolute trust in Stephen through her faith in Rachael's judgement. This in turn prompts Rachael's solemn reassertion of faith in Stephen; she *does* know him, and has never for one moment doubted his truth.

It is tempting to see this passage as sentimental, or even conventional, but this would surely be a mistake. Sissy is not just propping up a sister-woman with easy reassurances; her profession of belief in Rachael is as serious and considered as Rachael's reply. The confidence Rachael holds in her heart against all discouragement is not *likely* to be wrong. Rachael

caps this careful phrasing with a claim still more positive:
'God knows my heart, I have never once left trusting Stephen
Blackpool!'

In Dickens's world, as in everyday reality of course, this is a
striking claim. Dickens's is a world where evil can *seem* good,
and where appearances can sometimes deceive even the virtuous and loyal. Yet certain of his good characters – not all of
them – are endowed with a special insight beyond false appearances to the truth. Little Nell trusts Kit Nubbles, just as Jenny
Wren later trusts Old Riah, and both are right. Perhaps Dickens
is suggesting that though in an evil world hypocrisy can take in
nearly everyone, there is still an area where good can talk to
good. Some mysterious quality speaks from one to the other:
it is possible for Rachael to trust Stephen even though – this is
the most remarkable aspect – she knows of his momentary
temptation to murder his wife. The reason we endorse Dickens
is that he has the unusual power of making real this trust,
elusive and irrational as it might seem. At the same time it
seems to me to be authenticated by experience. While most
of us would not guarantee, no doubt, to be proof against a
thoroughly evil hypocrite, would we not agree that one or two
people known to us – *just* one or two – are quite certainly good?
Hard Times chooses to assert this irreducible area of virtue at
its grimmest moment, with two women sitting in shadow and
proclaiming their faith. This is why the rationality of Sissy's
faith in Rachael is important, and must be insisted upon. She
feels that Rachael is not a woman bolstering herself with illusions, but a woman who would never have befriended Stephen
Blackpool without first judging his worth.

VII

There are some novels that press us inwards, towards their
truth as artefact, others which refer us sharply back to real life.
Hard Times groups itself more strongly than most of Dickens's
novels among the latter, perhaps because of its powerful relevance to its own age. We recall John Stuart Mill brought to the
verge of suicide by unrelieved logic, and saved only when fancy

found its healing way back to his life. Coketown was a real factor of mid-nineteenth-century England, and Dickens was never more consciously messianic than he was here. Even so, the novel survives in its own right as a powerful fiction, striking and authentic even when its point has been won. In the later twentieth century England is very differently situated, with welfare services proliferating at the expense of sturdy independence, and education given to self-expression at the expense of fact. If Dickens were alive today to write an angry, topical novel, it would clearly not be this one. But *Hard Times* triumphantly survives.

9 *Little Dorrit*
a Dickens first chapter

I

'THIRTY years ago, Marseilles lay burning in the sun, one day.'
A typical Dickens opening. 'Thirty years ago' pushes us back
into history, 'one day' arrests us. Between the two, 'Marseilles
lay burning in the sun', the focus of life.

The description which follows resembles a symbolist poem.
Our most personal memories seem to be touched off by it, as
when childhood memories come back with uncharted intensity:

> Everything in Marseilles, and about Marseilles, had stared
> at the fervid sky, and been stared at in return, until a staring
> habit had become universal there. Strangers were stared out
> of countenance by staring white houses, staring white walls,
> staring white streets, staring tracts of arid road, staring hills
> from which verdure was burnt away. The only things to be seen
> not fixedly staring were the vines drooping under their load of
> grapes. These did occasionally wink a little, as the hot air barely
> moved their faint leaves.

There is an hypnotic clarity in so much staring. It is partly
physical: 'The universal stare made the eyes ache.' But notice
how active the stare is, oppressive and ominous, yet almost
godlike. The landscape is more active than the 'strangers', who
are stared out of countenance. Perhaps it is the introduction of
'glaring' to go with 'staring' which implies menace; perhaps it is
'drooping', and 'faint', with their suggestion of life drained of
energy.

The next paragraph introduces more physical images of heat.

> Boats without awnings were too hot to touch; ships blistered at
> their moorings; the stones of the quays had not cooled, night
> or day, for months. Hindoos, Russians, Chinese, Spaniards,
> Portuguese, Englishmen, Frenchmen, Genoese, Neapolitans,
> Venetians, Greeks, Turks, descendants from all the builders of

Babel, come to trade at Marseilles, sought the shade alike –
taking refuge in any hiding-place from a sea too intensely blue
to be looked at, and a sky of purple, set with one great flaming
jewel of fire.

But this heightened world is surrounded by nightmare, the arid
plain and the terrible sea. The waters of the harbour are immu-
tably separated from the pure sea beyond the harbour, yet both
are terrible to mortal eyes.

There was no wind to make a ripple on the foul water within
the harbour, or on the beautiful sea without. The line of
demarcation between the two colours, black and blue, showed
the point which the pure sea would not pass; but it lay as quiet
as the abominable pool, with which it never mixed.

So Marseilles becomes cursed, a place where the polluted waters
are segregated from the pure, but where the pure waters are 'too
intensely blue to be looked at'; by a powerful displacement, it
is suggested that to the exotic collection of humanity, all
seeking refuge, beauty and purity might be as unbearable as
the 'abominable pool'. The next two paragraphs continue the
powerful flow of evocations:

The universal stare made the eyes ache. Towards the distant
line of Italian coast, indeed, it was a little relieved by light
clouds of mist, slowly rising from the evaporation of the sea,
but it softened nowhere else. Far away the staring roads, deep
in dust, stared from the hill-side, stared from the hollow, stared
from the interminable plain. Far away the dusty vines over-
hanging wayside cottages, and the monotonous wayside
avenues of parched trees without shade, drooped beneath the
stare of earth and sky. So did the horses with drowsy bells, in
long files of carts, creeping slowly towards the interior; so did
their recumbent drivers, when they were awake, which rarely
happened; so did the exhausted labourers in the fields. Everything that lived or grew, was oppressed by the glare; except the
lizard, passing swiftly over rough stone walls, and the cicala,
chirping his dry hot chirp, like a rattle. The very dust was
scorched brown, and something quivered in the atmosphere as
if the air itself were panting.
  Blinds, shutters, curtains, awnings, were all closed and
drawn to keep out the stare. Grant it but a chink or keyhole,

and it shot in like a white-hot arrow. The churches were the
freest from it. To come out of the twilight of pillars and
arches – dreamily dotted with twinkling lamps, dreamily
peopled with ugly old shadows piously dozing, spitting and
begging – was to plunge into a fiery river, and swim for life to
the nearest strip of shade. So, with people lounging and lying
wherever shade was, with but little hum of tongues or barking
of dogs, with occasional jangling or discordant church bells and
rattling of vicious drums, Marseilles, a fact to be strongly
smelt and tasted, lay broiling in the sun one day.

When reading T. S. Eliot's poetry I am continually haunted by
his debt to Dickens. This is not acknowledged in the Notes to
The Waste Land or in the critical writings, and perhaps Eliot
was not specifically aware of it, but the first chapters of *Bleak
House, Little Dorrit, Our Mutual Friend* must have run in his
mind. They pervade *The Waste Land* not in exact verbal echoes,
perhaps, but in the evocations – aridity, sterility, spiritual oppression – and in the vividly hallucinated images, rich with suggestion. By the time of *Four Quartets*, the affinities are still more
striking. There are lines in 'East Coker' that are near to contain-
ing verbal echoes of the opening of *Little Dorrit*; and the
marvellously precise description of Eliot's own poetry near the
opening of 'Burnt Norton' comes as close as perhaps words
can to indicating the quality of Dickensian evocation in the
passage now concerning us, and in all similar moments in
Dickens's work:

> Footfalls echo in the memory
> Down the passage which we did not take
> Towards the door we never opened
> Into the rose-garden. My words echo
> Thus, in your mind.
>   But to what purpose
> Disturbing the dust on a bowl of rose-leaves
> I do not know.
>   Other echoes
> Inhabit the garden. Shall we follow?
> Quick, said the bird, find them, find them,
> Round the corner. Through the first gate,
> Into our first world . . .

By their nature, such echoes are private as well as public, resonant and open in what they 'mean'. A critic cannot dogmatise on such matters; he can merely point to the kinds of richness there might be. There are directions of mood, and directions of imagery; an unparaphrasable clarity, akin to music and the non-literary arts. Dickens's Marseilles is a refuge as well as a cesspool, yet a refuge actively under attack. Blinds, shutters, curtains, awnings, all reject the glare, but it leaps murderously through, a 'white hot arrow', where it can. These two paragraphs end, like the first sentence of the book, with the words 'one day', circling round with suggestions of finality as well as return. But the suggestions have all been of continuity, of life going on in endless and ageless secretive ways. The 'ugly old shadows' in the dim recesses of churches are decrepit, but somehow magic; the slow movements and distant sounds are a tidal music; the lizard, alone of living things, is at home in the heat. Life goes on in whatever shadows form as the heat deepens, with the promise of resurrection towards dusk. The next paragraphs seem, however, to reverse these suggestions – or to enrich them with a new dimension of oppression within oppression, depths where different laws hold :

In Marseilles that day there was a villainous prison. In one of its chambers, so repulsive a place that even the obtrusive stare blinked at it, and left it to such refuse of reflected light as it could find for itself, were two men. Besides the two men, a notched and disfigured bench, immovable from the wall, with a draught-board rudely hacked upon it with a knife, a set of draughts, made of old buttons and soup bones, a set of dominoes, two mats, and two or three wine bottles. That was all the chamber held, exclusive of rats and other unseen vermin, in addition to the seen vermin, the two men.

It received such light as it got through a grating of iron bars fashioned like a pretty large window, by means of which it could be always inspected from the gloomy staircase on which the grating gave. There was a broad strong ledge of stone to this grating where the bottom of it was let into the masonry, three or four feet above the ground. Upon it, one of the two men lolled half sitting and half lying, with his knees drawn up, and his feet and shoulders planted against the opposite sides of the aperture. The bars were wide enough apart to admit of his thrusting his arm through to the elbow; and so he held on negligently, for his greater ease.

A prison taint was on everything there. The imprisoned air, the imprisoned light, the imprisoned damps, the imprisoned men, were all deteriorated by confinement. As the captive men were faded and haggard, so the iron was rusty, the stone was slimy, the wood was rotten, the air was faint, the light was dim. Like a well, like a vault, like a tomb, the prison had no knowledge of the brightness outside, and would have kept its polluted atmosphere intact in one of the spice islands of the Indian ocean.

Marseilles has been a tainted place, but a place of refuge; the prison is now its tainted heart. Here, the arrows of light cannot penetrate; but their absence brings no relief. The very air is constraint and degradation: if the church brought a welcome escape from too much whiteness, too much staring, the dungeon is final, intolerable dusk. And, like Tom-All-Alone's, the dungeon dominates, reducing its inmates, good or evil, to verminous brutes.

Already, much of *Little Dorrit* is here. Prison: the prevailing image. And oppression: that heaviness of spirit, so typical of this novel and of the two novels on either side of it, which broods over the creative vitality itself. Oppression radiates (the verb seems hardly paradoxical) from the prison in Marseilles; from the Marshalsea; from the Circumlocution Office; from Mrs Clennam's House; from Bleeding Heart Yard; from Merdle's business empire; from the Convent of the Great St Bernard; eventually, in Venice, from the most colourful and exotic city in the world. And it radiates from the sterile, destroyed consciousness of the prisoners – William Dorrit, Mrs Clennam, Miss Wade, Tattycoram, Henry Gowan and his mother, Mr Merdle, Mrs General, Rigaud, Flintwinch, Mr F's Aunt. Above all, it radiates from those consciousnesses deteriorated by prison *though* inherently virtuous, from Arthur Clennam and Amy Dorrit, the twin victims and redeemers at the heart of the tale. For in *Little Dorrit* the virtuous are certainly victims, who pay for their moral role with much of their lives. It is the absence of energy, abdication of hope which haunts us: we

recall Arthur watching the faded hopes of his life float down the
river, and Amy, alone and desolate on the balcony in Venice,
when the *raison d'être* of her life is gone. Though virtuous,
they are – or seem to be – derelict: yet it is through them that
redeemed energy, redeemed hope might flow. Almost intolerable oppression, with faint hints of meaning: no wonder the
first chapter echoes in the book.

It is undeniable, I think, though perhaps also unprovable,
that the London of *Little Dorrit* is not Dickens's London elsewhere. The London of *Our Mutual Friend* is certainly a waste
land in many particulars, but it has charm, colour, humour as
well. The *Little Dorrit* London is bleak, even at comic moments,
a place of weary streets, grey housetops, slanting rain. It is
Arthur Clennam's return to his mother's house on a darkened
Sunday; it is Amy Dorrit's night locked out – her night of
freedom! – on London Bridge. The prison taint does indeed fall
on everything, and the virtuous, in all except their virtue, are
not exempt. If Louisa Gradgrind and Stephen Blackpool were
wreckage on a blackened landscape, Arthur and Amy are
pilgrims in the shadow of death.

Pilgrims as well as prisoners: and indeed *Little Dorrit* is
a novel of wide spaces, long wanderings, lonely voyages, as well
as of claustrophobic prisons and stifling airs. Its prisoners are in
some ways more imprisoned (if we except Mrs Clennam) in
their journeyings than they are when physically confined.
What are Miss Wade's wanderings, or Rigaud's, or William
Dorrit's when he leaves the Marshalsea, but expressions of
their tortuously imprisoned souls? The characters all meet,
seemingly by chance, in the course of voyaging, on that
stifling 'one day' in Marseilles. And if they are not travelling,
they are waiting for travellers – Affery, her wits scared out of
her, in the night watches, Mrs Clennam, grim and defiant, in
her room:

Strange, if the little sick-room fire were in effect a beacon fire,
summoning some one, and that the most unlikely some one in
the world, to the spot that he *must* come to. Strange, if the little
sick-room light were in effect a watch-light, burning in that
place every night until an appointed event should be watched

out! Which of the vast multitude of travellers, under the sun
and the stars, climbing the dusty hills and toiling along the
weary plains, journeying by land and journeying by sea, coming
and going so strangely, to meet and act and react on one another, which of the host may, with no suspicion of the journey's
end, be travelling surely hither?

The wording here is an echo of the end of chapter 1; and the
first chapter hints in other ways at this theme of imprisoned
wanderings, destined encounters, which are like labyrinthine
tunnels under the tale. We hear first, then see, the gaoler and
his little daughter, winding their way up stairs to the prisoners
in their cell. Just as the child prefigures the novel's heroine, in
her golden innocence, so she prefigures spontaneous (but less
costly?) heavenly love. 'Adieu, my birds!' says the child,
echoing her father, and the passing song recedes into the
texture of the book:

> Who passes by the road so late?
> Compagnon de la Majolaine!
> Who passes by this road so late?
> Always gay!

II

The first chapter of *Little Dorrit* moves on to the sinister
conversation between Rigaud and John Baptist Cavalletto, and
to the theme of false gentility, another obsession of the author
here as elsewhere. Of all Dickens's 'gentlemen', Rigaud is the
most purely evil, yet he is evil – it is a paradox not confined to
Little Dorrit – with an exuberance elusive to the virtuous and
good. The characterisation is by no means as melodramatic as it
has often been said to be; Rigaud's use of his own theatricality
rings sufficiently true. His insolent panache has affinities with
Browning's famous dramatic monologue 'My Last Duchess';
he may even be a seedy parody, dangerous enough to the late
Madame Rigaud, of Browning's murderous duke. Rigaud
creates himself a 'gentleman' to extract homage, knowing that
confidence is nine-tenths of the game. The tawdry sham gets
him through life more or less as intended: so we are prepared

not only for Rigaud himself in the rest of the book, and for poor William Dorrit, but also for all those other more-or-less successful impostors in polite society – Mrs Gowan and Henry Gowan, Mrs General, Mr and Mrs Merdle, and the rest. We are also prepared for Mr Meagles's Achilles' heel, his fatal snobbery, and for the false values of wealth and gentility which underlie so many of the sufferings we are to witness.

Little Dorrit centres, more than any other Dickens novel perhaps, on the virtuous sacrifice of a daughter to her father in a setting where hardly any hope can be seen. There could be few sorrows more harrowing than Amy's daily knowledge that the very qualities which make for dignity and honesty in life could only achieve her father's death. It is not only the ordinary desires and hopes of life that she has to surrender, but the intelligence and sensitivity of her innermost self. William Dorrit's one defensive weapon is the shield of gentility : take that away – all its shame, all its pettiness, all its hollowness – and he would die. Might death be better, even, than life in the Marshalsea? Self-knowledge, which might be painful redemption in the outside world, would be destruction there. There is no possibility of self-knowledge leading, through crisis, to renewal; self-knowledge is the enemy always to be feared. It is not even therefore as though Amy's sacrifice was made to redeem her father : a stern moralist might even condemn the pretence. More simply, her duty as she sees it is to keep him going. In an intolerable situation she can make life barely tolerable for him from hour to hour. But to do this she has to shore up the ruins of his snobbery, to make his survival from the stuff of decay. All moral realities must be concealed from him as far as concealment is possible – even when he solicits testimonials; even when he treats old Nandy with patronage and contempt. Amy must bear with him when he pretends that his daughters are not wage-earners, she must bear with him in his vicissitudes towards herself. Perhaps this is the heart of the horror for Amy Dorrit, the knowledge that her own sacrifice is continually exploited by her father, and in areas where his weakness is least to be condoned. And it is not even – given all this – that she can really deceive him; the most she can hope is to keep up the conditions where pretence remains just barely possible and practical, to the people who surround William Dorrit and to himself.

Nowhere else does Dickens produce for virtue a role so inherently exhausting and unrewarding. Even Little Nell had the practical side of her grandfather's dilemma to distract her, she was not left with nothing to *do*. Nowhere else is his psychological insight into virtue so harrowing: it is a probing of the *good* of good at its most sensitive point. There is also a particular irony in the enforced nature of Amy's sacrifice in this particular novel, where the folly and even evil of moral obtuseness is so much stressed. Whereas most of the sins and sinners cry aloud for intelligent analysis as a prelude to reformation, William Dorrit has passed beyond the stage where intelligent analysis would help. Amy has, therefore, to crucify even her desire to make a better man of her father; she has to assert her love and respect for him as homage to some remaining reality, which in this world, at least, will have no showing forth. Little wonder that her virtue seems like almost total self-immolation: the wonder, rather, is that the virtue is so authentic and true. At some level hard to articulate, *Little Dorrit* is a hopeful novel; like *Bleak House* and *Hard Times* it achieves this miracle against the most massive odds. The oppression so strongly realised in its first chapter pervades the novel, and is even virtue's consciousness, yet Amy is truly Christlike – in very marked contrast to Florence Dombey – in an unanswerable sense.

But if the novel has hope, then hope is driven, as so often in later Dickens, quite literally out of *this* world. This is no doubt why the final paragraph of chapter 1 appears as a final symbolist statement. As the drama winds on through the dark night of human experience, it is by the remotest hints only, hints and guesses, that hope lives on:

The wide stare stared itself out for one while; the sun went down in a red, green, golden glory; the stars came out in the heavens, and the fire-flies mimicked them in the lower air, as men may feebly imitate the goodness of a better order of beings; the long dusty roads and the interminable plains were in repose – and so deep a hush was on the sea, that it scarcely whispered of the time when it shall give up its dead.

10 *A Tale of Two Cities* recalled to life

A Tale of Two Cities proceeds chronologically, like most historical novels, but when we revisit it in memory certain passages seem to detach themselves and dance on their own. Their rhythms are frenzied and nightmarish – Mr Lorry's vision of the grindstone, La Carmagnole passing, the knitting women at La Guillotine; or chill and ghostly – the château of Monseigneur on the night of his murder, Charles Darnay's eerie encounter with the cream of France :

Through the dismal prison twilight, his new charge accompanied him by corridor and staircase, many doors clanging and locking behind them, until they came into a large, low, vaulted chamber, crowded with prisoners of both sexes. The women were seated at a long table, reading and writing, knitting, sewing, and embroidering; the men were for the most part standing behind their chairs, or lingering up and down the room.

In the instinctive association of prisoners with shameful crime and disgrace, the new comer recoiled from this company. But the crowning unreality of his long unreal ride, was, their all at once rising to receive him, with every refinement of manner known to the time, and with all the engaging graces and courtesies of life.

So strangely clouded were these refinements by the prison manners and gloom, so practical did they become in the inappropriate squalor and misery through which they were seen, that Charles Darnay seemed to stand in a company of the dead. Ghosts all! The ghost of beauty, the ghost of stateliness, the ghost of elegance, the ghost of pride, the ghost of frivolity, the ghost of wit, the ghost of youth, the ghost of age, all waiting their dismissal from the desolate shore, all turning on him eyes that were changed by the death they had died in coming here.

It struck him motionless. The gaoler standing at his side, and the other gaolers moving about, who would have been well

enough as to appearance in the ordinary exercise of their
functions, looked so extravagantly coarse contrasted with
sorrowing mothers and blooming daughters who were there –
with the apparitions of the coquette, the young beauty, and the
mature woman delicately bred – that the inversion of all experience and likelihood which the scene of shadows presented,
was heightened to its utmost. Surely ghosts all. Surely, the long
unreal ride some progress of disease that had brought him to
these gloomy shades!

From the moment when its motto theme sounds to the drowsy
Mr Lorry on his night-ride to Dover: 'You know that you are
recalled to life?', the novel is pervaded by ghosts and ghostli-
ness. Manette is a shade of himself, set apart from his fellows;
Charles Darnay is in the dock of the Old Bailey on trial for his
life. The whole atmosphere is uncanny, as though the leading
actors drifted neither dead nor alive, in no-man's-land, confronting unreal reflections of themselves. Darnay sees himself
in the infamous mirror of the Old Bailey:

Over the prisoner's head there was a mirror, to throw the light
down upon him. Crowds of the wicked and the wretched had
been reflected in it, and had passed from its surface and the
earth's together. Haunted in a most ghastly manner that abominable place would have been, if the glass could ever have rendered
back its reflections, as the ocean is one day to give up its dead.
Some passing thought of the infamy and disgrace for which it
had been reserved, may have struck the prisoner's mind. Be that
as it may, a change in his position making him conscious of a bar
of light across his face, he looked up; and when he saw the glass
his face flushed, and his right hand pushed the herbs away.

And minutes later, an unlooked-for *Doppelgänger* and rescuer
peers insolently back at him from the courtroom, strangely like
and unlike. After the acquittal, Sydney Carton takes Darnay
aside, and comments: 'This is a strange chance that throws you
and me together. This must be a strange night to you, standing
alone here with your counterpart on these street stones?'
Darnay is still dazed by his deliverance, and half-believing. His
strange rescuer goes out of his way to be unpleasant, seeing in
the man he has rescued himself, honourable and undepraved as

he might have been. What can Carton feel for such a vision but hatred? Yet he has saved Darnay on this occasion, as if by instinct, and will die later in his place.

These mirror-images are paralleled by others no less significant: the two cities London and Paris, reflecting each other before the Revolution in corrupt court and monarch, corrupt pleasure in the public spectacle of death. The crowd who come to see Charles Darnay in the dock of the Old Bailey are drawn by the terrible death which is to be his.

The sort of interest with which this man was stared and breathed at, was not a sort that elevated humanity. Had he stood in peril of a less horrible sentence – had there been a chance of any one of its savage details being spared – by just so much would he have lost his fascination. The form that was to be doomed to be so shamefully mangled, was the sight; the immortal creature that was to be so butchered and torn asunder, yielded the sensation. Whatever gloss the various spectators put upon the interest, according to their several arts and powers of self-deceit, the interest was, at the root of it, ogreish.

As in London, so in Paris. One of the Jacques tells of the occasion when Damiens was executed in the streets of Paris for his attempt on the life of Louis XV. Boiling oil, melted lead, hot resin, wax and sulphur into wounds made in his arms, breast and legs, and he was torn limb from limb by four strong horses. '. . . nothing was more noticed in the vast concourse that saw it done, than the crowd of ladies of quality and fashion, who were full of eager attention to the last – to the last, Jacques, prolonged until nightfall, when he had lost two legs and an arm, and still breathed.' But these two episodes are not self-cancelling. A further mirror offers reflections back to both of them, when the knitting women of the Republic count their fellow-beings away into heads.

II

These scenes, horrible enough in detail, are miniatures of the larger image given back by the Terror to the Old Régime. In its broad outline, the novel concerns itself with the psychology of revolution, corruption breeding corruption, cruelty breeding cruelty, death breeding death. The ordinary people are reduced to vermin by the Monseigneur, and the Monseigneur is reduced by the vermin to a head. On both sides there is hideous brutalisation and depersonalisation. The nobleman's 'honour', the republican's 'justice' turn to travesty; it is dignity, gentleness, civilisation that fall. Dr Manette is diminished to a mindless creature, knowing himself only as 'One Hundred and Five, North Tower'. The strong forces of the Republic become in triumph Jacques Three, The Vengeance, the wood-sawyer – no other names. Ordinary people hurl themselves into the revolution, losing all concern for life and value. In St Antoine 'every living creature there held life as of no account, and was demented with a passionate readiness to sacrifice it'. Blood lust becomes a sadistic compulsion, parodying creativity, with women turned to vengeful Bacchae as they whirl in the frenzied new dance of death along the streets. The very virtues throw up hideous distortions. Pity becomes the petulant tears shed by The Vengeance because Madame Defarge unexpectedly fails to turn up for La Guillotine: 'Bad Fortune!' cries The Vengeance, stamping her foot in the chair, 'and here are the tumbrils! And Evrémonde will be dispatched in a wink, and she not here! See her knitting in my hand, and her empty chair ready for her. I cry with vexation and disappointment!' The strong, cruel face of the Monseigneur achieves its own true reflection in the strong, cruel face of Madame Defarge.

The epiphany of evil is familiar to Dickens's readers, but nowhere is it so total as here. In its bare bones the novel is a polemic addressed to his own England of Poor Law, *laissez faire*, urban slums. Dickens says – like Orwell later in *Animal Farm* – that repressive conservatism, devoid of humanity and hardened against every prompting of love or justice, must face its nemesis in this frightful form. The insight is summed up explicitly: 'There could have been no such Revolution, if all laws, forms, and ceremonies, had not first been so monstrously abused, that the suicidal vengeance of the Revolution was to scatter them all to the winds.' We are told that this can and will happen again, given similar conditions: 'Crush humanity out of shape once more, under similar hammers, and it will twist itself into the same tortured forms. Sow the same seed of rapacious licence and oppression over again, and it will surely yield the same fruit according to its kind.' Unlike Orwell nearly a hundred years later, Dickens was unable to foresee the possibility of a police state so powerful and effective that oppression and injustice might be stabilised for ever. He assumed that in the end crushed humanity always would revolt successfully, though in these horrible and terrible ways.

Dickens's sense of the precariousness of civilisation is one which many Victorians fearful of revolution must have shared. Of all the modern errors about Victorianism, the oddest is that which ascribes to the period a more or less universal optimism. *A Tale of Two Cities* would not have seemed odd to Newman, or to Matthew Arnold; Dickens was playing on fears which to these and many other Victorians were familiar enough. There was great fear of socialist subversion or conspiracy, and a most uneasy consciousness of explosive potentials in the working-class. It was hoped, no doubt, that 'progress' would so increase prosperity that Arnold's 'raw, unkindled masses of humanity' would be softened, or damped-down even, with time. But the problem was huge, and the prognosis daunting; the forces of anarchy were much to be feared. Meanwhile, the French Terror operated on Victorian memories much as Belsen and Auschwitz do upon our own.

Dickens adds a new note of warning, however, in his sharp reminder that no society, however ancient and apparently immutable, is more than a few weeks safe. The most enduring foundations are as ice if the fires in even one human breast are fully kindled. Just as an individual man – a Tulkinghorn, Bradley Headstone or John Jasper – can dissolve into nightmare, so can a whole order of things. Overnight, the chateau goes up in flames. The peasant sheds the chains of authority worn for a lifetime. In a very few weeks, the new order makes a dream of the old :

A revolutionary tribunal in the capital, and forty or fifty thousand revolutionary committees all over the land; a law of the Suspected, which struck away all security for liberty or life, and delivered over any good and innocent person to any bad and guilty one; prisons gorged with people who had committed no offence, and could obtain no hearing; these things became the established order and nature of appointed things, and seemed to be ancient usage before they were many weeks old.

This vision is in tune with Christianity and, of course, with Hobbesian realism; social law is whatever rulers decree and can enforce. Dickens sees clearly enough that while the consistent violation of justice and humanity produces revolution, revolution produces a more dreadful violation of justice and humanity in its turn. There is an absolute rebuff in this novel to any revolutionary idealism, especially to the romantic primitivism with roots in Rousseau and the eighteenth century (Milton had learned similar lessons from the Old Testament), which has sustained optimistic revolutionists before and since. As we have seen in earlier novels, Dickens's political beliefs were chiefly Carlylean, and in no perceptible sense left-wing. He was not the kind of conservative who revered the past uncritically; the word 'conservative' he rejected indeed, many times. But he was conservative in his belief that social forms and laws should not be simply overthrown or rejected, but criticised and reformed from within. As a precursor of the welfare state he was a radical conservative, and the radical colour of his thought was its clearest aspect, to his readers, and of course to himself. He did not believe that economic miracles of *laissez faire* would greatly help matters; on the contrary, the rich would grow richer, and the poor merely stay as they were. He saw the need rather for society to become responsible for a whole range of services – sanitation, health, education, a properly human standard of living for the least fortunate – and was bitterly aware of the tremendous and relentless battles to be fought if such things were to be. Normally, we stress, rightly enough, the burning humanity which kindled him. His love and concern for the suffering were relentless, and he can fittingly be named with men like Wilberforce and Shaftesbury among the great political conscience-bearers of the past. But we have encountered also his reservations about specific panaceas for human suffering, originating in his mistrust of human nature as

a force to mend the world. His most virtuous characters – Little
Nell, Stephen Blackpool, Amy Dorrit – are strangers and
pilgrims, seeking a city that is to come. Dickens was never a
man to let such views excuse social inaction, but no reformer
has ever been less utopian than he. *A Tale of Two Cities* reminds
us that the other spur to Dickens's conservative radicalism, fear
of revolution and violence, was equally operative and urgent in
his work.

It is also clear that though his vision of evil had deepened
since *Pickwick*, it was different now in degree, not in kind.
Public cruelty remains here, as in *Barnaby Rudge*, among the
worst symptoms of disorder to be feared. Though his own penal
ideas had grown harsher, and he now supported capital punishment for murderers, he remained implacably opposed to the
public spectacle of death. Public executions and savage penal
laws are the prime sicknesses pointed to in both Paris and
London, and the Terror is seen as a fit, if terrible, punishment
for these. He regarded cruelty as something of a virus infection,
and civilisation as incompatible with cruelty in every form. If he
were alive now, he would undoubtedly mistrust the degree of
visual violence depicted on television, and particularly the
reintroduction of the public spectacle of death.

III

So much is easy to see, but *A Tale of Two Cities* is no simple
tale. Dickens's depiction of virtue is as concrete as ever, and
concentrated here in a beleaguered quintet. Lucie : whose love
and courage brings 'back to life' her father, and the two men
who love her. Charles Darnay : a gentle and strong man, whose
finely sensitive and rational humanity, the fruit of a civilisation
which its other representatives travesty, is so wholly alien in a
revolutionary setting that he is regarded as a traitor both by
the class he renounces and the class he pities, and stands trial
three times for his life. Sydney Carton : the dissolute idealist,
whose will is atrophied, so that residual virtue can lead only,
in his own view of things, to despair. Manette : the central
figure in the drama of vengeance, victim first of the Old Régime

and then of the New. And Mr Lorry: a true-hearted, valiant old man, less idiosyncratic than Wemmick or Grewgious, who does his duty quietly and firmly, and with more heart than his profession properly speaking encourages, and lives honourably on to a great old age.

To list these five is to sense an almost musical structure, as they interweave like variations, astonishingly inverted sometimes, on a theme. 'Back to life': this is the novel's motto in Mr Lorry's uneasy dozing, as he lurches on his way to Dover at the start.

> 'Buried how long?'
> The answer was always the same: 'Almost eighteen years.'
> 'You had abandoned all hope of being dug out?'
> 'Long ago.'
> 'You know that you are recalled to life?'
> 'They tell me so.'
> 'I hope you care to live?'
> 'I can't say.'

This austere and eerie dialogue circles its way into the upper hemisphere of the book. Again and again we seem to hear echoes of it, now ironic, now poignant, as the leading characters follow their destiny. 'You know that you are recalled to life?' 'They tell me so.' 'I hope you care to live?' During the Terror, Dickens notes how some people rush upon their death, almost with pleasure. 'In seasons of pestilence, some of us will have a secret attraction to the disease – a terrible passing inclination to die of it.' Is this true of Manette or Darnay? No: they do care to live, it seems, though the question cannot fail to hover above their lives. Is it true of Carton? He goes to his death unnecessarily, yet death is the one affirmation of life left open to him. The famous last words – thoughts Carton *might* have had if gifted with prophesy – are triumphant; and the greatest of all the texts of Christian hope – that text which by an odd coincidence Dickens was to write again into a novel, on the last day of his own life – rings through his mind: 'I am the Resurrection and the Life . . . He that believeth in me, though he were dead, yet shall he live: and whosoever liveth and believeth in me shall never die.'

In Carton, then, the choice of death is not a death-wish, but something like its reverse, though the choice itself seems founded on despair. Darnay's apparent choice of death is much simpler. After his recall to life at the Old Bailey and his happy marriage, he returns to France only in the spirit of a soldier going to battle. He chooses life, but this includes duty; and his duty, it seems, is to die. Manette, of course, is the theme itself rather than a variation; his recall is the most difficult and costly of them all. Yet despite his wounds, he returns to life fully, and it seems that this must be his inner choice.

My more detailed comments will stem from these simple observations; but it must be observed how omnipresent the theme is. In his usual fashion, Dickens rings grotesque variants on it in his comedy: Mr Cruncher's gruesome night-life as a Resurrection Man, Miss Pross's unexpected encounter with her lost Solomon, Cly's reappearance after his turbulent burial. In a dozen references the dead come back, or the living shuttle ghost-like between two worlds:

Far and wide lay a ruined country, yielding nothing but desolation. Every green leaf, every blade of grass and blade of grain, was as shrivelled and poor as the miserable people. Everything was bowed down, dejected, oppressed, and broken. Habitations, fences, domesticated animals, men, women, children, and the soil that bore them – all worn out.

IV

This desolate land is France under the Monseigneur, awaiting its baptism of blood. It is also, imagistically, Sydney Carton, who seems oddly akin to the wasted spirit of France:

Waste forces within him, and a desert all around, this man stood still on his way across a silent terrace, and saw for a moment, lying in the wilderness before him, a mirage of honourable ambition, self-denial and perseverance. In the fair city of this vision, there were airy galleries from which the loves and graces looked down on him, gardens in which the fruits of life hung ripening, waters of Hope that sparkled in his sight. A moment, and it was gone.

Carton suffers less danger, less cruel treatment at the hands of his fellow men, than Manette or Darnay, but he lacks their strong will to live. Until he meets Lucie, he suffers less than they do emotionally, lacking the power of commitment to duty and loyalty which gives unselfish meaning to life and death. He is somewhat akin to the whisky-priest in *The Power and the Glory*, and would be more at home than any other Dickens character in Greeneland (though he does not appear in Dickens's world, of course, in Greene's Catholic terms). As libertine, he resembles a number of Dickens's most interesting bachelors – Steerforth, Harthouse, Eugene Wrayburn – but is curiously disqualified from any satisfaction in his sins. Like Steerforth he has talent, promise, charm, good-looks, all squandered, but he lacks whatever it is in Steerforth that half-compensates for the desolation within. His way of life is more dissolute than Steerforth's, more akin, therefore, to Harthouse's, but he is not equipped for Harthouse's measure of success. Both his virtues and his vices conspire against him. He is too idealistic to settle for cynical depravity, yet lacks the will to cultivate hedonic ease and an urbane façade. He differs also, of course, from Eugene Wrayburn, whose boredom disguises steady determination and alert intelligence, and who has the self-respect and discipline required for amendment when he finds it worthwhile.

Carton is tormented beyond any of these with a sense of unredeemable depravity, as though abandoned to damnation in a Jansenist or a Manichaean world. The combination of high idealism and eroded willpower is the key to his dilemma, a classic formula for unhappiness in life. What does his depravity actually consist in? There must be more to it than sitting up all night preparing Stryver's briefs for him, with steaming towels round his head and continual refreshments of punch and port (a bad mixture, though Stryver stands up to it without steaming towels). Presumably Carton lives promiscuously and this is the source of his anxieties. It would be in keeping with the idealisation of Lucie which spurs his self-contempt beyond his ambition, and with his consciousness of being utterly unfitted to make her happy in life. Dickens's reticence, however 'Victorian', at least allows each reader to supply convincing depravities, and so to apprehend the psychological torment of Carton's trap. There remains an enigma, however, in his fatalism. Is it frank and accurate self-knowledge, or the crowning sin of despair? Carton makes no real effort to cure himself, and fatalism may be merely a rationalisation for depleted will. But it could also be a courageous tribute from impurity to purity over the barren and irrevocable ruins of self. Either possibility would ring true psychologically.

As usual, Dickens's portrait impresses chiefly by its truthfulness, which includes the teasing ambiguities which we hardly expect to solve about such a person in 'life'. Carton blames his 'luck', and announces himself to Darnay as a malcontent: 'I am a disappointed drudge, sir. I care for no man on earth, and no man on earth cares for me.' Other late Dickens characters who complain in similar terms are Bradley Headstone and John Jasper, but whatever his sins Carton does not belong with these. Unlike most malcontents, in fact, he blames not society but himself for his misfortunes. His anger with Darnay is in no sense personal; it is merely that Darnay cannot help mocking him with the image of loss.

What is indisputable is that Carton does not settle for hatred or bitterness, but submits to death in homage to his ideal. In this he achieves also the one consummation with Lucie left to him, becoming her *Doppelgänger* bridegroom indissolubly as his head falls. He perceives, of course, that he has no other way of winning her. Since his uncorrupted image alone can bring her happiness, his personal role must lie on the negative side. Though he loves her as deeply and tenderly as Darnay – he is sure of this, at least – in no normal sense is he a rival for her love. Dickens's clairvoyance in these odd byways is conveyed through brilliant touches. It is surely right that when in the hour of death Carton's temptations are over, he can at last possess the self he has otherwise lost. In becoming to the little seamstress who dies alongside him all that Darnay could have been to her, he becomes too, for the one possible moment, the man he acts. The possibility – never to be wholly exorcised in such a situation – of something profoundly morbid in Carton's vicarious substitution is balanced, then, by a healthy triumph of morality and tone. It is a triumph of life through death, the most paradoxical variation on the motto theme: 'You know that you are recalled to life?' 'They tell me so.' 'I hope you care to live?'

v

Darnay's recall to life is more orthodox. His sufferings originate wholly in a disordered society, and neither arise from nor reflect disorders within. Just as Carton's consciousness images the desolation of both Old Régime and Terror, so Darnay's images all that is gentle and civilised, exiled and persecuted in his political world. In this aspect, it is profoundly hopeful that Carton should die to give life to Darnay, a promise beyond their individual destinies to the values they share.

The central figure of the novel is, however, Manette, one of the most masterly fusions of psychological insight and symbolism in Dickens's work. The prime instance of 'recall to life', he is recalled successfully, and lives on to honoured old age. The recall is not easy, and not without inevitable regressions under strain. 'He was now a very energetic man indeed' (this a few years after his rescue, but before further trials) 'with great firmness of purpose, strength of resolution, and vigour of action.' Salvation comes from within and without. Reduced to premature senility by his sufferings, he would be lost without Lucie's loving companionship. He depends upon her wholly for his first steps back to life. But alone among Dickens's fathers in this position, he does not abuse it; salvation comes also and equally from the will to survive. He is able to resign Lucie to the man she chooses as husband, even though this turns out to be the one man in the world most calculated to stir his fears. His words to Lucie are – among other things – an insight glancing back to *Little Dorrit*:

'Consider how natural, and how plain it is, my dear, that it should be so. You, devoted and young, cannot fully appreciate the anxiety I have felt that your life should not be wasted – '

She moved her hand towards his lips, but he took it in his, and repeated the word.

' – wasted, my child – should not be wasted, struck aside from the natural order of things – for my sake.'

The shoemaker's bench is one of Dickens's most interesting accounts of a natural life-instinct asserting itself against the heaviest odds. Manette's reversions to it are occasioned only by very particular reminders of his sufferings, and it is his fate to have these old associations outrageously renewed. Why, after his first recovery, does he keep the bench? Mr Lorry is rebuked by Miss Pross for wondering this, but Mr Lorry still feels that keeping it may be a mistake. After the ten-day relapse, occasioned by Darnay's conversation with him on Lucie's wedding morning, Manette discusses himself with Mr Lorry, in a remarkable scene. By tacit agreement they discuss his symptoms in the third person, and Manette, analysing his own condition in the role of doctor, as though some entirely different person were in question, exemplifies a fine triumph of the rational over the irrational mind. He expresses very clearly the place of the shoemaking in his own survival:

'You see,' said Doctor Manette, turning to him after an uneasy pause, 'it is very hard to explain, consistently, the innermost workings of this poor man's mind. He once yearned so frightfully for that occupation, and it was so welcome when it came; no doubt it relieved his pain so much, by substituting the perplexity of the fingers for the perplexity of the brain, and by substituting, as he became more practised, the ingenuity of the hands, for the ingenuity of the mental torture; that he has never been able to bear the thought of putting it quite out of his reach. Even now, when I believe he is more hopeful of himself than he has ever been, and even speaks of himself with a kind of confidence, the idea that he might need that old employment, and not find it, gives him a sudden sense of terror, like that which one may fancy strikes to the heart of a lost child.'

This reasoning is lucid, and because lucid optimistic; it has its own healing power. Manette has clung to reason even in his grimmest days, seeking escape from suffering not in drugs or defeatism (the contrast with Carton's alcoholism is inescapable), but in creative release for his tortured mind. The shoemaking is his salvation, and when he later breaks down he instinctively reverts to it, as to a lifeline in the most literal sense. The occupation is mental crutches for a cripple bent on recovery; yet Lorry still feels that at a certain stage in the recovery the crutches should be cast aside. Though Manette cannot quite bring himself to do this, he agrees medically with Mr Lorry's reasoning, and authorises it to be done on his behalf. The scene of the destruction is remarkably authentic. Though Lorry and Miss Pross are affirming Manette's strength, there is an element of risk, and what they destroy has been infinitely precious in his life. As they go about their task, they look and feel almost like murderers: 'So wicked do destruction and secrecy appear to honest minds, that Mr Lorry and Miss Pross, while engaged in the commission of their deed and in the removal of its traces, almost felt, and almost looked, like accomplices in a horrible crime.'

The ensuing twists of Manette's destiny make him increasingly central to the book. During the Terror he takes on symbolic status for the Republicans, and his previous sufferings qualify him at this horrible moment for unique power. As he senses his role as Darnay's saviour, his sufferings seem to him justified, and he recovers self-confidence, even pride, to a new degree. He becomes happy, and in one touching moment of arrogance reverts with Lucie to the normal role of father protecting a helpless child. This phenomenon strikes Mr Lorry as odd, but healthy: ' "All curious to see", thought Mr Lorry, in his amiably shrewd way, "but all natural and right." ' And indeed it is, since it represents a moral victory the full extent of which we only later grasp. It is not pride of place in the Republic that gives Manette his new confidence, but gladness that he, and he alone, can save Darnay's life. In the Bastille, after ten years of imprisonment, he had succumbed to near despair, and denounced Darnay in a secret document to the vengeance of God and of man. Darnay's sin was his name, the sin of the fathers; in anguish Manette had wished the very name of Evrémonde to perish on earth. Now, many years later, his humanity recovered, his old sin of bitterness is also erased. Darnay is a real person to him, a beloved son-in-law, not a symbol of suffering from the past. The moral victory is costly

H

and decisive. Though Manette's irrational self still panics at the
name Evrémonde, his life is no longer passed under its cloud.
In achieving the high Christian law of forgiveness, he has found
it the law also of restoration and peace.

The contrast between Manette and his society could scarcely
be sharper, and it carries the main moral weight of the tale.
Manette's forgiveness is at an equal remove from the Monseigneur and from Madame Defarge, as they reflect one another
in the savage mirror of their lives. That the sins of the fathers
should be visited on the children is one conviction linking the
Old Régime and the New. Manette's transformation of Charles
Darnay from an object of instinctive dread and aversion to a
beloved and respected son-in-law is an opposing enchantment
to all that surrounds his life. It contrasts with the Monseigneur's
reduction of men to vermin. It contrasts with Madame Defarge's
reduction of men to heads.

VI

Manette wins this great victory, but his most ironic test is still
to come. Just as his original letter denouncing the Evrémondes
recoiled upon him in the ordeal of imprisonment, so the secret
document written in prison becomes the leading accuser of
Darnay after all. No wonder he reverts again under this blow
to near madness; it is altogether too much to bear. But nothing
could more concretely dramatise the inner meaning of the
Terror, corruption breeding corruption, cruelty breeding
cruelty, death breeding death. For all the republican talk of
liberty, equality, justice, Madame Defarge values Manette only
as an occasion for hate. By making him Darnay's chief accuser
she directs the moment of extreme weakness to which he had
once been reduced by their common enemies *against* the love
and sanity to which he had later returned. 'You know that you
are recalled to life?' 'They tell me so.' 'I hope you care to live?'
The word 'life' in Dickens is never left vague; *this* is the test,
for Madame Defarge as for Manette himself. Vital and strong
in her energy, fanatic in willpower, she is devoted utterly
to hatred and death. In her grisly conversation with The

Vengeance, Jacques Three and the wood-sawyer after Darnay's sensational condemnation, it is agreed that Lucie and her child should be sacrificed to La Guillotine – the child for aesthetic reasons partly – and that Manette himself is not to be spared. Why should Madame Defarge spare him, she wonders? Her husband would wish it, but this is his weakness; her husband is not after all as strong as she. And far in the past, Manette has championed her family against the Evrémondes and lost his liberty; but what is that to her? The fire which Manette saw flashing out long before in her dying brother is indeed become a consuming power. By now, La Guillotine herself has taken over. With his role as symbol suitably concluded, Manette's chief usefulness to the Revolution is now as another head.

VII

The tale is dramatised then not satirically, like Orwell's similar tract for the times *Animal Farm*, but in richly human terms. When writing of *Bleak House*, I remarked on this : that the girl who for her godmother is a misfortune, for her mother a guilty secret, for Tulkinghorn a handle for torture, exists also in the book as a centre of sanity and health. Much the same contrast works in this book, though in its own very different terms. In Manette, Darnay, Lucie, Carton, Mr Lorry – nor should Miss Pross be forgotten – we have the flesh-and-blood beyond the vermin and the heads. At the end of the tale, the final scene commences as follows : 'As The Vengeance descends from her elevation . . . the tumbrils begin to discharge their loads. The ministers of Sainte Guillotine are robed and ready. Crash! – a head is held up, and the knitting-women, who scarcely lifted their eyes to look at it a moment ago when it could think and speak, count One.' Nor did they lift their eyes a few minutes later – but the novel has made us lift ours – when Darnay/ Carton arrives for the ceremony. The last word of the Terror – though Dickens goes on to give us the prophetic and triumphant epilogue – is simple and characteristic : 'Twenty-three.'

11 *Great Expectations*
the immolations of Pip

'It was much on my mind that I ought to tell Joe the whole truth. Yet I did not, and for the reason that I mistrusted that if I did, he would think me worse than I was.' This was Pip's reason for concealing the traumatic incident of his childhood even from Joe. A child's fear, but a sound instinct, since Joe, although saintly, is not very bright.

Pip is naturally less reticent with his readers, yet these have sometimes condemned him in close accord with his childhood fears. All literature is a tempting occasion for cant and humbug, but as a catalyst for these qualities Pip stands almost alone. It is as if Dickens had succumbed, improbably enough, to some Jamesian teasing of his readers, and designed *Great Expectations* as a rare trap. If I am right – and a critic sensing traps cannot ignore the possibility of boomerangs – the trap is to read the novel so exclusively as a social account of Pip's snobbery, that the altogether unusual features surrounding and altering this are scarcely seen. It is said, for instance, that the novel concerns Pip's corruption by good fortune, and his belated redemption by a proper act of love. As, of course, it does; yet abstracted from the novel and heavily moralised over, this is surely false to the total effect. It is not even as though we were first with the discovery. Pip's capacity for self-accusation is developed to the verge of morbidity, as Mrs Joe has lovingly trained it to be. His circumstances, moreover, are highly unusual, and we might ponder what kind of boy could be expected to respond impeccably to Mrs Joe, Pumblechook and Wopsle, let alone Magwitch, Miss Havisham, Estella, and Pip's curious fate. These implications will be explored in what follows, but I start with a general summary of my view. To read *Great Expectations* as a moral *exemplum* concerned chiefly with snobbery is to disperse its rich concreteness into abstraction too readily, too unimaginatively, and too soon.

II

In chapter 27 Joe makes his first visit to Pip's new London chambers, and Pip is not at his best. He loves and admires Joe, but dreads his visit; a shameful and uncomfortable frame of mind. His particular fear is that Bentley Drummle will bump into Joe and be amused by him, a disgrace which Pip's precarious aspirations to gentility might not survive. The meanness of this is so tormentingly clear to Pip, that he exposes it with classic clarity himself: ' . . . so throughout our life our worst weaknesses and meannesses are usually committed for the sake of people whom we most despise'. But this knowledge, which only someone far less sensitive than Pip could escape from, does not make for greater ease when the moment comes. The very sound of Joe's footsteps on the stairs (later he will hear other footsteps mounting) is dismaying. 'I knew it was Joe by his clumsy manner of coming upstairs – his state boots were always too big for him.' From before its start the reunion is a disaster and, characteristically, Pip sees all the blame as his own. Yet Joe's extreme awkwardness and gaucherie helps neither of them; nor does Joe's saintly understanding and self-accusation at the end. How can Pip fail to feel Joe's noble words as coals of fire heaped on him, even if they are entirely without reproach? How can he fail to make resolutions to see Joe more often in future, to be kinder to him, while dismally knowing he will do no such things?

These mishaps are the stuff of everyday life, not of high drama, and it would take a rarefied reader to expect them easily solved. Which of us has not been ashamed of parents and loved ones if only in schooldays, and heartily wished them elsewhere? Which of us has completely escaped the guilt of growing away from family and home background, even in the common and irreducible form of growing up? When the process is accompanied, however, by different and better interests in life, different and better worldly prospects, the tension is bound to be great. When it is further accompanied by consciousness of

simplicity and virtue in parent or guardian not to be equalled or
successfully emulated, much self-accusation is certain to arise.

Though Pip's ingratitude to Mrs Joe does not greatly bother
him, he is much tormented by his ingratitude to Joe. But what
should he do to relieve it? Should he solve matters by staying on
at the forge despite his good fortune, and abandoning all desire
to get on in life? This course is urged on him by Biddy and
is certainly tempting, since it would bring immediate, if not
lasting, peace of mind. There would be the consolation of Joe's
happy face and Biddy's approval; and of the thought that he had
not, after all, succumbed to Estella's contempt. Much of the
condemnation of Pip's snobbery seems to imply the rightness
of some such solution, but can this really be what the novel says?
Pip is no Tom Pinch or Tim Linkinwater; nor was Dickens,
who to some degree identifies himself with Pip. He cannot know
his place humbly, despise opportunity, retreat to a backwater;
he has to embrace good fortune, with all its risks. It falls to us
as readers, then, to follow him imaginatively in his destiny. And
this requires more than an easy endorsement of misgivings and
fears.

There is an important further strand to be discerned in Pip's
temperament before we plunge into the troubled moral waters
of the book. This concerns his early upbringing, and its indelible
imprint for ill on his later life. Mrs Joe has 'brought him up by
hand' with such extreme insensitivity that he is almost a text-
book occasion for repression and neurotic guilt. She has even
ganged up with other silly and insensitive adults like Pumblechook and Wopsle to cultivate guilt in him about existing at all.
He hears that he has been saved from the churchyard by Mrs
Joe's munificence, and that she would 'never do it again!' At
Christmas the reminders of unworthiness are intensified; he has
to survive his sister, Wopsle and the preposterous Pumblechook, as well as the convict who terrorises him on his father's
grave. Like many other Dickens characters, in fact, he has a
blighted childhood, and carries the scars irrevocably through
life. Even Esther Summerson is crippled, despite her heroic
virtue, while Arthur Clennam has abandoned all hope of love
or happiness in life. Pip is in some ways more 'normal' than

Esther and Arthur – less virtuous than the one, less morbidly crushed and introspective than the other – and his situation is less spectacular than theirs. Whereas Esther's godmother, and Mrs Clennam, blight their respective charges with religious severity, Mrs Joe is a more humble and usual example of human sin. Yet this does not make Pip's situation notably easier. On the contrary, he is made to feel that the blight is not even at one degree removed from him through the sins of fathers, but fairly and squarely his own.

It is precisely here that Joe fails Pip, despite his virtue. Even if Joe can alleviate Pip's sense of being totally unloved and isolated, he is powerless to prevent Mrs Joe's violation of the home. Pip values Joe's love, simplicity and physical courage, but knows that Joe cannot be depended upon for long-term help. Joe himself is a child in the young Pip's view of him, and the boy's intuition is not far from the truth. Joe is more child than husband to Mrs Joe certainly, since he cannot stand up success-fully to what he knows to be wrong. 'Lookee here, old chap,' he tells Pip much later, in Pip's serious illness,

'I done what I could to keep you and Tickler in sunders, but my power were not always fully equal to my inclinations. For when your poor sister had a mind to drop into you, it were not so much,' said Joe, in his favourite argumentative way, 'that she dropped into me too, if I put myself in opposition to her but that she dropped into you always heavier for it. I noticed that. . . .'

But Joe also failed in a more serious way, that he does not know about; though he could conspire reassuringly with the young Pip as fellow-child when Mrs Joe was on the rampage, he could never enter Pip's private world of need and guilt. And he was far too innocent even to be a good conspirator, all too often be-traying Pip to Mrs Joe by awkward hints. When Pip was confronted with the truly awful secret of the marshes, Joe was no use at all. Consciously, Pip was afraid of shocking him and losing his affection; less consciously, he must also have feared to be let down.

All of this the mature Pip naturally cannot write up to the credit side of his childhood. To do so would be to betray Joe further, and in leaving home he has already betrayed Joe enough.

Possibly he never reflects consciously on Joe's inadequacy, though the evidence is presented clearly enough for a reader of the tale. There is great poignancy indeed in Pip's personal sense of the dilemma : 'It was a most miserable thing to feel ashamed of home.'

The interest in this aspect of Pip's situation is its comparative normality. Miss Havisham, Magwitch, Estella are highly unusual people, but we do not have to search far for a Mrs Joe. Her cruelty to Pip with Tickler, and her more important mental cruelty, are common enough in the world. She is not an evil woman, merely a somewhat more than average bad one, shrewish, unimaginative, self-centred, unappreciative of Joe and of such good things as life has brought her, unwilling to offer more than sourness back to life. She enjoys martyrdom only a shade less theatrically than Mrs Wilfer, and is equally willing to sacrifice to it her husband and Pip. It is thoroughly in keeping that she should inculcate in Pip both morbid introspection – whatever he does is wrong and selfish by definition – and a morbid obligation of gratitude to herself. We are not surprised to find her begrudging answers to Pip's childish questions, and resenting the first halting steps in literacy of Pip and Joe. She mistrusts education because it might help Pip to escape from her, a trait typical (Gaffer Hexam is a fuller study of it) in many bad working-class homes.

From such an upbringing it would be strange for any boy to emerge unmarked; but Pip is to be further demoralised by his peculiar fate. He is destined to fall in love with precisely the woman educated to continue Mrs Joe's brand of contempt for his manhood, and to be taken up by the one benefactor in the world most certain to accentuate guilt feelings to Joe (by appearing in the role of second father) and to flood his whole being, through memories of the traumatic childhood encounter, with aversion and fear. The data of the novel go far beyond some average drama of snobbery, and Pip's various records of anguish ('In a word, I was too cowardly to avoid doing what I knew to be right, as I have been too cowardly to avoid doing what I knew to be wrong . . .') require correspondingly more of us than a self-righteous nod.

There is a further reason why Pip's situation might expect sympathy from a modern reader. Not only is the mechanism of guilt better understood since Freud than it was by many Victorians, but the actual terms of Pip's conflict are far more familiar now than they used to be. In the late 1850s, when the novel was written (its setting is of course earlier), few boys in Pip's station would have either had his chances, or known the kinds of anguish involved. Forster's Education Act (1870) was still in the future, and even then would have been of little help to a boy like Pip. Pip's educational opportunities were restricted to Mr Wopsle's great-aunt's Dame School, which opened no glittering prospects to the son of a forge. Even Hardy's Jude, created in the 1890s, has no true hope of bettering himself, and for Pip there would be no escape from home by this route. His escape rather is by way of a most unusual benefaction, 'great expectations' from an unknown and therefore exotic source. The possibility must have been common in the 1850s only in daydream, and remote enough for Pip to present to his first readers, and indeed to most of his readers for the next half-century or more, a highly original and entertaining case.

Today, when we order things differently, a boy of Pip's ability would be plunged into something like his situation as by right. Grammar or comprehensive school, followed by university; then respectability, and a professional job. Except that our modern offer of great expectations carries no secret obligations, Pip's situation is a common one with us. But have the patterns of tensions changed all that much since *Great Expectations*? It must be particularly familiar to many of Pip's undergraduate critics, this iniquity of having more interests than the folk at home, more money and prospects, different friends. For every student whose home is fully attuned to the situation there is possibly another whose difficulties oppress his heart and life. How many students in whom guilt has been planted and watered by a latter-day Mrs Joe do better than Pip – avoiding misunderstandings, rebukes, high melodrama, escaping the relentless accuser within? Yet social conditions are on the side of a student in our own time just as certainly as in the early nineteenth century they were against Pip. How many modern

students indeed are wholly unfamiliar with Pip's further temptations, when under very great stress and then serious illness he
regresses, at the end, to the forge?

III

Joe's visit to Pip is a social disaster, whoever we blame for it;
Magwitch's visit nearly drives him out of his mind. Chapter 39
of *Great Expectations*, one of Dickens's greatest pieces of
writing, is a terrible discovery and reversal for Pip. It comes,
like Edwin Drood's disappearance later, on a night of exceptional wind and storm. There are few scenes in literature more
ineffaceable than the picture of Pip working in his high chamber
on this dire night, and his first intimation of a visitor on the
stair.

To describe Pip's shame for Joe as 'snobbish' is true, if oversimplified : to describe his aversion to Magwitch in such terms
is surely untrue. The point needs making, since hypocrisy takes
various forms in various ages, and the hypocrisy of middle-class
progressive radicalism is virulent today. Fewer Pecksniffs and
Podsnaps there may be, but Dickens would recognise their
successors if he were here. I have in mind the kind of progressive
radical who assumes that because love for one's fellows is
desirable it is also normative, and who feels himself free to
stigmatise all efforts of realism on this matter as 'fascism',
reaction or sheer lack of concern. His attitude to opponents is one
of contempt and amazement, perhaps because he holds them guilty
of so many crimes. Everyone is guilty of the world's crimes
except their actual perpetrators; everyone is guilty of the latest
sensational murder except the murderer himself. Every criminal, indeed, is 'our' responsibility, by the remarkable law which
removes responsibility for evils from the people enacting them
to Society (progressive radicals somewhat naturally excepted)
at large. For readers holding such views, Pip's aversion to
Magwitch is self-evidently blameworthy, and his recovery from
it a lesson too belatedly learned.

For smugness and lack of imagination our current progressive
radicalism is unbeatable, an excellent match for Podsnap's

Podsnappery in its day. And such opinions are seldom more depressing than when there is a grain of truth in them, since the process of reasoning is so despicably wrong. Naturally Pip *is* right to help Magwitch, and exemplary to love him; but this is heroic virtue – a great triumph of will over instinctive loathing – and nothing like belated recovery from a contemptible mistake.

The whole area of Pip's relationship to Magwitch was, of course, a personally sensitive one for Dickens, for more reasons than one. In the blacking factory at the age of twelve he had shuddered away from vulgar small boys, and it was the boy who showed him the most personal kindness whose name was later bestowed on Fagin in *Oliver Twist*. We can readily believe that much of Dickens's later championing of Kit Nubbles, Tom Pinch and their like was a lesson intended, as much for himself as for his readers, on the sacredness and frequent moral superiority of the virtuous poor. Yet Dickens was nothing like these grotesque figures he celebrated, and he spent his life escaping from their world. From the first, moreover, he was ruthless to men of criminality and violence. As he grew older, his belief in punishment and deterrence increased.

Magwitch is created, therefore, in a most sensitive area for Dickens, a criminal violent and horrible enough for us to shudder away from, yet with unusual simplicity and generosity of heart. Even if Pip had been free of childhood memories, his aversion to Magwitch would be understandable. But given the whole story – the traumatic associations; the sudden overthrow of every hope Pip has been building, not least of Estella; the uncouthness of Magwitch's person, and the strange obsessions which have led him to entwine himself so ruinously in the young Pip's life – there is in this enough, and more than enough, to overthrow Pip, at least for a period, as a rational man.

There are, of course, further ironic items in Magwitch's epiphany, notably the idea of a 'gentleman' which conditions the delusions he has built. This links us back, rudely enough, with Pip's snobbery, but is not an easy stick for detractors to use. What was a 'gentleman'? Dickens quarrelled often enough with

the idea in his novels, perhaps because he had never been fully
accepted as one himself. Urbanity is usually shown as a façade
for cold self-centredness – bad enough in Chester or Gowan,
worse in Rigaud – and as the mode in which such men impose
themselves on a credulous world. Again, it is often presented
as a superficial veneer bought by money and accepted by money
in a world where the gentleman is no longer chiefly, even, a
creature of birth. Wealth has won a battle over breeding: and
if it turns out that Chester, Gowan, the Veneerings and Lammles
are not really moneyed after all but are merely impostors, this
is simply a further refinement of the joke. Dickens sees the poison of such falsely upper-class urbanity spilling over into the
large world of gentility and genteel pretension just beneath. His
perception is that gentility has its own kind of vulgarity to
match against Magwitch's. From the Kenwigs, Mrs Nickleby,
Mrs Snagsby, Mrs Wilfer (a wide spectrum with a great many
women), there is a descent to still more shaming and unbearable
levels – the deportment of William Dorrit, for instance, in his
long ordeal.

Against so many instances of perverted gentility we find also
in all his novels, and particularly the later ones, a pressure to
wrest the word 'gentleman' away from a class description and
refurbish it acceptably as a moral ideal. Herbert Pocket's father
believes that 'no man who was not a true gentleman at heart ever
was, since the world began, a true gentleman in manner', and
this is clearly endorsed by the novel's tone. This notion of the
'true gentleman' would (of course) make Tom Pinch a 'truer'
gentleman than Pecksniff, and would force even Sir Leicester
Dedlock to earn the title by behaviour (as he does) as well as by
birth. If we are prepared to accept it, the discrepancies between
snobbery and true virtue are sharply pointed, and satire has a
ready instrument to hand.

Joe, then, is a 'better' gentleman than Pip – as Lizzie Hexam
is a better lady than old Tippins – and if we take this point, as
we are expected to, Magwitch's whole enterprise of making a
gentleman with money, owning him, showing him off proudly
in the circus of conspicuous consumption becomes a just, if
horrifying, mirror to debased ideals. The shock to Pip could

hardly be more effective, since Magwitch operates by his own, and Estella's, most debased ideals.

Yet even at this obvious level, Dickens strains his terms slightly. The word 'gentleman' has never been accepted in ordinary speech simply as a synonym for 'good and honourable', and there remains a sense in which Chester and Rigaud are truer gentlemen, even in evil parody, than, say, Joe. Joe is a good and kindly man, but not a gentleman; Magwitch is a coarse and dreadful, redeemable and sincere man, but not a gentleman; Pip, after his refurbishing with Magwitch's money, *is* a gentleman, or on his way to becoming one: to this degree Magwitch is right. It is a matter of safeguarding normal language against too much distortion, since certain ideals of social manner and speech, certain kinds of reticence and politeness, certain appearances remain part of the 'gentleman', and no amount of virtue or indeed wealth will quite do instead. In *David Copperfield* there was a strain about Ham's status as a 'true' gentleman. Joe Gargery seems a still more intractable case.

On this matter Dickens succumbed either to slight confusion or to linguistic juggling, but his basic values remain clear. It has always been one of Pip's tormenting pieces of self-knowledge that his gentlemanly aspirations come not from the best but the worst in him: 'Her contempt for me was so strong,' he says of Estella, 'that it became infectious, and I caught it.' His hatred of vulgarity and criminality, which derives largely from his childish fright on the marshes, turns to self-abasement before an idealised Estella from the first. When Miss Havisham sends Estella to be educated as a 'lady', the gulf between them fills him with despair. It is torture to be shown Newgate by the friendly Wemmick just when Estella is due to meet him; he cannot bear to think of her tainted even at one remove. All the more certain that when Pip does at length discover the true nature of his expectations, his sharpest pain is for Estella, and the impossibility of his even thinking of her now, across the gulf. Dickens's own purpose, of course, is to pose other sharp realities against Pip's anxieties: the man who creates himself as Pip's second father is Estella's real father; Estella's mother is a criminal more violent and lost than Magwitch himself. This strange whirligig involves the further scrutiny of the sources of money; in what sense can Magwitch's money, earned honestly and independently and in a process of self-rehabilitation, be more shameful than Miss Havisham's inherited and sterile wealth?

My chief concern is to suggest that Dickens's story is no simple *exemplum*, even if we see it chiefly in social terms. But Magwitch is no abstract embodiment of satiric concepts; he is a most complex, unusual and touching man. When we consider his project for Pip in relation to his own needs and hopes in life, it is hard to know what moral bearings to take. Are we to approve of it, as an honourable means of his own redemption? Or to condemn it, as a violation of Pip? Or is it to be regarded as an aspect of delusion, and so beyond moral appraisal of a normal kind? It starts in Magwitch's misreading of the young Pip's fear of him as pity, from the minimal evidence that Pip and Joe have not exulted in his arrest. Or did the misreading establish itself even earlier, at the first moment of their encounter? – perhaps because Magwitch desperately wanted to escape from the consciousness of terrifying a child deliberately, or from his more chronic consciousness of being abhorred and unloved. At some stage, anyway, he has persuaded himself that the episode has the same kind of reality for Pip that it has for him, and he has made a myth of it at the centre of his life.

In this aspect it seems hard to censure Magwitch, and easy to discern the seeds of good. When he at last renounces criminality for the great Victorian virtues of hard work, self-help, thrift and successful capitalism, he does this unselfishly, thinking only of Pip. It is true of course that even for Magwitch this is only part of the story; gratitude to Pip is balanced by a plot for social revenge. Magwitch knows that he is not himself a gentleman, by any stretch of imagination, but he believes that money can buy a successful gentleman in his stead. The world which has judged him and found him wanting will, then, be duly confounded by a gentleman created *ex nihilo* by Magwitch, yet fully up to the standards prescribed by itself.

In this devious plot, what if anything can be said for Magwitch, who so disastrously usurps Joe's place as second father to Pip? The small Pip had confided to him the loss of his father – indeed, Pip was attacked on his father's tombstone – so Magwitch at least knows, or thinks he knows, Pip's parental void. Further, he persuades himself that his undertaking is wholly unselfish; he chooses for his adopted son not some new name, as Betsey Trotwood had done for David, but the name 'Pip' that the child had given to himself. Here is an almost humble sense of Pip's identity, which Magwitch will respect, consciously at least, at every turn. There is the further sense that in giving Pip money and status he is rescuing him from his own former predicament, and giving the boy a unique chance of freedom and happiness in life. It must be admitted also that, misreading the young Pip's fear as pity, Magwitch has at least responded to pity with love instead of hate. His project compares not unfavourably with Miss Havisham's plans for Estella. Both adopt a child, and offer education, the one for making a lady, the other a gentleman, after the way of the world. Both are genuinely concerned for the child – in her way Miss Havisham loves Estella – and both use the child in a personal and delusional dream of revenge. But whereas Miss Havisham's 'revenge' is born of hatred, Magwitch's comes from a comparatively innocent pride. Estella is to provide for Miss Havisham the spectacle of males in agony; Pip is merely to charm himself, and society, and so to justify Magwitch's ruined life. The consciousness of for once in his life doing good sustains Magwitch, and helped along with oaths sworn on his pocket Bible, he achieves that most unusual thing in Dickens's novels or, indeed, in life as we know it, a genuine conversion from criminality in his middle age.

At root, it seems, Magwitch has always been decent; and it is part of Dickens's greatness to demonstrate just the psychological spur required to change him to the extent that we see. Yet it hardly needs adding that Magwitch's plan, in the aspects hidden from him, is a terrible violation of Pip, and at exactly that precious point – Pip's identity – which Magwitch thinks he respects. Pip is used as a thing in Magwitch's own strange fight for salvation, and from any perspective outside Magwitch the terrible consequences cry aloud to be seen. But it is of a piece with the delusional mentality that Magwitch cannot see from any other angle; and, moreover, that despite the stringent condition of secrecy laid upon Pip about his benefactor, he is privately convinced that Pip 'must know'. If it is so central to Magwitch's life, how can it be less so to Pip's? The boy will naturally and joyfully have detected his second father from the first.

Dickens nowhere makes these implications explicit, but embodies them in vividly brilliant scenes. They are unmistakeable in Magwitch's manner of revealing himself, and in the tone of affectionate ownership and complicity, unbearable to Pip, which he instinctively adopts. The lesson of Pip's snobbery to Joe, real and painful enough in such a horrible denouement, is one aspect only of a confrontation which Pip's reason barely survives. Little wonder that Pip conceives an almost unconquerable aversion to this man, when even Herbert, unimplicated in Magwitch's wealth (as he fondly believes), shrinks away. Pip's subsequent willingness to detect and honour the goodness in Magwitch's conduct is not a simple recovery from snobbery, but courage of a rare and fine kind. But Pip is dazed by his own misfortunes during this period and enveloped in a nightmare; and when all is finished, he sinks into a fever and almost dies.

IV

What should Pip have done about his great expectations? Before we look at the third of the episodes which are to be examined here, Pip's regression to the forge after his serious illness, the roles of Miss Havisham and Orlick require to be related to his life. Fortunately, Miss Havisham has been excellently discussed by Dorothy Van Ghent in her well-known essay on the novel, which concerns itself more directly than this present reading can find space for with the novel's mythic suggestiveness and power. Satis House is instinct with the atmosphere of folklore and fairytale: in its timelessness, struck still and dark one morning at twenty minutes to nine; in the frozen beauty of Estella; in the ruined wedding feast, where a disappointed bride will be laid out one day for burial; in Miss Havisham's tireless walks through the darkened rooms where the clocks stand still. All these images converge with eerie potency as we see the young Pip leading Miss Havisham in solemn circles round her gruesome feast. Is he the Prince destined to awaken Sleeping Beauty? For unknown purposes, he is encouraged to think so; but we are reminded also of two children trapped, for ogreish purposes, in a witch's house. To see and respond to this is, I think, to discover an important constructional feature of the novel which is by its nature concealed from the narrator, Pip's tribulations from delusional and dangerous minds. From Pip's viewpoint his tale is a linear narrative, his own history and progress, which he relates chronologically and attunes to normality as he goes along. He is indeed a normal enough boy given his abnormal capacity for guilt and self-accusation, and tends to take his destiny, naturally enough, as a matter of course. We follow him along this path, somewhat inside his assessment; yet as the novel unfolds, another pattern, beyond that perceived by Pip, becomes clear. It is as though there were a series of traps poised over Pip, always threatening him, all emanating from highly unbalanced minds. The first and least culpably motivated we have examined, from its origin in Magwitch's first encounter with Pip, to its disastrous epiphany in chapter 39. The second and more consciously malign trap is Miss Havisham's, as she chooses Pip, or Pip is chosen for her, for her revenge. Miss Havisham is an obsessive like Magwitch, but more corrupt and abnormal; she exists at one of the final blind ends in the maze of bitterness and hate. She is the extreme case, however, of a familiar evil, in which Mrs Joe is also implicated, the use of a child for selfish and personal needs. She persuades herself, not wholly implausibly, that she 'loves' Estella, and that indifference to men is cultivated for the girl's own good. The memory of her own sufferings possesses her so completely that she barely sees the reality of the people she harms. Pip rightly diagnoses her wickedness in his last interview with her as lack of imagination, and generously accepts the harm she has done him without answering revenge. It is understandable that she is more totally locked in her self-imposed darkness than Estella or Pip are, and that when at last she sees in Pip the mirror of her own former agony, she repents, without being able to expiate, her crime. The portrait is of a woman near, but not over, the brink of incurable madness. Though cut off from reality, her delusions are pursued with rational, and even grimly humorous, will. There were more women like her in Victorian England (one suspects) than in our own society – rich, bitter, isolated and eccentric, turning life into a grim drama subservient to their wills.

Estella is the product of Satis House, a victim of eccentric education, just as Louisa Gradgrind was victim in Gradgrind's more orthodox school. She is nurtured to be 'unnatural' in the sense now most often given to the word : sexually frigid to men, and repaying their love with contempt. This warping of sexuality seems psychologically possible, and it is a just, if harsh, nemesis for Miss Havisham to discover that her training extends back, from its intended victims, to herself :

'Soon forgotten!' moaned Miss Havisham. 'Times soon forgotten!'
'No, not forgotten,' retorted Estella. 'Not forgotten, but treasured up in my memory. When have you found me false to your teaching? When have you found me unmindful of your lessons? When have you found me giving admission here,' she touched her bosom with her hand, 'to anything that you excluded? Be just to me.'
'So proud, so proud!' moaned Miss Havisham, pushing away her grey hair with both her hands.
'Who taught me to be proud ?' returned Estella. 'Who praised me when I learnt my lesson ?'
'So hard, so hard!' moaned Miss Havisham, with her former action.
'Who taught me to be hard ?' returned Estella. 'Who praised me when I learnt my lesson ?'
'But to be proud and hard to *me*!' Miss Havisham quite shrieked, as she stretched out her arms. 'Estella, Estella, Estella, to be proud and hard to *me*!'

Estella is trained as *belle dame sans merci*, and Pip, who, knowing this, has been unable to believe it, suffers the consequences of his disbelief. Miss Havisham's training and Estella's scorn are after all his portion; he is their victim, their chief victim even, and not a favoured exception as he supposed. It is an aspect of Pip's insensitivity or ignorance that he should delude himself; yet he blames himself as resolutely and uselessly for his infatuation with Estella, even while he suffers it, as he blames himself for his treatment of Joe.

The weight of guilt is his destiny, as the novel's music, brooding and introspective, sad and autumnal, attests. Graham Greene speaks of 'Dickens's secret prose, that sense of a mind speaking to itself with no one there to listen', and again of 'the delicate and exact poetic cadences, the music of memory, that so influenced Proust'. Dickens shares with Shakespeare, and with few other writers, the gift of creating a music peculiar to each masterpiece, and it is this, the rarest and least analysable of literary gifts, that takes us to the heart of the book. *Great Expectations* is not, in its inner vibrations, a comedy of social manners, but the tragedy and triumph of a sensitive, ill-fated man. Pip's incidental cruelties – to Biddy for instance – are surface aspects, but they are not what haunts us in the prose. There, it is the immolations of Pip which we always return to, and the inner worlds of those strange beings who surround and oppress his life.

This, I believe, is why the attempt on Pip's life by Orlick *feels* so inevitable, even though in plot terms it looks almost dragged in. Pip has suffered immolations at the hands of Mrs Joe and Pumblechook, Magwitch, Miss Havisham and Estella; now he suffers a further immolation at the ultimate shore. Behind all the other people who have engulfed him in their dreams and revenges has been one more evil and mad than them all. Orlick traps Pip and renders him helpless, and tells him to prepare for his death. He calls Pip 'wolf' and 'enemy' – terms which Pip has earned almost in passing, with little sense of their festering growth in another mind. Orlick's mad logic plays with extraordinary subtlety on Pip's guilt. Mrs Joe was felled with the leg-iron saw from Magwitch's leg through Pip's complicity, and Pip has always felt obscurely guilty of her death. In telling him that Mrs Joe's death was Pip's murder for which he must now pay the penalty, Orlick plays on his most deep-rooted fears. In a marvellous way the madness of Orlick and the morbidity of Pip lock together, as though here, in Pip's death, is the sudden illumination of his life. Orlick's plans for Pip are extreme and final. 'You was always in old Orlick's way since ever you was a child,' he tells him. 'You goes out of his way, this present night. He'll have no more of you . . . You're dead! . . . More than that . . . I won't have a rag of you, I won't have a bone of you, left on earth.' It is against this that Pip must defend himself and fight for survival. His fight and victory are the moral centre of the tale.

v

The final episode I wish to refer to is that which follows Pip's serious illness, when Joe nurses him back to health, and, his expectations gone, he returns to the old relationship of trusting dependence that he knew as a child. Immediately after this, he comes to a resolution, and sets off back to the forge with 'a settled purpose'.

The purpose was, that I would go back to Biddy, that I would show her how humbled and repentant I came back, that I would tell her how I had lost all I once hoped for, that I would remind her of our old confidences in my first unhappy time. Then, I would say to her, 'Biddy, I think you once liked me very well, when my errant heart, even while it strayed away from you, was quieter and better with you than it ever has been since. If you can like me only half as well once more, if you can take me with all my faults and disappointments on my head, if you can receive me like a forgiven child (and indeed I am as sorry, Biddy, and have as much need of a hushing voice and a soothing hand), I hope I am a little worthier of you than I was – not much, but a little. And, Biddy, it shall rest with you to say whether I shall work at the forge with Joe, or whether I shall try for any different occupation down in this country, or whether we shall go away to a distant place where an opportunity awaits me, which I set aside when it was offered, until I knew your answer. And now, dear Biddy, if you can tell me that you will go through the world with me, you will surely make it a better world for me, and me a better man for it, and I will try hard to make it a better world for you.'

Mercifully, this does not come to anything, since Joe and Biddy have married one another just in time. But what an escape for all three of them! As usual, Dickens shows us precisely how Pip comes to this resolve. Just as his pursuit of gentility was the result, in Pip's guilty assessment, of Estella's contempt for him, so this resolve presents itself as chastened insight and amendment of life. Pip has learned the lesson of snobbery and will return now to the gentler, truer life of earlier times. He scarcely perceives that Biddy presents herself in these tender reflections as a mother, or that the forge beckons with the lure of lost innocence before the Fall.

X   Those who read the novel as Pip's redemption from snobbery might even endorse this decision, as a lesson learned correctly from experience, but sadly too late. It is in tune, certainly, with Joe's simple moral absolutes, and with the position stated earlier by Biddy herself. The temptation to leave well alone! To reconcile oneself to one's station in life : to give up the hope of betterment, with all its suffering, and to carry on the tradition from father to son. Surely this way will avoid *hubris*, and please the gods? – especially the great and jealous god of *status quo* :

> The rich man in his castle,
> The poor man at his gate :
> God made them, high and lowly,
> And order'd their estate.

It is the choice of serenity 'far from the madding crowd's ignoble strife', a quiet life and a quiet death. Who will approve of it, apart from Joe and Biddy? Certainly the 'haves' in a competitive world, who do not like to look back down their ladders and see strangers from Pip's class on the lower rungs. Certainly Mrs Joe – her ghost, or her natural heirs – who will hate to relinquish martyrdom and power. Certainly the voices implanted in Pip and those like him by early upbringing : the voice of guilt, whispering of disloyalty; the voice of fear, telling of unseen dangers and threatened innocence; the voice of apathy, urging the comforts and virtues of staying still. Biddy has said to Pip before he left the forge 'You know best, Pip; but don't you think you are happier as you are?' and there was the following exchange :

'Biddy,' I exclaimed, impatiently, 'I am not at all happy as I

am. I am disgusted with my calling and with my life. I have
never taken to either, since I was bound. Don't be absurd.'

'Was I absurd?' said Biddy, quietly raising her eyebrows;
'I am sorry for that; I didn't mean to be. I only want you to do
well, and to be comfortable.'

'Well then, understand once for all that I never shall or can be
comfortable – or anything but miserable – there, Biddy! –
unless I can lead a very different sort of life from the life I lead
now.'

'That's a pity!' said Biddy, shaking her head with a sorrowful
air.

Now, I too had so often thought it a pity, that, in the singular
kind of quarrel with myself which I was always carrying on, I
was half inclined to shed tears of vexation and distress when
Biddy gave utterance to her sentiment and my own. I told her
she was right, and I knew it was much to be regretted, but still
it was not to be helped.

This prompting to virtue, or temptation, however one sees it,
is likely enough to circle round again. When Pip is shorn of his
expectations and weakened by illness, repentance and amendment can present themselves in such terms. On a simplistic
view of the book, this is Pip 'coming to his senses', and being
suitably punished by coming to them just too late. Immediately
after the conversation just quoted, Pip had gone on to say to
Biddy – it is his worst moment of thoughtless cruelty –

'If I could only get myself to fall in love with you – you don't
mind my speaking so openly to such an old acquaintance?'

'Oh dear, not at all!' said Biddy. 'Don't mind me.'

'If I could only get myself to do it, *that* would be the thing for
me.'

'But you never will, you see,' said Biddy.

Biddy is a good woman, sane, kindly and long-suffering, and
here at least she sees the truth. If Pip *had* returned at the end
and found her a free woman, would she have had the courage or
the insight to say 'no'? She is not put to this particular test, by
great good fortune, and lives on in happiness with Joe. Pip is
freed therefore for the proper ending of the book, which is surely
the second ending as we have it now. The assertion that Dickens
feebly gave in to Bulwer Lytton's pleas for a happy ending does

not convince me in the least. Dickens seldom allowed friends to influence him unless he secretly agreed with them, and his first ending was oddly brutal and flat. Pip's final sentence in the original version also seems insensitive and even selfish: 'I was very glad afterwards to have had the interview; for, in her face and in her voice, and in her touch, she gave me the assurance, that suffering had been stronger than Miss Havisham's teaching, and had given her a heart to understand what my heart used to be.' The revised ending turns this from an unspoken assurance into words, and gives the words, far more suitably, to Estella herself.

The revised ending is not a happy ending; it is ambiguous in meaning, yet not in tone. Perhaps Dickens had in mind the conclusion of Charlotte Brontë's *Villette*, though if so, his effect is not quite the same. The end of *Villette* is more desolating than an explicit statement, since who but the shallowest optimist would adopt the escape provided by Lucy Snowe for readers unable to bear *her* fate? What happens at the end of *Great Expectations* is less certain. It is barely possible that Pip and Estella marry, barely possible that they are happy if they do. The final words are profoundly satisfying not because they give certainty about what happens, or any clear moral judgement, but because they complete the peculiar music, silvery and autumnal, of the tale:

I took her hand in mine, and we went out of the ruined place; and, as the morning mists had risen long ago when I first left the forge, so, the evening mists were rising now, and in all the broad expanse of tranquil light they showed to me, I saw no shadow of another parting from her.

12 *Our Mutual Friend*
poetry comes dearer

W E all have our favourites, and this is mine; it is the novel I go
back to with greatest pleasure. But I am not wholly sure why.
It is not, I think, Dickens's greatest novel. *Bleak House* or
David Copperfield would be my choice for that. It is not his least
flawed. Readers who set their highest value on artistic compression and homogeneity will prefer *Great Expectations, A
Tale of Two Cities, Hard Times*. It is not as charming as *David
Copperfield*, not as funny as *Martin Chuzzlewit*, not as tragic as
Little Dorrit, not as haunting as *Edwin Drood*. Is the secret
somewhere outside art, and back in 'life'? There is much serious
social commentary in *Our Mutual Friend*, and the theme of
corruption by money is pursued through intricate analogies
which belie any first impression that geniality has ousted art.
Yet to my mind it can be made to sound along these paths
altogether too sombre. Though sinister, it is also funny, a real
recovery of Dickens's great comic form.

In humour, in fact, it seems to me superior to everything
since *Martin Chuzzlewit*, though there are no close similarities
between the two. *Our Mutual Friend* develops none of that sense
of a holiday of evil which I pointed to in *Martin Chuzzlewit*;
the high spirits are more disciplined than of old. Those notes of
the grotesque, the macabre, the downright wicked which were
there as early as *Pickwick* and *The Old Curiosity Shop* are
vibrant now, and none of the humour of *Our Mutual Friend*
is untouched by them. Mrs Wilfer is surely one of Dickens's
funniest people, but the sacrifice she makes of husband and
children to her ego is as reprehensible as Mrs Joe's sacrifice of
Joe and Pip. The scenes in Mr Venus's shop are vintage
Dickens, yet Mr Venus is enigmatic and rather alarming in his
watery way. When our minds wander back over the Dickens

world, no longer pondering individual works of art but visiting
the whole universe in that timeless and haunting dimension it
then assumes, the shop in Clerkenwell will often be revisited.
There Mr Venus is, his little red eyes winking vindictively,
upbraiding the boys who are making a mock of him. 'Don't
sauce *me*, in the wicious pride of your youth; don't hit *me*
because you see I'm down. You've no idea how small you'd
come out, if I had the articulating of you.' And there he is,
pushing Mr Boffin into concealment behind the alligator's yard
or two of smile, with the encouraging comment: 'He's a little
dusty but he's very like you in tone.' And there too is Silas
Wegg, brooding over Mr Venus's habit of floating his powerful
mind in tea, and steadily pursuing the proper Wegg humility:
'I am not so haughty as to be above doing myself a good turn.'
All this is splendid, but it is unquestionably sinister; and Wegg,
like Venus, is not 'simply' funny in the last resort. In literary
terms, he must be among the ancestors of the tramp in Pinter's
The Caretaker, though the mode of presentation is more ruthless.
Dickens is not concerned to explore the chronic uncertainty
which would make it understandable, though not forgivable,
that Wegg should reward his innocent patron with bleak
treachery. He is not concerned to remind us of the horrors of
losing a leg in the days before anaesthetics, or the pains as well
as the disadvantages of a wooden leg. Wegg's mean stupidity
is exploited chiefly for comedy, with the wooden leg an astonishing and sometimes horrible joke. Perhaps Wegg is freed to
be comic because he is not, after all, likely to do much real
damage, and because in the larger scheme of the book he is only
one variation among others on a leading theme. Yet Wegg
rings true, and is truly despicable. Dickens does not metamor-
phose him right out of the normal moral world.

There is a bitter edge again to the humour of Veneerings and
Podsnappery, and to the absurd predicament of the Lammles,
while the situation between Jenny Wren and her deplorable
father has the kind of really black humour which challenges us
(along with Eugene) to laugh if we dare.

The humour, though memorable, does not account then for
the curious spell of the book. This exists rather, in my view, in

a combination of virtues, the unique marriage of the complex structure and high social seriousness of Dickens's later work with the expansive extravagance, often the sunlit quality, of his earlier tales. The characters, of course, are memorable, equalling those other vintage casts of *David Copperfield* and *Bleak House*. *Our Mutual Friend* has its share of the Immortals – those creatures of whom Pecksniff and Mrs Gamp remain unchallenged exemplars and who seem to be eternally creating themselves – this impression will not be resisted – somewhere beyond the covers of the book. I would count Silas Wegg among the Immortals, despite the qualifications already touched upon, and also Mrs Wilfer, Mr Podsnap, Mr Boffin, Jenny Wren. There are other minor people tinged with this most Dickensian of qualities – Old Riah, Lady Tippins, Mr Venus, Abbey Potterson, Mrs Boffin. And among the major people, even Rogue Riderhood has a hint of it – though if he *is* an Immortal, he is much the nastiest of the lot.

Such impressions run counter to the normal trend of modern criticism, which has praised the darker side of the book. *Our Mutual Friend* is called Dickens's 'sinister masterpiece' by Robert Morse, and compared by Edgar Johnson with Eliot's *Waste Land*: 'Even more than in *Great Expectations*, this society is a society of monetary barbarism, devoid of culture, and emptier still of sincerity, generosity, integrity, and warmth of feeling.' And I would by no means disagree with these judgements: *Our Mutual Friend* is indeed sinister, with its opening scene of bodies recovered from the river to be robbed by Hexam, and a suggestion, borne out later, that the *Tale of Two Cities* theme 'back to life' is to be heard again. A major grouping of characters acts out a very grim drama. It could be said, I think, that almost everyone directly concerned with Lizzie Hexam and her story – her father and brother, Rogue Riderhood, Eugene Wrayburn and Bradley Headstone – takes on that brooding intensity, ominous and strongly realistic, which in the other three of his four last novels Dickens distilled into quintessence rather than spreading through a larger, ramifying book. In this novel Lizzie meets Betty Higden, fittingly, only at the moment when Betty's story ends; and she meets Bella Wilfer and

influences her without, however, at all inhabiting the same
world. The treatment of Bella, whilst being more realistic than
is always acknowledged, operates in a mythic and happier frame.
She is one of the lucky ones of life, a Perdita not a Cordelia in
the Dickens world. At the same time it remains true, as Edgar
Johnson says, that the world of this novel is predominantly
treacherous and ungenerous, and that the good characters have
the appearance, familiar by now in this reading of Dickens, of
aliens in a darkened place.

Before I pass on from this preamble – not strictly critical, and
perhaps self-indulgent – I can pin down one further reason why
this presents itself to me as the favourite work. Several of the
characters seem to come straight from my own childhood, and
take on a special resonance from that. As a boy in Paddington
in the 1930s, in a street of much the same time and style as
Holloway, I have seen Mrs Wilfer time and again in her doorstep aspect, head tied in a handkerchief for a mysterious
toothache, gloved hands (I would swear to them) at the
rhetorical ready, radiating inner martyrdom and disdain. *Our
Mutual Friend* came on first reading as a revelation of what
went on behind the doorstep, a mystery often pondered, and
here solved. A street or so away Mr Wegg hung out, in a dingy
second-hand shop, his nose missing as well as his leg (Mr Wegg
was at least spared this), but with dreadful damp gingerbread
traps still baited for the neighbouring young. In the canal area
were Riderhoods – they looked like Riderhoods – and Miss
Patience Riderhood was not unknown. The scene was completed
by Jenny Wren, that strangely authentic creation with her
twisted back and legs and her golden bower of hair, her sharp
pride and anger, her imagination ranging between heaven and
hell. As always, Dickens conveys his people in their prime
reality – speech and gesture, relationships at home, the world
they move in – and it is for us to make of them what we can as
adults, as we did when young.

Our Mutual Friend is also the crowning novel about London.
That long tale of love and hatred which is Dickens's London
reaches a perfect climax in this mysterious world – all sordidness
in its details, the River, the Dust Heaps, the mean home of

Mrs Wilfer, Mr Venus's gruesome shop, yet haunting and
ineffaceable: London as it must have been for its author, as he
tramped its streets obsessively by day and night.

Dickens has been accused too often of exaggeration, caricature,
psychological improbability, but *Our Mutual Friend* presents
two classic occasions of this kind. Best to begin with these and
get them over, since they can be real stumbling-blocks. The
most difficult is no doubt Old Riah. Does the old man's willingness to be degraded by Fledgeby ring true? It is easy to conclude
that for once Dickens really is exaggerating, or at the very
least that in his anxiety to produce a good Jew to balance Fagin
(accusations of anti-semitism upset him) he failed to scrutinise
his creation with due care. Riah after all is not deluded about
Fledgeby, as Tom Pinch was about Pecksniff, but is the actual
instrument of evil used by the man he serves. This is hard to
reconcile with Riah's own perception (articulated, it is true,
only when he leaves Fledgeby) that the whole Jewish race
tends to be judged, however unfairly, by each individual Jew.
We see that Riah's bondage to Fledgeby is Gratitude, but what
is Gratitude? Can it cease to be blind virtue and become blinkered
vice? Yet Dickens presumably understood the risks he was
taking and accepted them, and did not overlook the discrepancy
himself.

The clue perhaps is in Riah's extreme simplicity. He accepts
his role in life as unquestioningly as he accepts his strange
Jewish garb. It is stressed that his way of life seems to be forced
upon him by society – the Jew was still to some degree pushed
into professions such as money-lending, which then perpetuated
aversion – and when at the end we see him under Jenny Wren's
protection he looks a little anxious, like a man who has lost his
way. Dickens may be suggesting, as he had already done with
Tom Pinch, that certain kinds of virtue can have a touch of the
childish as well as the childlike, and that a truly good man can
lack the kind of moral imagination required to analyse and
reject a situation like Riah's. Riah's gentleness certainly appears

as the reverse side of his passivity, and he is the Good Samaritan (in sharp contrast to the Poor Law, which hounds Betty Higden) because he responds instinctively, not calculatingly, to human need.

The combination of gentleness and simplicity, kindness and vulnerability may or may not explain Riah's relationship with Fledgeby; every reader will confront this problem for himself. What *is* undeniable is the vividness of his presence. Like the people who pass him in the fog, we rub our eyes, wondering: is he conjured up by fancy? – can he be real? Yet if on a certain foggy evening of indeterminate date we had been on that route from Smith Square in Westminster to the Six Jolly Fellowship Porters in Limehouse, we should surely have seen them – that improbable pair, Jenny Wren and Old Riah, passing together over the two bridges across the river, along the dangerous Ratcliffe Highway in Wapping, on their journey to clear the name of the late Gaffer Hexam with Miss Abbey Potterson. The dreamlike vividness of the image is irresistible and ineffaceable, in that area of fantasy where Dickens is most assuredly himself.

The other grave difficulty is the testing of Bella, which is less detachable from the main structure of the tale. Can we accept that Bella would, or should, accept the tricks played upon her with gratitude? The difficulty in part arises from a mingling of romance conventions with psychological insight (in this, it resembles old Martin Chuzzlewit's role in *Martin Chuzzlewit*, and Jarndyce's role at the end of *Bleak House*), but it is aggravated by the great changes brought about in our attitude to paternalism and charity by the welfare state and other major new factors in the past century; and we cannot overlook the fact that problems about 'gratitude' not only link this crux with the one I have just been discussing, Old Riah, but also with modern difficulties felt about the heroine of *Bleak House*. The mingling of romance and realism is, however, central; whether Old Riah is or is not Jenny Wren's fairy-godmother, Bella Wilfer is Cinderella beyond a doubt. A reluctant Cinderella, when we meet her first as pseudo-widow, but more reconciled to the part as she rides in triumph to Holloway in the Boffin

coach. Later, when it is 'black midnight' with the Golden
Dustman, she is duly bereft of her finery, and returns home in
her old (comparative) rags. Later again, she is carried off after
all by Prince Charming, and brought home to the house of her
purest dreams.

In such a tale we expect the heroine to be tested. To put love
before money, heart before head, is the inalienable rule of her
luck. The testing is admirably contrived for this purpose, since
if Bella really were the mercenary wretch she proclaims herself,
the plan would never have worked. She is rescued not from
herself but from a false view of herself, which she comes
dangerously close to mistaking for truth. To this degree she is
in no way violated, and the happy ending deprives her of no
fruits more palatable than angry pride and bitter revenge. The
Golden Dustman's charade shows to Bella what we, as readers,
have never wholly doubted. She is not to be numbered with Mr
Veneering and Mr Podsnap, Mr Lammle and Mr Fledgeby,
Mr Wegg and Mr Riderhood, among those who deride, sell or
kill their fellows for gold. She always has belonged with the
uncorrupted Boffin, whose apparent overthrow reveals to her
the true state, the true existence even, of her heart.

To see this is to see that she is not tricked into marriage; but
there remains an unhappy tinge of deceit. It is unfortunate that
Bella comes to admire Rokesmith for his manliness before the
wrath of Mr Boffin when she should really have been admiring
his acting skill. In this she is treated a little like one of Jenny
Wren's dolls, a role in life which she explicitly rejects; and we
remember that there are other characters in the novel, like
Fledgeby, who also can act. It is also notable that when Bella
marries Rokesmith, blind trust is the further virtue he expects
of her. After she has sacrificed wealth for him, she must sacrifice
the faculty of rational doubt. The evil love outside reason of
Bradley Headstone must be balanced, it seems, by the good
love outside reason of married trust. Modern readers might find
this perverse, but Dickens, who understood the ramifications of
deceit and evil as well as any man, seems to have endorsed it
himself. Bella joins that *élite* in his novels who, marrying for
love, are thereby ennobled: an *élite* among whom the most

unlikely, paradoxical, touching and ill-fated member is Sir Leicester Dedlock, and the most favoured member Bella herself. Sir Leicester is let down in his trust, and suffers greatly; Bella is justified, and earns her reward. The domestic happiness at Blackheath is not the last word (just as well for readers who are allergic to it) : because she is Cinderella, she is also to have the Prince and his golden coach.

Is this possible? In my view, certainly. Some people have all the luck. Dickens is no anti-capitalist, puritanically at war with pleasure; it is the corruptions of money, not money itself, he rejects. Because Bella marries for love and wins happiness, she can afford to acclaim Mr Boffin 'the dearest and kindest finger-post that ever was set up anywhere'. In these ways Dickens brings psychological realism into harmony with romantic parable, as Shakespeare had also done in his last plays. He reasserts the belief that strong, good virtues can bring rewards on earth for the lucky ones. It is Bella's luck that those real flaws in her nature – coquetry, petulance, vanity, thoughtlessness – are not destined for nemesis in the tragic mode. It is supremely her luck that she is tested not in the furnace of life like Amy Dorrit or Lizzie Hexam, but in the play of Boffin's golden affection and love.

III

The web of analogy in Dickens's art was never more complex, as J. Hillis Miller and Edgar Johnson have shown. The theme of money and corruption by money is so omnipresent, that hardly a character escapes some variation on the theme. There is a spectrum from the Boffins, who survive good fortune so triumphantly as to become the real benefactors of Harmon and Bella, to the total scoundrels and swindlers – the Lammles, Silas Wegg, Fascination Fledgeby, above all Riderhood. The Rogue sells Gaffer Hexam's life for money, and robs Betty Higden just before she dies. The novel's symbols give gruesome colouring to such villainy : dead bodies yielding their treasure to birds of prey, sailors murderously assaulted in dockland, Silas Wegg's wooden leg disgustingly stuck in the great Dust

Heap. In the end Wegg is chucked into a scavenger's cart by
Sloppy, and declines and falls in rubbish, upside down. There is
the polished thin ice of the Veneering world, where the Voice of
Society sounds loud and clear and seems to prevail. In this
Veneering world, Shares: and though Dickens leaves the time-
scale of *Our Mutual Friend* deliberately vague, the famous
Shares passage belonged to the 1860s and was right up to date:

As is well known to the wise in their generation, traffic in
Shares is the one thing to have to do with in this world. Have
no antecedents, no established character, no cultivation, no
ideas, no manners; have Shares. Have Shares enough to be on
Boards of Direction in capital letters, oscillate on mysterious
business between London and Paris, and be great. Where does
he come from? Shares. Where is he going to? Shares. What are
his tastes? Shares. Has he any principles? Shares. What
squeezes him into Parliament? Shares. Perhaps he never of
himself achieved success in anything, never originated anything,
never produced anything! Sufficient answer to all; Shares. O
mighty Shares! To set these blaring images so high, and to
cause us smaller vermin, as under the influence of henbane or
opium, to cry out night and day, 'Relieve us of our money,
scatter it for us, buy us and sell us, ruin us, only we beseech ye
take rank among the powers of the earth and fatten on us.'

Money in *Our Mutual Friend* begets conspiracy: Wegg against
Boffin, the Lammles against each other, Riderhood against
Hexam; Fledgeby, the Veneerings and the Lammles against the
world. Prices rise perceptibly in a seller's market. The price of
orphans goes up when Mrs Boffin is casting around for one, the
price of poetry rises with Mr Boffin's literary sights:

'As to the amount of strain upon the intellect, now. Was you
thinking at all of poetry?' Mr Wegg inquired, musing.
  'Would it come dearer?' Mr Boffin asked.
  'It would come dearer,' Mr Wegg returned. 'For when a
person comes to grind off poetry night after night, it is but
right he should expect to be paid for its weakening effect on his
mind.'

The conspiracies of the novel (not all deriving from money:
there is also Bradley Headstone) are allied to multiple disguisings of various kinds. Here the actual process of physical

disguise blends with the disguising of identity. The chief instance is the novel's hero, John Harmon, alias Julius Handford, alias John Rokesmith, who is also Mrs Wilfer's lodger, Mr Boffin's secretary, and the anonymous, oakum-headed, oakum-whiskered sailor in Limehouse. Bradley Headstone disguises himself as Riderhood, and seems more at home in that part than in his own. Names are changed, as so often in Dickens. Fanny Cleaver rechristens herself Jenny Wren, and who remembers Fanny Cleaver? – Mr Cleaver is irrevocably turned into Mr Dolls. There is a wide confusion of roles, with Boffin as miser, Riah as grasping money-lender, the Lammles as people of fortune, Bella as mercenary wretch, Silas Wegg as literary man *with* a wooden leg, Miss Pleasant Riderhood as *belle dame sans merci*, Fledgeby as anxious friend of Riah's victims, the Veneerings as Veneerings (whatever under the Veneer that might be). It will be seen how varied in style and function these changes are, some adopted under pressure from society or from inner need. Closely linked to them are the roles which people play out as their public *personae* – Mrs Wilfer's Tragedy Queen, Podsnap's Podsnappery, Eugene's and Mortimer's bored cynicism, Jenny Wren's maternity, Bradley Headstone's respectability, old Tippins' flirtatious young siren and the rest. Against this, Mrs Boffin's display of fashion is pure innocence, honoured by an author who could be savage enough with false gentility when he chose. There are, also, more extreme examples of Dickensian transformation – Mrs Podsnap to rocking-horse, poor Twemlow to 'an innocent piece of dinner-furniture that went upon easy castors and was kept over a livery stable-yard in Duke Street.' Through this maze of confounded identity we are guided surely and exuberantly. Dickens savours the sheer unexpectedness and diversity of disguisings, even while he probes the reality, or the vacuum, concealed.

IV

In so vast a canvas, all one can do is to alight on a few themes of interest. As always, Dickens is fascinated by the manner in which people drift or erupt into each other's lives. There is the

I

permanent possibility of interest or danger. Whose footsteps
out of the endless footsteps of humanity will pause at our
doorstep? Whose ship, storm-tossed and still distant, will
embark at our port? From his earliest writings Dickens had
often pondered this; in *Little Dorrit* it is a guiding thread. In
Our Mutual Friend he reverts to it, as his huge cast of characters
bump into one another with incalculable possibilities for good
and ill. Thus: Eugene Wrayburn drifts into Lizzie's life by a
mere accident, and starts to circle, interestingly but obscurely,
on the edge. A little later, Bradley Headstone drifts into it. 'He
is a very strange man,' Lizzie muses. 'I wish he was so very
strange a man as to be a total stranger' is Jenny Wren's reply.
Wegg and Boffin come together in a chance encounter, made
possible by Boffin's aspirations and Wegg's skills. The
Veneerings collect oldest and dearest friends like vultures,
while poor Mr Twemlow clutches his head. There are some
grim encounters, meaning murder: John Harmon with his
simulacrum on the voyage back to England, Bradley Headstone's
with Riderhood late one night outside Temple Bar. As a dark
undertow there is the encounter with which the novel opens,
Gaffer Hexam and his prey, the newly dead, drifting in polluted
waters to its latter end.

These chance meetings and encounters are the stuff of life,
the stuff of drama. Dickens is marvellous at showing those
elusive yet powerful tones which pervade all our encounters;
there are no egalitarian relationships in his tales. Among
apparent equals, even, power swings to the stronger or more
unscrupulous of the two. Whereas it is sometimes held today
that even sexual relationships can be switched on and off
casually among 'sensible people', Dickens failed to perceive
much good sense in human affairs. Any relationship in his novels
is dramatic and open. From the 'spare a bob, Guv' wheedling,
two-thirds ingratiating, one-third menacing of casual encounter,
up or down to total personal involvement for good or ill,
Dickens remains sensitive to the mesh of demands, obligations,
guilts, pleas, jealousies, needs, sufferings, embarrassments,
revenges, joys, loves, hates, fears, despairs that can overtake
anything rationally planned or clearly foreseen. The salesman

with his foot in the door is no more practised than Silas Wegg
when he inserts his literary wooden leg into Mr Boffin's life.
Dull though he is, Wegg knows how to make Boffin feel
awkward and indefinably guilty in direct proportion to the
kindness bestowed. The blackmail of the compassionate by the
bitter, the healthy by the ailing, the donor by the recipient all
shape themselves by instinct in Wegg's tone. Unfortunately for
him, he underestimates Mr Boffin, and like the tramp in Pinter's
The Caretaker oversteps all possible bounds. But the will to
pitiless exploitation is strong in him, and not less odious because
we sense the hopeless aridity of his normal life.

Most relationships in *Our Mutual Friend* survive because
people play parts consonant with their circumstances and talents.
When a character steps right out of role, there is danger : for
Bradley Headstone when he abandons hard-won respectability
for dubious passion, for Eugene Wrayburn when he allows love
to prevail over class.

Dickens is especially good at noticing the precarious power
balance among rogues and outlaws when, stripped of the
pretences and protections of convention, they fight it out by
their wits. Alfred Lammle appears to win supremacy over
Fledgeby when he threatens to pull his nose and Fledgeby's
bluster turns to cringing, but Fledgeby is financially and morally
set for a sneaking revenge. Wegg and Venus pursue a precarious
alliance, hilarious for the reader, with mutual suspicion, mutual
treachery, and for Wegg, at least, twinges of fear. The relationship between Riderhood and Headstone is a stage further in the
wilderness. Bradley in his dull, plodding way casts Riderhood
first as his tool and then as his victim, little imagining how
Riderhood's sharper wits and more practised wickedness will
turn the scale. Bradley is characteristically too self-preoccupied
to see Riderhood clearly, and he makes the fatal error, natural
to him as a schoolmaster, of confusing illiteracy with slowness
of mind. Riderhood's cat-and-mouse appearance in the school-
room is frighteningly realistic : here is the chance he has always
been looking for. He cannot bully Miss Abbey Potterson, who
is not afraid of him; he cannot bully Eugene Wrayburn, who
treats him like dirt. Here at last is a victim really in his power,

and one whom he has a positive right to torment, since they are
at war outside all pity by Bradley's choice. But Riderhood
miscalculates Bradley Headstone's desperation, just as Wegg
had miscalculated Mr Boffin's virtue, and they fittingly go
clasped together to death.

v

A recurring theme in the Dickens world is the limits of freedom;
how free is Charlie Hexam? Much that is morally wrong with
him is explained by his background, but if we simply blame him
upon his father, his illiteracy in early years, the Limehouse
water life, then Lizzie Hexam is there to point the lie. Since
Lizzie is equally understandable in terms of this background,
some other important factor must have intervened.

But it is easier to deduce from this what Dickens's views of
freedom were not, than what they were. He was certainly not a
mechanical determinist. Like most energetic creators, he prized
his freedom to co-operate with fate. It is the dignity of his evil
characters to be responsible, no less than it is the dignity of the
good. *Hard Times* is the only novel where determinism seems
at all possible, and even there Tom and Louisa Gradgrind
remain poles apart.

The moral differences between people coming from the same
unpropitious background : this theme fascinated Dickens all his
life. Some characters respond to adversity with bitter selfishness,
like Charlie Hexam; some respond with Lizzie's selfless and
dedicated love. Both reactions require some kind of a struggle.
Just as great virtue does not mature without severe discipline,
so great evil must be struggled towards. The famous passage
concerning Bradley Headstone's descent into violence I am
holding back for my next chapter, but its purport will be readily
recalled. Evil is never merely the product of inertia. It requires
will as well as feeling to bring it to fruit.

Clearly, then, Dickens is not a primitivist, or an optimistic
humanist. He does not trace evil by predetermined steps to
poverty, bad laws or dogmas, nor does he suggest that ideal
circumstances must promote good. Yet the realism of his

depictions is unquestionable. We all know that moral opposites do grow in one soil, like Charlie and Lizzie. We all know that though both plants can be retrospectively accounted for by clear chains of causation, the organic divide remains splendidly unexplained. (This remains true of *Our Mutual Friend* even if we concede that Lizzie's speech habits are more refined than could normally be expected, and that Dickens, who was not usually wrong about speech habits, was wrong here.)

But where, then, does Lizzie differ from Charlie? Though both are free agents or seem so – to themselves and their readers – is freedom illusory after all? We can see how easy it would be to interpret Dickens as a concealed Calvinist, or Jansenist, or even as a concealed Manichee, particularly since he so seldom shows a good man becoming convincingly evil or an evil man good. The nearest we get to this is the moral redemption of people like Miss Havisham and Magwitch: but then, we tend to feel that they are after all redeemable people who have been pushed terribly out of shape by suffering, and that they have never belonged with Sikes and Rudge, Chester and Carker, Tulkinghorn and John Jasper, the real wanderers in the dark. In the two most famous moral reformations, those of Scrooge and Mr Dombey, an unresolved difficulty remains. Mr Dombey's change of heart may be essentially (I have argued) an aspect of his ruin and breakdown, while Scrooge was always a case apart. One explanation of Scrooge is Chesterton's: 'Scrooge is not really inhuman at the beginning any more than he is at the end. There is a heartiness in his inhospitable sentiments that is akin to humour and therefore to humanity; he is only a crusty old bachelor, and had (I strongly suspect) given away turkeys secretly all his life.' An alternative possibility is that by New Year's Day Scrooge's clerk will be crouching over a fire only a shade less extinguished than it was on Christmas Eve. Either way, the change of heart vanishes; and do we really believe – did Dickens? – in the change of heart?

In the novel we are now considering, it is notable that Mr Boffin is never really miserly, Bella never really mercenary, Eugene Wrayburn never really a Harthouse deep down. Eugene is in fact like Bella, though in a more sombre mode of realism, in that he is not so much changed by his experiences as revealed to himself by them, just in time, as he really is. If we think back over Dickens's novels, it seems true to say that though fundamentally good people are shown sinking into sin and squalor through specific faults, and notably through failure of willpower, they are never transformed into active agents of ill. Little Em'ly, Richard Carstone, Louisa Gradgrind, Sydney Carton are defeated in life and cut off from happiness, but they never gladly take to sin. Characters like Tom Gradgrind or Charlie Hexam are notably different. In them, some commitment to self, profound and untouchable, extinguishes whatever might have been noble or selfless at source. If their actual evil falls short of its potential, this scarcely redeems them. In their self-regard there is a touch of prudence, perhaps of cowardice; it is this, not any virtue, which separates them from Rogue Riderhood's world. And beyond Tom and Charlie there are those still more evil characters whom we have often encountered, where evil seems almost inseparable from the principle of life.

It appears therefore that while Dickens does full justice to the fact that people seem to themselves and to others to be making free choices, he does not usually show his people developing through a notable moral change. Pip is not an exception to this, in my reading; he is simply a man forced by circumstances to become either very flawed or unusually good. Dickens's characters do indeed develop, but in other particulars. They develop by working out their inner logic, like Pecksniff or Micawber; or by the scenes and places which take colour from them – Coketown or Cloisterham; or by the degree to which enveloping circumstances bring good or evil into the open and write them large. But the corollary is that these moral tendencies are all apparent very early. We know them – Uriah Heep, Rosa Dartle, Skimpole, old Mr Turveydrop – from the very first speech rhythms we hear.

This returns us, then, to the mystery; what makes them moral agents, and the people they are? Not heredity; Dickens propounds no physiological answer; not environment, in any determinist reading; not in any declared manner the will of God. But (of course) such explanations always *are* mere explanations, as enigmatic and difficult in life as they are in art. Which of us expects to make definitive judgements on complex people, or to achieve a generally coherent theory of fate and free will? I would suggest that the most important key to Dickens's depiction is simple realism; all he does, morally, is to tell the truth.

This may seem a perverse or eccentric suggestion, given Dickens's people; are they not more individualistic, as a group, than most groups would be? But people *are* highly individual when we look at them closely; and their moral consistency is very much, by and large, as Dickens says. The mystery of conduct in Dickens's typical people and situations is the mystery we encounter daily, with equal bewilderment, in friends, neighbours, strangers, and not least in ourselves. There are indeed people as dynamic as Varden, as good as Amy Dorrit; there are indeed people as cold as Carker, as slimy as Heep. And such people seldom change much; they are revealed more fully in the stress of dangerous or difficult circumstances; they grow or deteriorate with practice and age. They have, as Dickens shows, some clear moral colouring; some tug of generosity or malice, love of life or rejection of life, operates in their choices, their gestures and tone. Just occasionally we meet a person so good that we are totally surprised and humbled; just occasionally we meet someone wholly corrupt. This is the real world, and it is Dickens's world. The mystery which prompts widely different and conflicting moral theories in formal philosophy retains its mystery in his art.

But, as I have hinted already, Dickens is not neutral in his interpretation, even though he does not force his views. All that he shows of humanity seems consistent with Christian doctrine, including the perception that final judgements are not man's to make. If there is any classic statement of the view of human virtue shown in his novels, it is surely this, from the Epistle to the Hebrews: 'For whom the Lord loveth he chasteneth, and scourgeth every son whom he receiveth. . . . For here have we no continuing city, but we seek one to come.' We live in a world where dynamic virtue exists, and has peculiar attractions and unmistakable authority; but where evil is rampant, and in actual situations may well come off best. Dickens would no

doubt have felt the force of this great passage from Newman's
Apologia, though it was written too late to have any direct
influence on his thought :

To consider the world in its length and breadth, its various
history, the many races of man, their starts, their fortunes, their
mutual alienation, their conflicts; and then their ways, habits,
governments, forms of worship; their enterprises, their aimless
courses, their random achievements and acquirements, the
impotent conclusion of long-standing facts, the tokens so faint
and broken, of a superintending design, the blind evolution of
what turn out to be great powers of truth, the progress of
things, as if from unreasoning elements, not towards final
causes, the greatness and littleness of man, his far-reaching
aims, his short duration, the curtain hung over his futurity, the
disappointments of life, the defeat of good, the success of evil,
physical pain, mental anguish, the prevalence and intensity of
sin, the pervading idolatries, the corruptions, the dreary hopeless irreligion, that condition of the whole race, so fearfully yet
exactly described in the Apostle's words, 'having no hope and
without God in the world' – all this is a vision to dizzy and appal;
and inflicts upon the mind the sense of a profound mystery,
which is absolutely beyond human solution.

What shall be said to this heart-piercing, reason-bewildering
fact? I can only answer, that either there is no Creator, or this
living society of men is in a true sense discarded from His
presence.

It is evident that though the leading of Newman's kindly light
was not the leading of Dickens's, in vision and ultimate optimism they were not unlike. Dickens never made the darkness
a text for despair or inaction; vision and common sense were
not at war in him. Though the original taint of our nature is
too deep to be cured by merely political action, political action
can and must cope with particular harms. It was Dickens's
common sense to see that even if slums and poverty are not the
seeds of criminality, they are at least the most propitious possible soil for its growth. It was his common sense to see that the
lives of people would certainly be happier, and therefore
probably more virtuous, if the evils of social injustice and
oppression were removed. Again and again in his novels the
men and women degraded in prisons or rotting in tenements are

compared with vermin: not because Dickens himself sees them
as vermin, but because he sees that if society treats them as
vermin they will be more, not less, verminous as a result. The
other side of the picture is that even ordinary virtue becomes
heroic in adverse circumstances; old Betty Higden shines no
less brightly for her poor lot in life.

But Dickens's activism was not simply inspired by common
sense, though that was part of it; he would have been active
even if he had seen no possibility of winning his wars. Like
Newman, he found his real energy in religion; since poverty and
squalor were absolutely incompatible with the Christian profession, their continuance in a society supposedly Christian
could never be anything other than cruelty or cant. If inhumanity
comes naturally enough to a Fascination Fledgeby or a Riderhood, this is no reason why it should come naturally to us all.
Dickens was determined to arouse and act upon every propensity to humanity in his readers, since he really believed in
the 'heavenly compassion' born in most of their hearts. The
outcome was that moral militancy, exemplified here chiefly in
the Betty Higden chapters, which is as much a feature, we know,
of the Dickens novel, as the equally characteristic image of good
at bay in an alien world.

A very striking instance of this other characteristic image is,
however, to be found in *Our Mutual Friend*. Fledgeby thrives
on ill-gotten gains, and his city house is his to dispose of; but on
the roof, amid the smoke and grime of London, Old Riah makes
a small garden for himself and his friends. There, Riah, Lizzie
Hexam and Jenny Wren escape their miseries in a small but
creative oasis. Nothing could be more symbolic of Dickens's
world.

No less typical of this world is Jenny Wren, though the
strange co-existence of good and evil in her small person may at
first appear to set her apart. She is a touching, curious person,
suspended between great moral opposites, just as her twisted
body is crowned by the golden bower of hair. The heavenly and
hellish alternate in her imagery as they do in·her love for
Lizzie, her hatred of Fledgeby and his works. Some of her
fantasies are strikingly sadistic, while at times she has the

12

celestial imagination of a child. The reversal of roles forced upon
her by her father has clearly warped her; more obviously than
in one of Dickens's 'angel' women, we see the fruits in a
profound and apparent harm. Yet the self-pity of her references
to herself are chiefly defensive, and so is her habitual wariness of
insult or slight. The perpetual guard is needed for survival, as
indeed is her power to arouse answering wariness in those she
mistrusts. And with all this, Jenny is pure gold when tested; the
scourge of Eugene, Bradley Headstone and Fledgeby, the patron
of Lizzie Hexam and Old Riah. She is also one of those rare
people in Dickens with an almost unfailing nose for true and
false. A sharp, dangerous, very vital person, unlike anyone else
in Dickens (except perhaps Susan Nipper to some degree), yet
no-one but Dickens would have drawn her like this.

In conclusion I must note that Riderhood's return from near
drowning seems to me centrally Dickensian; the spark of life
is sacred, whatever the man. Riderhood alive is a hateful presence, Riderhood dead a hateful memory; Riderhood suspended
between life and death is a mystery to be looked on with awe.
The simple men in the Six Jolly Fellowship Porters, labouring to
revive the spark of life and rejoicing as it returns to them, are
very close to Dickens himself.

13 *Edwin Drood*
a horrible wonder apart

ON the morning of 8 June 1870 Dickens went into his chalet at Gad's Hill as usual, to continue work on *The Mystery of Edwin Drood*. He spent the whole day with it, breaking only for lunch, and at some time during the afternoon wrote the following words :

A brilliant morning shines on the old city. Its antiquities and ruins are surpassingly beautiful, with a lusty ivy gleaming in the sun, and the rich trees waving in the balmy air. Changes of glorious light from moving boughs, songs of birds, scents from gardens, woods, and fields – or, rather, from the one great garden of the whole cultivated island in its yielding time – penetrate into the Cathedral, subdue its earthy odour, and preach the Resurrection and the Life. The cold stone tombs of centuries ago grow warm, and flecks of brightness dart into the sternest marble corners of the building, fluttering there like wings.

    Comes Mr Tope with his large keys and yawningly unlocks and sets open. Come Mrs Tope and attendant sweeping sprites. Come, in due time, organist and bellows-boy, peeping down from the red curtains in the loft, fearlessly flapping dust from books up at that remote elevation, and whisking it from stops and pedals. Come sundry rooks, from various quarters of the sky, back to the great tower, who may be presumed to enjoy vibration, and to know that bell and organ are going to give it them. Come a very small and straggling congregation indeed : chiefly from Minor Canon Corner and the Precincts. Come Mr Crisparkle, fresh and bright, and his ministering brethren, not quite so fresh and bright. Come the Choir in a hurry (always in a hurry, and struggling into their night-gowns at the last moment, like children shirking bed), and comes John Jasper leading their line. Last of all comes Mr Datchery into a stall, one of a choice empty collection very much at his service, and glancing about him for Her Royal Highness the Princess Puffer.

The service is pretty well advanced before Mr Datchery can discern Her Royal Highness. But by that time he has made her out, in the shade. She is behind a pillar, carefully withdrawn from the Choir-master's view, but regards him with the closest attention. All unconscious of her presence, he chants and sings. She grins when he is most musically fervid, and – yes, Mr Datchery sees her do it! – shakes her fist at him behind the pillar's friendly shelter.

Mr Datchery looks again, to convince himself. Yes, again! As ugly and withered as one of the fantastic carvings on the underbrackets of the stall-seats, as malignant as the Evil One, as hard as the big brass eagle holding the sacred books upon his wings (and, according to the sculptor's representation of his ferocious attributes, not at all converted by them), she hugs herself in her lean arms, and then shakes both fists at the leader of the Choir.

And at that moment, outside the grated door of the Choir, having eluded the vigilance of Mr Tope by shifty resources in which he is an adept, Deputy peeps, sharp-eyed, through the bars, and stares astounded from the threatener to the threatened.

The service comes to an end, and the servitors disperse to breakfast. Mr Datchery accosts his last new acquaintance outside, when the Choir (as much in a hurry to get their bed-gowns off as they were but now to get them on) have scuffled away.

'Well, mistress. Good morning. You have seen him?'

'*I*'ve seen him, deary, *I*'ve seen him!'

'And you know him?'

'Know him! Better far than all the Reverend Parsons put together know him.'

Mrs Tope's care has spread a very neat, clean breakfast ready for her lodger. Before sitting down to it he opens his corner-cupboard door; takes his bit of chalk from its shelf; adds one thick line to the score, extending from the top of the cupboard door to the bottom; and then falls to with an appetite.

This was the point where he broke off to write a few letters before dinner. During dinner, he was obviously in pain, and towards the end he pushed his chair back, announcing that he must go to London at once. Almost immediately he fell into a coma, from which he never recovered. He died the next day.

Dickens's last words as a novelist are, then, in front of us, the very end of the Inimitable stream of novels and tales. The final seven words take on an air of appropriate if partial epitaph, even while they tease with their permanent mystery. What had Datchery seen or deduced, to justify his 'one thick line to the score' and his excellent appetite? Who is Datchery? What is he doing there?

It is worth remembering that Dickens's unfinished novel had very nearly been not this one but the one before it, where the 'mysteries' had been proclaimed too obvious for some critics' taste. Dickens was writing *Our Mutual Friend* when he survived the terrible train disaster of Friday 9 June 1865, five years to the day before his death. He had helped other survivors as far as he could – the loss of life had been heavy – and then climbed back into his overturned carriage to retrieve the manuscript: Rogue Riderhood surveying the sleeping Bradley Headstone; Mr and Mrs Boffin at breakfast with the Lammles; Bella Wilfer marrying her mendicant in Greenwich. If he had died, would a question mark have hovered permanently over Mr Boffin, Eugene Wrayburn, John Harmon, or would we have clearly enough foreseen the end? Hard to say now; but the next novel was deliberately designed to baffle; and it is impossible not to acknowledge, all too ruefully, Dickens's success.

Robert Morse called *Our Mutual Friend* Dickens's 'sinister masterpiece', but the later novel has at least equal claims. In its genre a tale of mystery and sensation, it challenges us to pay attention to every detail, every notable inclusion or omission, every nuance of tone. In this aspect, the genre conventions co-operate with the proper demands of criticism, that whether a book is a 'mystery' or not in this formal sense, we should scrutinise most closely all its effects. Longfellow called it the most 'beautiful' of Dickens's novels, and one readily sees what he meant. The psychological probing is at least as fascinating and surprising as the plot mechanism, while the structure has all the rich suggestiveness of symbolist verse.

The final paragraphs of *Edwin Drood* take place (like most of its action) in Cloisterham, which of course is Rochester, set back in time and weirdly transformed. Rochester was always numinous for Dickens, especially when associated with his own childhood years. He had been born in near-by Chatham, and lived most happily there until his clouded tenth year. Certain romances had nourished his young imagination – *The Arabian Nights, Tom Jones, Peregrine Pickle, Roderick Random, Humphry Clinker* – and his father, pointing out the fascinating house on the hill called Gad's Hill, had told him that if he worked hard, he might grow up to live there one day. The family fortunes collapsed, and Dickens moved to London with his family, and to the wounding experience of the blacking factory in his twelfth year. Rochester receded in imagination as a paradise of lost innocence and happiness, while remaining, through his father's words, a New Jerusalem perhaps one day to be won. On later visits he was comically dismayed by the shrinkage; *could* the Corn Exchange clock ('as inexpressive, moon-faced, and weak a clock as I ever saw') really be the magnificent childhood clock of his dreams? But his obsession with Rochester survived all such disappointments. On 14 March 1856, while he was writing *Little Dorrit*, his father's spur became prophecy, and Gad's Hill was made his home. It was in Gad's Hill that he was writing about Rochester at the time of his death.

In his fiction there had been what Mr Venus would have called Rochesters Warious, but no Rochesters lit by the light of common day. 'Bright and pleasant was the sky, balmy the air, and beautiful the appearance of every object around, as Mr Pickwick leant over the balustrades of Rochester Bridge, contemplating nature, and waiting for breakfast.' Thus Mr Pickwick, at the beginning of chapter 5 of the great novel of innocence. Yet even he is destined to meet the dismal man before his breakfast, and to be asked : 'Did it ever strike you, on such a morning as this, that drowning would be happiness and peace?' David Copperfield passes through Rochester on his journey of escape to his aunt's house at Dover, and has his dismaying adventure with the Goroo man. Pip is born and brought up in the forge near Rochester, and there encounters the strange figures – Magwitch, Miss Havisham, Estella, Orlick – who surround his life. In *Great Expectations* the cathedral appears only once, but on that occasion (chapter 49) it becomes intermingled with Pip's melancholia, and is ready, even to the rooks, for its apotheosis in *Edwin Drood* :

The best light of the day was gone when I passed along the quiet echoing courts behind the High-street. The nooks of ruin where the old monks had once their refectories and gardens, and where the strong walls were now pressed into the service of humble sheds and stables, were almost as silent as the old monks in their graves. The cathedral chimes had at once a sadder and a more remote sound to me, as I hurried on avoiding observation, than they had ever had before; so, the swell of the old organ was borne to my ears like funeral music; and the rooks, as they hovered about the grey tower and swung in the bare high trees of the priory-garden, seemed to call to me that the place was changed, and that Estella was gone out of it for ever.

In *Edwin Drood* the mingling of nightmare and idyll in descriptions of Cloisterham, impregnated now with Jasper's consciousness, now with Crisparkle's, becomes a vision of heaven and hell, the saved and the damned. We come upon it first as an ancient city :

An ancient city, Cloisterham, and no meet dwelling-place for anyone with hankerings after the noisy world . . . A drowsy city . . . whose inhabitants seem to suppose, with an inconsistency more strange than rare, that all its changes lie behind it . . .

In a word, a city of another and a bygone time is Cloisterham, with . . . its hoarse rooks hovering about the Cathedral tower, its hoarser and less distinct rooks in the stalls far beneath.

Suspended, this Cloisterham, between two kinds of timelessness, the timelessness of childhood memory which haunts and beckons, and the timelessness of social stagnation which Jasper so hates. Confronted with Mr Sapsea, it is possible almost to agree with Jasper – yet the novel does not *feel* like social observation and criticism; it feels, rather, like a shifting dream. Jasper, for whom Cloisterham is a prison, himself infects it. The more mouldering and dank the cloisters, the more sinister the tower, the more ominous the rook calls, by so much the deeper are we engulfed in the Jasper mind. Jasper's rebellion takes him to opium, and through opium to murder, as he rejects reason, religion, all that Crisparkle's Cloisterham celebrates, for the dark intensities of his innermost self.

In this very last passage that Dickens wrote, however, Cloisterham seems suspended between the Jasper darkness,

which still infuses it, and the timeless idyll of summer days.
Even the cathedral reaches out from its habitual dankness to
preach, like the religion supposedly sustaining it, the Resurrection and the Life. Yet there is Jasper, the respectable choir-
master, still in the cathedral among the human adornments, and
in fine voice for his service to greet the day. Is he watched
without knowing it (like Rosa earlier) by sly gargoyle faces
'carved on spout and gable'? Sly human faces there are in
plenty, notably that of the Princess Puffer, who had patiently
tracked him there on some shadowy mission not yet clear.
There she is, lurking behind a pillar, shaking her fist – both her
fists – at him as he sings. And there by the door is another
watcher – the imp of Satan, Deputy, also Jasper's enemy, who
sharp-eyed and appreciative 'stares astounded from the threatener to the threatened'. There too is Datchery, watching all
three of them : the mysterious stranger, come to spy on Jasper,
who takes in the whole scene of menace and mystery before his
eyes. As the service ends and the odd congregation disperses
in the sunlight, the Princess confides that *she* knows Jasper,
better than all his reverend colleagues in the cathedral town.
So Datchery goes off to score his thick notch; Dickens lays
down his pen, and the day closes. We are left with this image of
spying and watching, obscure threats and fears from person to
person; a not unfitting conclusion to the novel, or to its author's
life.

It is, indeed, a quintessence of Cloisterham, far removed
from the social trivialities or the saving reasonableness of
'normal' life. There is little respite from such themes from the
first page onwards, when we make out the cathedral, dimly and
surprisingly, through the swirling images of Jasper's mind.
Jasper watches Edwin with his strange, fixed look that never
changes or wavers; he watches Rosa in a manner that petrifies
her with aversion and fear. When he sets off for his night expedition with Durdles and pauses to spy on Neville and Crisparkle, he watches Neville 'as though his eye were at the trigger
of a loaded rifle, and he had covered him and were going to fire.
. . . A sense of destructive power is so expressed in his face
that even Durdles pauses in his munching and looks at him,

with an unmunched something in his cheek.' When Edwin disappears, Jasper proclaims Neville the murderer, and sets a
watch on Neville in his retreat at Staple Inn.

But Jasper is watched (as we have seen) as well as watcher,
hunted as well as hunter, like Neville himself. The Princess
Puffer dogs his footsteps, for some reason not disclosed but
clearly hostile; she turns up on the afternoon of Edwin's
disappearance, and here she is again, on the last pages that we
have. Why does she come from the opium den, where Jasper
is only one among her many customers, to menace him from
behind a pillar in his respectable life? Datchery is there, of
course, to keep his eye on Jasper, and Mr Grewgious is no
doubt behind him in some undisclosed way. Durdles adopts a
tone of complicity towards Jasper which is not accounted for,
but seems somehow disquieting. The sharp Deputy has his eyes
open most of the time.

But watching and spying in *Edwin Drood* are not simple
activities; they use strange modes of communication – hypnotism, intuition, telepathy – and seem instinct with destructive
passions and aims. Jasper writes in his diary of 'dark intangible
presentiments of evil', and records : 'I have a morbid dread upon
me of some horrible consequences resulting to my dear boy, that
I cannot reason with or in any way contend against. All my
efforts are vain. The demoniacal passion of this Neville Landless, his strength in his fury, and his savage rage for the destruction of its object, appal me.' Perhaps so; perhaps not so : but
Jasper himself inspires much irrational fear. Rosa's dread extends to horror lest he should 'pass in through the wall when he
is spoken of', and she claims that he has made a slave of her
without uttering a word. Either Rosa is subject to delusion –
and the general tenor of the book is wholly against this – or
Jasper really is subduing her by some hypnotic power.

The theme of one mind's ascendancy over another extends
to the comic scenes, a sure sign that it is at the heart of the book.
There is Bazzard's odd relationship with Mr Grewgious, a
matter which would clearly have had some amiable explanation
though it is hard to guess precisely what Dickens had in mind :
'A pale, puffy-faced, dark-haired person of thirty, with big dark

eyes that wholly wanted lustre, and a dissatisfied doughy
complexion that seemed to ask to be sent to the baker's, this
attendant was a mysterious being, possessed of some strange
power over Mr Grewgious.' Mr Sapsea's marriage consisted of
finding another worthy to look up to him, and his ambition to
absorb his wife's mind in his own was so successful that her only
effective communication – so he tells us – was an adoring
'O Thou!' Mr Honeythunder is by no means alien to this
pattern, in that his abominable bullying in the name of charity
passes like a steamroller over all other minds.

These comic variants parody without in any way alleviating
the frightful intensity of will which Jasper unleashes whenever
he drops that mask of sombre respectability which is all that
Edwin (who *can't* be warned) ever sees. At the same time, Mr
Crisparkle accepts the challenge to rise from his good-natured
diffidence for a war against evil, and begins to establish over
Neville – at the boy's own eager request – a moral authority
which will tame the 'tiger' in his blood. We have in the making
here the power struggle which the novel will develop, with
Rosa the centre, much against her wish and indeed against her
comprehension, of a fearful battle of passionate wills. How far
this theme was to do with Dickens's own affair with Ellen
Ternan we cannot know, and perhaps need not speculate; what
is certain is that in his last three novels he depicted three times
and with agonising intensity the darker sides of love – Pip's
relationship with Estella, Bradley Headstone's with Lizzie
Hexam, and now the dark forces surrounding Rosa Bud. Both
Jasper and Neville entertain for Rosa a passion which they
describe as madness, and profess in terms of the darkest violence
and hate. The difference is that Neville submits to Mr Crisparkle, acknowledging wickedness in himself and accepting
discipline, while Jasper encourages his own passion with the
commitment to intense experiences which characterises him,
and becomes the diabolical figure glimpsed by Durdles and
revealed in full horror at the sun-dial to Rosa herself. It is clear
enough that Jasper murdered Edwin chiefly to win Rosa, and
that his fainting fit before Mr Grewgious testifies to the discovery, so soon after his crime, that he murdered in vain. He

remains determined to hound his other rival, Neville, and warns
Rosa that any other man she favours will be killed.

These dark forces are made additionally terrifying by the
paranormal aspects of pursuit. Neville and Helena have an
understanding with each other which borders on telepathy, and
which would presumably have had some part in the denouement
of the tale. Jasper, as is now generally recognised, is a hypnotist,
with considerable power over other minds. There are small
indications throughout of his power to intuit and play upon
currents of feeling between other people, as though dominance
were an instinct in his life. His more particular ascendancy over
Rosa is associated with sound. Edmund Wilson has noted that
this was a common feature in Victorian speculation about
mesmerism : 'hence', he adds, 'the insistent keynote in the piano
scene and the swelling note of the organ that frightens Rosa
in the garden'. Mr Crisparkle is drawn by curious compulsion
to the weir where he finds Edwin's watch and shirt-pin, and
presumably some hypnotic suggestion has been implanted in
his mind. For his most striking effects, Jasper intensifies his
hypnotism with drugs which increase the mind's suggestibility
and lower its defences. Just as he is induced to reveal his own
secrets under opium to the Princess Puffer (she has by this time
discovered the correct mixture for this delicate effect), so
Jasper drugs Edwin and Neville on the night of their quarrel,
and their hostility spirals into a bitter scene. Jasper also drugs
Durdles on the night of their expedition, not trusting alcohol
alone to do the work. The result is that Jasper seems to Rosa to
possess supernatural powers, and the abandonment to evil which
she senses in him is made more terrifying by his mastery of
anger and fear.

Dickens's interest in hypnotism was long-standing, and he
possessed hypnotic powers himself. He had used them on Mme
de la Rue to alleviate her delusions, and was intrigued with the
possibility of mastering another mind. It seems likely that his
obsessive public readings included some measure of hypnotism
on suggestible members of the audience. He had always relished
his power of moving men to laughter or tears. For these reasons,
Jasper's will to dominate would have greatly fascinated him.

But we have to remember – and I shall be returning to this – the use Jasper makes of it. He is a man so devoted to evil that evil colours all he does.

II

The patterns apparent in the closing paragraphs of *Edwin Drood* are, then, very central to it: people watching and spying; people seeking to dominate and perhaps destroy others; devious paths converging for some still unknown end. There is one aspect which now requires special attention, and for this we can usefully return to the start. *Edwin Drood* opens with a paragraph which in literary terms was remarkably experimental (it incurred some of the odium and ridicule later attracted by 'modern' literature), since it introduces us directly and with no warning into Jasper's drugged mind:

An ancient English Cathedral tower? How can the ancient English Cathedral tower be here! The well-known massive grey square tower of its old Cathedral? How can that be here! There is no spike of rusty iron in the air between the eye and it from any point of the real prospect. What is the spike that intervenes, and who has set it up? Maybe it is set up by the Sultan's orders for the impaling of a horde of Turkish robbers, one by one. It is so, for cymbals clash and the Sultan goes by to his palace in long procession. Ten thousand scimitars flash in the sunlight, and thrice ten thousand dancing-girls strew flowers. Then follow white elephants caparisoned in countless gorgeous colours, and infinite in number and attendants. Still the Cathedral Tower rises in the background, where it cannot be, and still no writhing figure is on the grim spike. Stay! Is the spike so low a thing as the rusty spike on the top of a post of an old bedstead that has tumbled all awry? Some vague period of drowsy laughter must be devoted to the consideration of this possibility.

Shaking from head to foot, the man whose scattered consciousness has thus fantastically pieced itself together at length rises, supports his trembling frame upon his arms, and looks around.

Notice the strangeness which the 'well-known' cathedral tower takes on in its dream simulacrum ('How can that be here!'), and the exotic, timeless, yet sinister pageantry which passes through the questioning mind. There is the grim symbolism of the spike, strange in itself ('What is the spike that intervenes, and who has set it up?') and strange on account of something missing ('still no writhing figure is on the grim spike'). We learn later that Jasper has taken a fellow-traveller to murder many times in the course of his opium fantasies (chapter 23), and that this clash of colourful imagery is released only after the deed (' "Yes! I always made the journey first, before the changes of colours and the great landscapes and glittering processions began. They couldn't begin till it was off my mind." ') If the novel had started a few seconds before it does, the mystery of Edwin Drood would have been less a mystery; but as things are, we never do know the details of that drugged and murderous journey in Jasper's mind.

The first paragraph is recalled for us, however, by several things we do see later, and notably by Jasper's night with Durdles in chapter 12. The two ascend the cathedral tower in a passage as eerie, in its way, as Jasper's opium vision, and Durdles tells of the terrible shriek and howl which he heard there on the previous Christmas Eve, just a year before Edwin is to disappear. Jasper appears fiercely startled by this disclosure : ' "What do you mean?" is the very abrupt, and one might say, fierce retort.' Durdles does not reply directly, but there remains an old complicity in his tone. They then descend to the crypt, where Jasper goes about secret business, watched we may infer by Deputy, after Durdles has succumbed to drugged sleep. The mingling of reality and fantasy in an atmosphere charged with evil returns us to the mood of the opening while hinting at further revelations now permanently lost.

At the opening of chapter 1 the scene is one of 'scattered consciousness', from which Jasper returns to a reality of external sordidness and inward disgust. 'He rises unsteadily from the bed, lays the pipe upon the hearthstone, draws back the ragged curtain, and looks with repugnance at his three companions.' Further on in this first chapter, other hints of 'scattered consciousness' abound. There is the 'unclean spirit of imitation' set up by the opium, so that the Princess Puffer becomes 'a strange likeness of the Chinaman', and Jasper has to wrestle with a similar tendency in himself. Is the form taken by the 'unclean spirit' significant? Some secret oriental background may link Jasper and the Princess, and Neville and Helena Landless come from Ceylon. Then again, we see a fellow addict of Jasper's fighting and murdering in *his* scattered dreams :

As he falls, the Lascar starts into a half-risen attitude, glares with his eyes, lashes about him fiercely with his arms, and draws a phantom knife. It then becomes apparent that the woman has taken possession of this knife, for safety's sake; for, she too starting up, and restraining and expostulating with him, the knife is visible in her dress, not in his, when they drowsily drop back, side by side.

How clear can the borderline between reality and illusion ever be, for a drugged mind? On the day of Edwin's disappearance, we witness Jasper at the peak of his form, as if keyed up to perfection : 'It still seems as if a false note were not within his power tonight, and as if nothing could hurry or retard him.' When Jasper is questioned by the Princess Puffer under drugs after Edwin's disappearance, he says that when 'it comes to be real at last, it is so short that it seems unreal for the first time'. There are also suggestions that on this first re-enactment under opium after the disappearance Jasper lacks the proper satisfactions : 'No struggle, no consciousness of peril, no entreaty', and there is also something not prefigured : ' "Yet I never saw *that* before." With a start.'

Might it be that some unexpected action of the drugs thwarted his actual attempt on Edwin, perhaps because – as we see with the Lascar – phantom weapons can present themselves as real in a dream? Might it even be that the Princess Puffer, who has taken the Lascar's knife into custody, extends her protection to other victims of her clients? She was in Cloisterham on the day of Edwin's disappearance, presumably to try to save him, though she missed Jasper on that occasion (we discover this later), and she did not recognise Edwin as the man she had come to warn. If Jasper's attempt on Edwin was confused by some miscalculation of his drug, then Edwin might conceivably have escaped to Mr Grewgious, gone into hiding and reappeared as Datchery. (But on this showing, he would also have to suffer amnesia, since Datchery seems genuinely uncertain of Cloisterham's geography; and for reasons I shall return to, it seems to me much more likely that Edwin is dead.)

The first chapter ends with Jasper's return to Cloisterham in his normal *persona*, and with his entry into the cathedral (this was underlined in Dickens's notes) in time to participate as 'the intoned words, "WHEN THE WICKED MAN – " rise among groins of arches and beams of roofs, awakening muttered thunder'.

III

This brings us again to Jasper, who is indeed central. Just as we enter the novel through his scattered consciousness, so he permeates much of its mood and tone. In his distinctive manner Dickens projects Jasper into the world around him: into his room, where the congruence between the man and his surroundings goes beyond the fairly normal perception that a man may colour a room, or even that a room may symbolise a man, to some more dynamic sense of the man incarnating himself in his surroundings and possibly enjoying the revelation and the concealment of himself in such a way:

Mr Jasper is a dark man of some six-and-twenty, with thick, lustrous, well-arranged black hair and whiskers. He looks older than he is, as dark men often do. His voice is deep and good, his face and figure are good, his manner is a little sombre. His room is a little sombre, and may have had its influence in forming his manner. It is mostly in shadow. Even when the sun shines brilliantly it seldom touches the grand piano in the recess, or the folio music-books on the stand, or the bookshelves on the wall, or the unfinished picture of a blooming schoolgirl hanging over the chimney piece . . .

This blends in turn with the more sinister description of Jasper in his room, watching his nephew:

Once for all, a look of intentness and intensity – a look of hungry, exacting, watchful, and yet devoted affection – is

always, now and ever afterwards, on the Jasper face whenever
the Jasper face is addressed in this direction. And whenever it is
so addressed it is never, on this occasion or on any other,
dividedly addressed; it is always concentrated.

In a novel of the hunters and hunted 'the Jasper face' suggests a
degree of dislocation between reality and appearance that is
highly sinister ('There's no art/To read the mind's construction
in the face'). It is as though the look, 'hungry, exalting, watchful' were a cloak to cover whatever obsession underlies 'affection'; or as though only a constant effort, such as that required
to overcome the 'unclean spirit of imitation' under opium, could
keep the Jasper face from relapsing into other shapes – the
'strange and sudden smile' and the 'sense of destructive power'
which Durdles sees, or the even fuller revelation to Rosa at the
sun-dial: 'But his face looks so wicked and menacing, as he
stands leaning against the sun-dial – setting, as it were, his
black mark upon the very face of day – that her flight is arrested
by horror as she looks at him.' In the affinity between Jasper
and his room it may not be fanciful to discern a further suggestion: that just as the room appears dimly respectable, except
in such moments as it becomes a place of rage and violence
(Edwin's quarrel with Neville, and the night of Edwin's disappearance), so Jasper appears dimly respectable for much of
the time, to his own nephew (who 'can't' be warned) as to the
world.

As with Jasper's room, so with Cloisterham; it is as though
the darker undercurrents of morbidity to be discerned there, in
crypt and cloister, emanate somehow from this man. This may
be why Jasper's impatience with Cloisterham and hatred of its
deadness strikes us not as justification for his escape – we know
the terms of that escape, after all – but rather as the source of
infection, projecting what is seen. Just as the strange world of
The Ancient Mariner takes on aridity and horror for the guilty
mariner, so Cloisterham's evil seems strangely like Jasper's
consciousness in decay. Jasper's Cloisterham is at best a place of
sultry brooding, shot through with sharp flashes of fear and
terror, where Rosa's fear of the man, exaggerated though it may
be by aversion, is an index of his malign power for ill. Our

release from *this* Cloisterham, as readers, comes not from Jasper's own escape into opium, which merely turns the cathedral into a nightmare stage for ritual murder, but from a different consciousness altogether: that of Canon Crisparkle and his mother – for whom a closet can turn to paradise, and the very cathedral proclaim, on sunlit mornings, the Resurrection and the Life.

IV

The chief enigma for the reader is not then whether Jasper is malign and tormented – that is stamped on everything – but whether he is evil, or mad, or conceivably both. I want to return to this for my concluding remarks on the novel; but a few words are first required on the plot. As we know Dickens intended this to mystify, but he could not have foreseen such permanent success. We must accept, however reluctantly, that certain of his intentions remain inaccessible, and that areas of doubt about the projected denouement will always remain. There is in this (to digress a little) an accidental insight about 'inevitability', in so far as we often feel retrospective 'inevitability' about a major work of art in its finished state. If *Edwin Drood* had been completed, it would surely have struck us like this, since what we have of it demonstrates such a rare unity of mood and growth. Yet when it breaks off, conflicting possibilities remain very evidently open, as if to confirm the actual laws of organic growth. We can be as sure that the whole concept would have been prefigured convincingly and causally from the very beginning as we *are* sure that the final secrets will now never be known. In this the novel is not unlike a man who dies suddenly and unexpectedly, while some apparently momentous and logical pattern is unfolding but still incomplete.

Much literature has assembled around the Drood mystery in this shadowy world of speculation, and I do not propose to add to it here. Some of it is vitiated by failure to apprehend the mood and poetry of the novel; some by failure to see it as a novel by Dickens rather than by some other hand. To propose

Crisparkle as the villain (for instance) does not violate the
broadest laws of detective fiction, and is not without plausi-
bility: it *is* odd that he discovers Edwin's watch and shirt-pin
where he does. But it is an absolute absurdity to toy with any
such 'solution' for *this* novel: Crisparkle's virtue is sufficiently
apparent in the poetic texture and structure, even if we do not
bring in (and why shouldn't we?) what we know of Dickens
elsewhere. For the same reason, any whitewashing of Jasper
is out of the question, particularly if it involves the notion that
Rosa's fear of him is simply immature. The argument is not in
any scientific terms 'provable', though reference can be made to
psychological probability as well as to aesthetic structure in its
support. Naturally one could have a novel where a young girl's
fears were morbid or delusional, and a great injustice to their
object, but the girl would scarcely resemble Rosa Bud. Though
spoilt and silly in some ways, Rosa is neither mad nor cowardly;
and her fears are shared by all the characters who represent
sanity and good. Mr Grewgious clearly stands in a line of
Dickens characters which includes Mr Lorry and Wemmick,
while Mr Crisparkle and his mother are in Dickens's idyllic
mode. The scene at the sun-dial is too close, moreover, to Bradley Headstone's dreadful interview with Lizzie Hexam for us
to doubt that the same dark murderous passions are at work.
Not that the two scenes are identical – Jasper is a very different
character from Headstone, and Rosa from Lizzie – but the
emotional colourings are undeniably close.

My own view is that Dickens's intentions were precisely as he
explained them to Forster, and that the account in Forster's
biography is true as far as it goes. The outline fits with everything we actually have of the novel; and it is hard to imagine
Dickens risking Forster's future wrath by trifling with him,
though there might have been more twists and turns in his mind
than he chose to reveal. 'I laid aside the fancy I told you of,'
Dickens wrote to Forster, 'and have a very curious and new idea
for my story. Not a communicable idea (or the interest of the
book would be gone), but a very strong one, though difficult to
work.' Forster quotes this, and continues as follows:

The story, I learnt immediately afterwards, was to be that of the murder of a nephew by his uncle; the originality of which was to consist in the review of the murderer's career by himself at the close, when its temptations were to be dwelt upon as if, not he the culprit, but some other man, was the tempted. The last chapters were to be written in the condemned cell, to which his wickedness, all elaborately elicited from him as if told of another, had brought him. Discovery by the murderer of the utter need-lessness of the murder for its object, was to follow hard upon commission of the deed; but all discovery of the murderer was to be baffled till towards the close, when, by means of a gold ring which had resisted the corrosive effects of the lime into which he had thrown the body, not only the person murdered was to be identified but the locality of the crime and the man who committed it. So much was told to me before any of the book was written . . . Rosa was to marry Tartar, and Crisparkle the sister of Landless, who was himself, I think, to have perished in assisting Tartar finally to unmask and seize the murderer.

Strong hints of the two marriages alluded to can be found in the final chapters of the work as we have it, and Neville's vulner-ability may be sensed throughout. It is unlikely that Edwin would have survived to marry Rosa (though he might have survived to marry someone else: we should not forget that new characters tend to appear in Dickens's novels at a later stage than we have reached).

What else can we know more or less certainly? Jasper's long black scarf in the chapter 'When Shall These Three Meet Again?' sounds important (and Dickens's illustrator, Sir Luke Fildes, understood that Edwin was to be strangled with this). There are continual hints of strange happenings in Cloisterham – the cry heard by Durdles in the cathedral a year before, the Princess Puffer's mysterious arrival on the day of Edwin's disap-pearance, Jasper's night with Durdles – and I would not rule out the exotic possibility accepted by both Edmund Wilson and Edgar Johnson that Jasper would turn out to be a thug, and that his evil dreams would include the ritual murder of a guest. The importance attached to the gold ring entrusted to Edwin by Mr Grewgious fully bears out Forster's account. It is the one piece of gold on Edwin's person which Jasper does not know

about, and which is not removed before his disappearance or
death. We have heard Mr Grewgious wondering 'Will it come
back to me? My mind hangs about her ring very uneasily
tonight'; and the moment when Edwin decides not to let Rosa
know about the ring, for fear of hurting her further, but retains
it in his pocket for future restoration to Mr Grewgious, has
been established as a moment fraught with destiny:

Among the mighty store of wonderful chains that are forever
forging, day and night, in the vast iron-works of time and
circumstance, there was one chain forged in the moment of that
small conclusion, riveted to the foundations of heaven and
earth, and gifted with invincible force to hold and drag.

But if the ring was indeed to be found in lime in a manner clearly
identifying Jasper (perhaps with help from the watchful Deputy)
as murderer, it seems almost certain that Edwin's body must
have perished. The teasing chapter heading 'When Shall These
Three Meet Again?', with its hint of witchcraft as well as
murder, seems then to prefigure not Edwin's reappearance, but
some sensational confrontation of Jasper and Neville over
Edwin's grave.

   Who, then, is Datchery? If he is not Edwin, and this seems
almost certain, it remains most likely, from the nature of his
disguise and the general relish of mystery, that he is someone
already known to us in the book. A firm favourite for some
readers has been Helena Landless, mainly because Neville has
spoken of her prowess as a male impersonator. ('When we ran
away . . . the flight was always of her planning and leading.
Each time she dressed as a boy, and showed the daring of a man.')
But could Helena, even given these gifts, address a full coffee-
room with masculine confidence, and impress Mr Sapsea with a
grand, almost military air? Philip Collins has come down in
favour of Mr Grewgious, but this seems to me very unlikely.
Mr Grewgious seems far too idiosyncratic in appearance to be
readily disguisable, and unless the time-scale is deliberately
juggled, he is living in London while Datchery lives in rooms
at Mrs Tope's. The most plausible candidate in my view is
Bazzard. Bazzard promises to be something of a conundrum
in his own right, but there is nothing in the description of

Datchery – very minimal – to preclude him from the role. One of the few things clear about Datchery is that he appears to be a stranger in Cloisterham (this, if true, would also exclude Helena), but has come there for the purpose of watching Jasper. It is extremely likely that Mr Grewgious, who suspects Jasper from the first yet is not visibly active, is behind Datchery, and Bazzard would be his obvious first choice. Bazzard, moreover, has temporarily disappeared from Mr Grewgious's; and we know that he has theatrical ambitions of a grandiose kind.

But all of this is a matter of speculation. All we can be sure of is that the Princess Puffer and Deputy know more than we do, in that final chapter, but that they remain eternally suspended with their secrets beyond our reach.

v

Is Jasper mad? The question, perhaps no more finally solvable than the plot riddles, has fascinating interest in the Dickens world. To my mind he is mad only as he drives himself mad, and he drives himself mad through evil designs. In *Great Expectations* there is a most revealing insight of Pip's about Mrs Joe's rampages: 'I must remark of my sister, what is equally true of all the violent women I have ever seen, that passion was no excuse for her, because it is undeniable that instead of lapsing into passion, she consciously and deliberately took extraordinary pains to force herself into it, and became blindly furious by regular stages.' Mrs Joe is an ordinary callous woman, certainly not a 'horrible wonder apart' like Jasper, yet the process of degradation may be the same. A nearer instance is Bradley Headstone, who, although slower and stupider than Jasper, is like him in passion, and is described during the genesis of murder in these terms (*Our Mutual Friend*, chapter 44):

The state of the man was murderous, and he knew it. More; he irritated it, with a kind of perverse pleasure akin to that which a sick man sometimes has in irritating a wound upon his body. Tied up all day with his disciplined show upon him, subdued to the performance of his routine of educational tricks, encircled by a gabbling crowd, he broke loose at night like an ill-tamed wild animal. Under his daily restraint, it was his compensation, not his trouble, to give a glance towards his state at night and to the freedom of its being indulged. If great criminals told the truth – which, being great criminals, they do not – they would very rarely tell of their struggles against the crime. Their struggles are towards it. They buffet with opposing waves, to gain the bloody shore, not to recede from it. This man perfectly comprehended that he hated his rival with his strongest and worst forces, and that if he tracked him to Lizzie Hexam, his so doing would never serve himself with her, or serve her. All his pains were taken to the end that he might incense himself with the sight of the detested figure in her company and favour, in her place of concealment. And he knew as well what act of his would follow, if he did, as he knew that his mother had borne him.

We have only to think back over the great tormented minds in Dickens to notice that he regarded madness as almost self-induced, the final and worst stage of an evil will. At a certain stage the process may be irreversible, with the madman no longer accountable to himself or anyone for what he does, but this still remains a natural punishment for sin. There are certain energies which alienate from humanity, and enfold in torment: revenge for instance, as we see it in Carker, Edith Dombey, Alice Marwood, Rosa Dartle, Mrs Clennam, Miss Wade, Miss Havisham: and murder (where the men start to preponderate) – Bill Sikes, Rudge, Jonas Chuzzlewit, Tulkinghorn (who can be numbered here), Rigaud, Orlick, Headstone. All of these might be, or come to be 'mad' clinically, but Dickens finds wickedness at the core. These people do not belong with the deranged people who are victims of defects of birth (Barnaby), intolerable sufferings borne with gentleness (Miss Flite), or clinical disorders (Mr F's Aunt), and who deserve pity. They present themselves rather as the reverse of those characters who, responding to suffering with patience, courage, selflessness and other difficult virtues, become the salt of the earth.

Merely to reflect upon the men and women on both sides of this equation is to remember that Dickens never repeated characters or situations, and that his depiction of the endless byways of virtue and vice is as far-ranging as any in literature.

Yet it remains true that all his really wicked characters violate certain clear rules of virtue and reason, and bring their worst derangements upon themselves. Dickens's greatest fear, both touching individuals and society, was anarchy. No doubt he was led to this partly by self-knowledge; the capacities for destruction as well as creation in his own great energy are always clear. It is with this in mind that we can properly acknowledge his more remarkable villains as partial self-portraits; just as we might feel that Macbeth lurked in Shakespeare himself. 'Partial' is, however, the qualification, with all the difference implied in it between heaven and hell. If a writer can not only create a Macbeth but place him as Shakespeare does, the gulf cannot properly be described in lesser terms.

I make these observations because Jasper has actually been identified with Dickens by some critics (I shall return to this), and because others have seen him as pitiable because clinically mad. The confusion arises from the nature of the split in Jasper's character. Is he indeed one person, or two or more persons inhabiting one frame? When Mr Tope has been describing Jasper's 'daze' in the second chapter, the Dean replies 'And Mr Jasper has gone home quite himself, has he?' The 'daze' we know to be an after-effect of opium, and the mystery of what 'quite himself' might imply, with a man like Jasper, already obtrudes itself as cause for concern. James Wright has followed the critics who see the case as one of schizophrenia, with Jasper as a kind of Jekyll and Hyde. He quotes an innocent-seeming remark about Miss Twinkleton, and ponders whether Miss Twinkleton is the 'only one':

As, in some cases of drunkenness, and in others of animal magnetism, there are two states of consciousness which never clash, but each of which pursues its separate course as though it were continuous instead of broken (thus, if I hide my watch when I am drunk, I must be drunk again before I can remember where), so Miss Twinkleton has two different and distinct phases of being . . .

In my own view this passage undoubtedly conceals some hidden clue, possibly in the parenthesis (it would turn out to be relevant perhaps to whatever arts Jasper has practised on Crisparkle

which lead him to the weir), but I cannot see it as having any
analogy to Jasper's frame of mind. The 'split' in him is not
between two personalities, but between two deliberate *personae*
– the respectable public self of Cloisterham and the exotic
private self of the Limehouse den. At all times in his 'normal'
life Jasper commands both *personae*. The suppressed excitement
of his manner with Edwin comes of their ironic tension, and his
only forgetfulness is during the spell of the drugs. Indeed, he so
hates his public *persona* even while adopting it, that he tells
Edwin it is the merest façade.

It is the same with the main action of the novel, Jasper's plan
to make away with Edwin and Neville and to possess Rosa, to
which all his waking words and deeds are attuned. The 'warning'
he gives to Edwin, in the safe knowledge that Edwin will not
understand it, is true enough as far as it goes. Jasper is already
'madly' in love with Rosa, and determined to control her, while
murder is enacted as yet only in opium dreams. Jasper's attitude
to Edwin obviously reflects a dark obsession with him, but an
obsession which he consciously intensifies in his Limehouse life.
When Neville comes on the scene, Jasper organises their
quarrel, and takes care that the whole town shall be told. His
morbid 'fears' are clearly intended for Crisparkle, and his diary
exists chiefy – perhaps solely – to this end.

Jasper's plans for the murder of Edwin include the public role
which he builds up for himself as doting uncle, and his mysterious visit to the cathedral with Durdles, with its patent design
(there are no doubt other designs also) on Durdles's keys. On
the final day of Edwin's life we see Jasper wearing his long
black scarf in readiness, and fully tuned, almost certainly with
drugs, to his deed. Edwin also discovers on this day – too late
for him to understand the import or to profit from it – that his
uncle has a clear mental image of every scrap of his personal
jewellery, and, moreover, that there is a dire threat to someone
in Cloisterham called Ned ('not an inspiriting close to a dull
day').

In all these plans Jasper the choir-master is engaged most
fully, and there is no evidence of any 'self' in ignorance of what
he does. His careful planning is, rather, an expression of moral

deterioration, encouraged and accelerated in himself. The most
obvious example of this is his recourse to opium, and to the
Limehouse setting where we meet him first. In taking to drugs
he renounces reason and normal consciousness in favour of
'scattered consciousness' outside reason's writ. This in turn
follows his calculated rejection of the twin pillars on which his
civilisation remains stable, the respectability of Cloisterham,
and the demands and promises of the Christian faith. His
hypocrisy in remaining outwardly conformist has none of the
Pecksniffian panache; rather, its tone is sardonic and sultry, as
evidenced in his revelation to Edwin:

'You were going to say (but that I interrupted you in spite
of myself) what a quiet life mine is. No whirl and uproar around
me, no distracting commerce or calculation, no risk, no change
of place, myself devoted to the art I pursue, my business my
pleasure.'
'I really was going to say something of the kind, Jack . . .'
'Yes, I saw what you were tending to. I hate it.'
'Hate it, Jack?' (Much bewildered.)
'I hate it. The cramped monotony of my existence grinds me
away by the grain. How does our service sound to you?'
'Beautiful! Quite celestial!'
'It often sounds to me quite devilish. I am so weary of it. The
echoes of my own voice among the arches seem to mock me
with my daily drudging round. No wretched monk who droned
his life away in that gloomy place before me can have been more
tired of it than I am. He could take for relief (and did take) to
carving demons out of the stalls and seats and desks. What shall
I do? Must I take to carving them out of my heart?'

At the present time, Jasper's tone of social protest might seem
almost standard; and Dickens would not have been wholly out
of sympathy himself. He had no brief for the cloister and would
not have relished it, though on the other hand he would scarcely
have seen himself, as Jasper does, as a secluded drudge. But
Jasper's tone is at once too urbane and too elusive to be sympathetic; surely he *relishes* Edwin's failure to glimpse the
carvings in his heart? When he reveals himself more fully to
Rosa at the sun-dial, we see behind the mask of his tone:

'There is my past and my present wasted life. There is the

desolation of my heart and my soul. There is my peace; there is my despair. Stamp them into the dust, so that you take me, were it even mortally hating me!'

The frightful vehemence of the man, now reaching its full height, so additionally terrifies her as to break the spell that has held her to the spot.

Even if this torment is somehow familiar – especially if it is somehow familiar – we might as well pity a cobra about to strike. Jasper is so mad here, that we can merely hope his own destruction will be upon him before other victims fall to his despair. The rejection of restraint and reason has so far been accomplished in him, that he is incapable also by now of love and trust. It is apparent that the 'love' he now declares is nightmarish, and that surrender to egotism has made a horror of the word.

The fact that he *is* passing into real madness becomes first fully apparent in his night with Durdles. From the start, Durdles asserts a kind of complicity which ought to warn him; but, watching Neville and Crisparkle in the moonlight, Jasper gives way to a fit of uncontrolled laughter which leaves Durdles pale. As the novel progressed, Jasper's madness would have deepened, and the scene in the condemned cell would have revealed the total derangement of his mind. If Dickens had lived longer, he might have surpassed his previous summits in this depiction. As it is, the image of Jasper at the sun-dial remains impressed on our minds.

VI

There is surely then a curious irony in Edmund Wilson's famous suggestion that in important aspects Jasper is a final portrait of Dickens himself. His analysis of *Edwin Drood* is too long, and too deservedly famous, to quote fully, but the following sentences compress the case :

Mr Jasper is, like Dickens, an artist: he is a musician, he has a beautiful voice. He smokes opium, and so, like Dickens, leads a life of the imagination apart from the life of men. Like Dickens, he is a skilful magician, whose power over his fellows may be dangerous. Like Dickens, he is an alien from another world; yet, like Dickens, he has made himself respected in the conventional English community. Is he a villain? From the point of view of the cathedral congregation of Cloisterham, who have admired his ability as an artist, he will have been playing a diabolical role. All that sentiment, all those edifying high spirits, which Dickens has been dispensing so long, which he is still making an effort to dispense – has all this now grown as false as those hymns to the glory of the Christian God which are performed by the worshipper of Kali? And yet in another land there is another point of view from which Jasper is a good and faithful servant.

There is no major and seminal piece of literary criticism known to me – and Wilson's essay did more than any other piece of critical writing to introduce the modern world to Dickens's greatness – where a more damnable piece of nonsense can be found. I use the word advisedly, since the notion that Jasper's damnation should be justifiable from any valid point of view, and most of all from the author's, partakes of damnation itself. If Jasper worships Kali, and is regarded by the cult as a good and faithful servant, then are not Kali's worshippers a sect of murderous rogues? And is it not damnable to imagine that a murdering scoundrel like Jasper can in any serious manner be compared with one of the greatest creative minds of his own or any other age?

Wilson's error seems to me here so depressing, and yet so distinctively modern, that it is hard to know in what spirit it should be opposed. Who but a modern would imagine that the escape world of opium could have anything to do, except in the sickest parody, with the creative artist's power? Jasper's drugs are a rejection of consciousness for uncontrolled fantasy, not that union of consciousness and reason which fuse in all creative art. Drugs might be compatible with intelligent rubbish like the novels of William Burroughs, but never with the creation of a novel like *Edwin Drood*. As creator, Dickens confers beauty and significance of the kind which come only from the world of rational morality which Jasper spurns beneath his feet and kicks away. Wilson's suggestion is a melancholy reminder that Jasper is not only a wicked man but a surprisingly modern one;

an *exemplum* who has surprising relevance to our scattered consciousness today.

He is, to be more precise, a precursor of our own last-ditch romanticism, a condition more prevalent and dangerous at the centenary of Dickens's death than it was when the novel was new. The early Romantics had directed the mind of man inwards to his personal psyche and the quest for its fulfilment. The prognosis seemed excellent. Only cast off the old chains of law and custom and man might be free and noble, loving and joyful; might be a great hero; might be a god. Literature since has offered tragic overtones to this splendid optimism, yet its lure is as potent now as it ever was. The Victorian novelists discovered that a tragic destiny might attend such freedom; in the twentieth century the prospects have further declined. Through desolate tracts of waste land to absurdist nightmares, the modern romantic pilgrimage wends its way. Yet still they come : the poor whites and poor blacks of Baldwin's New York, imbibing its poison; the world of Moses Herzog; the *personae* of confessional poems by Robert Lowell, Sylvia Plath and Anne Sexton : and, if we leave these heights for the morass of intelligent pornography masquerading as literature, thousands of tormented seekers of fulfilment in thousands of modish novels and plays. Even the classics – Jan Kott's Shakespeare – are being duly locked up with ourselves in the madhouse, and if Shakespeare, why not Dickens as well? The only answer seems to be that both must sooner or later be released from a totally false imprisonment, since we need them, ourselves, to show the way.

The importance of *Edwin Drood* to an insane climate – its peculiar relevance, I am suggesting – lies then in Jasper's prophetic gropings towards ourselves. From inside his consciousness, he is naturally a victim, to be pitied all the more as he becomes a 'horrible wonder apart'. From anywhere outside his consciousness he is an extreme evil, to be locked up if at all possible, and perhaps even killed.

What could more justify Crisparkle, with his Christian cheerfulness, and when called upon for it his Christian sternness, than the nightmare loosed on and into Cloisterham in this tale?

Crisparkle holds out to Neville, also tigerishly tempted, the salutary hope of discipline and pure love. Love *itself* will not do : Jasper 'loves' Rosa, after all. For love to be purified, something else is needed. Decency, sanity, wisdom : these above all are the healing things.

If we consider *Edwin Drood* as a genre novel, it might seem a regression, a return beyond the moral realism of Jane Austen's dealings with cathedral cities to the wild world of gothic romance. A closer look dispels this notion. Eighteenth-century gothic pressed madness, drugs, unbridled passion and so forth into the service of sensationalism. With no pressure from realism, they arrived at 'mere entertainment', in a disabling sense. *Edwin Drood* looks not backward to this but forward, to our modern probing of madness, and our modern situation itself. It is as though Jane Austen's world becomes, in the light of *Edwin Drood*, the illusion, a mere dream of stable and decorous society in the human world. Dickens takes us to the battlefield where good and evil engage each other, and Cloisterham reflects the purities and nightmares of these rival worlds.

The wheel has indeed come full circle, when one can feel Jane Austen's as the world where a modern reader is likely to seek his escapism, and *Edwin Drood* as an image of life as it normally is. Dickens depicts in Jasper a path of despair and damnation which stands in its relevance to the individual much as the Terror in *A Tale of Two Cities* does to society at large. His final novel is his most striking picture of the human situation in its starkest relationship to good and evil. It is also his most striking justification of reason and sanity as the grounds for all human activity, the true pearls beyond price.

Index

Fictional characters are distinguished from real by the use of capitals for the latter.